Praise for
NEXT TO ME

"Many people live with Parkinson's. David Jones defies it. This story is inspirational to both those with the condition and those without it. Buy this book and David Jones may yet fall into the second of these categories."
Tom Isaacs, Trustee, The Cure Parkinson's Trust

"David Jones's story offers anyone living with Parkinson's the optimism and hope that great achievements – in business and in life – are still possible."
Michael J. Fox

David –
Let's get this job done!
all my very Best
Michael J Fox

NEXT TO ME

NEXT TO ME

Luck, leadership and

living with Parkinson's

David Jones

NICHOLAS BREALEY
PUBLISHING

BOSTON • LONDON

First published by
Nicholas Brealey Publishing in 2005

3–5 Spafield Street   100 City Hall Plaza, Suite 501
Clerkenwell, London   Boston
EC1R 4QB, UK   MA 02108, USA
Tel: +44 (0)20 7239 0360   Tel: (888) BREALEY
Fax: +44 (0)20 7239 0370   *Fax: (617) 523 3708*
http://www.nbrealey-books.com

© David Jones 2005

ISBN 1-85788-357-8

British Library Cataloguing in Publication Data
A catalogue record for this book is available from the
British Library.

Printed in Germany by GGP Media GmbH.

Contents

Foreword
by Philip Green

first met David Jones in the early 1980s. I could perhaps be for-given for not predicting then that I would one day be writing the foreword to the life story of one of the most admired men in British retailing.

In fairness, few could have foreseen that the young boy who left school with underwhelming A-level results would grow up to take the battered and almost bankrupt NEXT of the late 1980s and turn it into a multibillion-pound retail success story.

Fewer still would have backed him to do this while fighting a very private battle with Parkinson's Disease. His has been an incredible career, dominated by two traits: honesty and hard work.

David's career started as a temporary clerk at Kays of Worcester. From this lowly base he worked his way up to finance director at the age of 27. An obsession with the mail-order industry was born and after a spell as managing director of the British Mail Order Corporation – like Kays, a subsidiary of Great Universal Stores – he was headhunted to run Grattan, where he pulled off a dramatic turnaround.

Grattan merged with NEXT, the new star of the retail industry, and David was installed as deputy chief executive. He helped launch the NEXT Directory, which is today by far the most successful home shopping business in the UK.

But NEXT was in trouble after a period of massive over-expansion. With the recession biting, the business needed slimming down radically. David did just that. Having reported a huge loss in 1990, NEXT returned to profit in 1992 thanks to the sale of Grattan and a cost-cutting exercise in which he was prepared to halve his own pay packet.

Today NEXT is one of the best known names on the High Street, a retail powerhouse with a turnover of £3 billion, profits of over £400 million and a stock market value of £4 billion.

To get an idea of the esteem in which David is held, you only need to talk to his friends and competitors in the industry, such as Stuart Rose, chief executive of Marks & Spencer, who has said: 'He's a terrific man. He delivers. It's a fantastic track record – he is one of the unsung greats in retail.'

Adjectives such as 'modest', 'unsung' and 'quiet' are all too familiar in testimonials to David. This low-key approach has been a constant character trait whether his role has been that of finance director, chief executive, chairman or non-executive director.

But those who have thought that this was the sign of a man without determination or resolve have had cause to regret their lack of judgement.

Such is the respect in which he is held that David has always been happy to let the inaccurate image of the 'grey man' grow, satisfied that actions speak louder than the pushiest of public relations agents. The truth is that David is one of the wittiest and brightest people around, and I hugely enjoy our meetings and conversations.

The fantastic support of his lovely wife Ann through the 20 years he has battled with his health, with no fuss or mention ever made, tells you all about this really special man. The secrets that have led to his successes are revealed in the following pages, and they make great reading. David may not be a rock star, but when rock stars release their autobiographies it often signals the end of their creativity: the release of this book surely does not herald the end of David Jones's marvellous career.

Introduction

The doctor stopped writing up his notes. He walked over to me, took off my glasses, and gently tapped my forehead just above the bridge of my nose.

'You've got Parkinson's Disease,' he said, and left the room.

In that startling moment – at half past eleven on the morning of 25 July 1982 – the pattern of my life changed forever.

I was 39 years old. I had a wonderful family. I had always thought of myself as a lucky man, not in the sense that I had been born with any great material advantages or obvious natural gifts – I hadn't – but in the sense that at crucial moments in my adult life the dice always seemed to roll in my favour, and I made the most of my good luck. That was how I had risen in less than 20 years from unpromising beginnings as a teenage clerk, to become a leader of Britain's home shopping industry as chief executive of Grattan plc, one of the biggest and most respected names in the business.

But now my luck had suddenly turned for the worse. I had a horrible, incurable, progressive disease that was going to make leadership more and more challenging for me as time went on. From that day to this I have been living with Parkinson's, and from that day until 28 May 2001 I lived with it in secret.

My family and a small number of very close friends knew, but my colleagues and the world at large did not. Despite what the disease was doing to my body, I enjoyed a tremendously challenging business career – in which Grattan merged with NEXT to become part of the great retail revolution of the 1980s, and NEXT went from triumph to disaster and back again in the 1990s. This book is chiefly about those events, and about the lessons to be drawn from them about business leadership.

But wrapped around the business story is a deeply personal story about how I have coped with Parkinson's. I have done so partly by medication, partly by mental discipline and partly by sheer optimism. By telling my story now, after keeping it private for so long, I want to offer a ray of hope to fellow Parkinson's sufferers and those who care for them.

All of us with experience of Parkinson's know that it is about unpredictable ups and downs, about good days and bad. This is how it has been for me, not only in physical health but also in the fortunes of the companies with which I have been connected.

That is true most especially at NEXT, of which I am still chairman and which has provided one of the most turbulent sagas of modern corporate history. And it has been equally true in recent times at Wm Morrison, the supermarket group, where as deputy chairman I have helped steer the company through the difficulties that followed its takeover of Safeway.

Over these years there have been plenty of good days, and there has been plenty to learn from the bad ones. I have had a wonderful experience of life and business, and I am lucky – once again – to have this opportunity to share it.

It was a routine medical with the company doctor, who was known unkindly at Grattan as 'the butcher of Manningham Lane' (an area of Bradford in Yorkshire where the company was based) because of the rather rough way he administered the injections required for our regular buying trips to the Far East. The examination did not take long. I was waiting for the usual stern lecture that company doctors give busy executives about weight, booze and stress. Instead, he surprised me by asking, in a concerned tone: 'Is there anything else bothering you?'

Although I had not intended to mention a slight problem with my right hand, the tone of his question made me tell him that I had some stiffness that was making my writing a bit squiggly. That was mildly irritating, I said, but the more serious side effect was that it was interfering with my ability to hold a golf club properly.

I made a joke of it, but it really was beginning to concern me. I had first noticed it in the pub the previous Christmas Eve when we were having our usual end-of-year celebration. All my team were there – the valued colleagues who had come over to Grattan from Great Universal Stores with me, plus the best of Grattan's own people who had joined our crusade to revitalise the company.

It was a great celebration. In the year we had been together at Grattan we had made radical changes. We had really moved the business forward. We had a terrific sense of collective achievement. But when someone offered me a crisp, to my surprise I had difficulty picking one up. It was a simple, everyday action, but it was suddenly and noticeably more difficult.

Don't worry, I thought, you've just had too much to drink. It was Christmas, after all, and I wasn't driving home. But during the holiday I began to notice many more bouts of stiffness and difficulties with everyday actions.

Over the next few months these problems continued to get worse, but I was working so hard that I had no time to think about them. I never spoke about my concern to anyone, not even my wife Ann. Since the doctor had just asked whether anything else was bothering me, however, I mentioned it for the first time. And that was when he said it: 'You've got Parkinson's Disease.'

He had rushed out of the room before I had time to react. I was completely stunned. My first thought was: Why has he rushed out? Surely it isn't contagious?

He returned excitedly two minutes later with the other members of his practice. They looked at me as if I was a unique exhibit – apparently I was the youngest person any of them had ever seen diagnosed with Parkinson's.

But I can't have Parkinson's, I thought. From what little I knew of the disease, or of people who suffered from it, it was an old people's complaint. And I was only 39 years old – a bit unfit and overweight, admittedly, but not even in the prime of my life yet. I couldn't possibly have Parkinson's. And how could the doctor tell from such a cursory examination?

He despatched me to see a consultant at the Yorkshire Clinic in Bingley the following day. I tried to look unconcerned, praying for a different diagnosis. But the consultant confirmed it. I really did have Parkinson's.

Something that medical science still does not fully understand was preventing the nerve cells in my brain from manufacturing enough of a substance called dopamine to maintain the right balance of levels with another substance called acetylcholine. The results of this imbalance are tremors, loss of coordination, stiffness in muscles and joints, and various other unpleasant side effects including tiredness and depression.

Parkinson's doesn't kill you, but it does terrible things to your quality of life. It makes you different. It makes people think differently about you.

I left the clinic and walked round the car park. This could not happen to me. I was a workaholic with a big company, thousands of employees and a share price to worry about.

That particular week had started well: Grattan's orders from home shopping customers were running 22 per cent up on the previous year. Our profits for June had been double those of the previous year. Our shares were approaching a new high of £1, almost double the price when I had joined Grattan in Bradford in January 1981 after two decades of working for the Wolfson family's Great Universal Stores group. But I still had an awful lot to do to complete the task of turning Grattan around and driving it forward again.

And most importantly, I had a wife, three children, an elderly father and a yellow labrador called Jodie to support. As soon as I told everyone I had this crippling disease, they would surely tell me I had to give up the job I loved. Then what would I do? How on earth would I live?

The answer slowly dawned on me. I would ignore the disease, not because I hoped or believed that it would go away, but because I just could not allow it to interfere with my life.

It is one of my principles in business that whatever the problem may be, there is always a solution. You just have to think it through. That is what I did as I walked around that car park. From that day on, I decided, there would be two David Joneses: one the chief executive of Grattan, the other the one with Parkinson's Disease. The two had to be kept strictly apart.

And that meant, without exception, that no one must know about the second David Jones. I was not going to tell Ann, and I certainly was not going to tell even my closest colleagues at work.

For the next two years, no one knew except me, my consultant and the company doctor. To begin with, it was not difficult to hide the disease. If anyone spotted me taking tablets and asked what they were for, I would explain that I had arthritis and that the pills were painkillers. But then Ann started to notice that when I was tired, I dragged my right leg slightly and held my hands almost clenched in front of my body. Before very long I had to tell her.

It was an emotional conversation. She was angry that I had not told her straight away, but I think she understood that I had played it that way to try to protect her from worry. We agreed to keep the secret from the children – who had school exams to face – and from everyone else except my loyal secretary June, who had to know because she would have to organise my medical appointments and fetch my prescriptions from the chemists as the condition progressed.

The only good news was that I had a version of Parkinson's that causes very slow deterioration, so that during the most difficult times at NEXT in the late 1980s and early 1990s I was able to keep the condition under control and out of sight. It was most difficult to suppress the visible symptoms first thing in the morning, but I made a habit of getting up early and taking my first medication at 6.30 so that by 8 my body was ready for the day ahead.

In Part I of this book, I recall all the stressful confrontations and late-night negotiations that took NEXT to the brink and back. But you will find I rarely mention my illness or how it affected me. That may seem surprising. I thought about the disease every morning when I woke up and had to get my body to the starting line for the day – a process that I will talk frankly about in Part III. But the simple truth is that, thanks to medication and an element of mind over matter, it never affected my performance or my determination to find solutions to NEXT's problems and rebuild the company into a winning business.

Eventually, after many years of maintaining the subterfuge, I decided that the moment was right for the two David Joneses to meet in public – when I was about to move on from chief executive of NEXT to deputy chairman in 2001, and when I realised there was another career opportunity in front of me as a fundraiser for Parkinson's charities. But until that moment, the two really did lead separate lives.

And that made me, more than most senior executives of major high-street companies, very disinclined to step into the spotlight and talk about myself. In some ways it was a reticence that came naturally. In my early days, I had nothing much to shout about.

In the GUS group – first as finance director of Kays of Worcester, where my career began, then as managing director of the British Mail Order Corporation in Manchester – I did not consciously set out to make a name for myself. I was not especially ambitious, and I certainly had no sense of being destined for the top. I worked hard because it gave me a sense of achievement; I did not worry about what other people said or thought about me.

And my preference for a low profile was prompted by another medical problem, which I found out about some years before the Parkinson's diagnosis. I was hard of hearing in both ears. I have never worn hearing aids and have a self-taught ability to lip-read, but nevertheless I often avoided corporate banter and point scoring with competitors simply because I was not sure I could hear everything that was being discussed.

My attitude did not change when I moved from GUS to Grattan. I did not want to make a song and dance about success there until it had actually been achieved. The proof of that achievement was not to be found in glowing headlines, Sunday newspaper profiles and chat-show appearances, but in the fact that I managed to persuade George Davies, the creator of NEXT, to buy Grattan in 1986 for £350 million.

NEXT's founding philosophy was very different to mine. The runaway success of the brand had been built around the extraordinarily high profile of George Davies himself. That worked for a while, in the boom years of the mid-1980s. George was a star of the High Street, the City and the tabloid press.

But every business leader should learn that if the media build you up and place you on a pedestal, they will bring you down with a bang when it suits them to do so. The cult of George Davies created the NEXT phenomenon, but in the end it took the company to the edge of bankruptcy.

For a long time I was reluctant to talk in public about how we brought NEXT back from that edge. In the fiercely competitive world of retailing, there was no reason to give our rivals too much insight into what we were doing. I have declined any number of invitations to take part in seminars or make speeches at retailing conferences.

But there were other reasons to refuse, besides commercial caution. Speeches are time-consuming to prepare and, for me, not very enjoyable to deliver. I believe a chief executive's time should be used for the benefit of his company, not to enhance his own standing on the conference circuit.

And I declined many invitations simply because I did not want anyone in the audience to detect the symptoms of Parkinson's. The more I was exposed to the public, the more likelihood there was that people would realise I was not 100 per cent physically fit, and rumours would spread.

As much as I tried, as much as I felt on top of the job within myself, I could not always hide the effects of the disease: the shaking on my right side, the slow movements and the blank facial expression, which is particularly upsetting when I see myself in photographs.

So there were strong personal as well as business reasons to keep my profile low during NEXT's recovery period. That policy was so successful that if you ask most people today who they associate with NEXT they will still say 'George Davies', even though he left the company more than 16 years ago after a relatively short reign.

Nevertheless, I really did not mind that the wider public outside the retail trade and the City had no idea who I was. I was amused by one episode when I was asked by a director of a German printing company to speak about NEXT Directory – our home shopping catalogue – at a seminar in Düsseldorf. Against my usual instincts I accepted his invitation, because his company had done me a big favour when one of Robert Maxwell's printing companies had let me down.

I arrived at the conference in good time and took my seat in the front row, nervously awaiting my turn. My nerves got decidedly worse when I realised that there were 2000 people in the hall. When it was time for me to go on, the chairman of the conference introduced me: 'I would now like to welcome a man from the United Kingdom who began his career in Kays of Worcester in 1960...'

He summarised my CV very precisely, in German-accented English, and ended with a flourish: 'Please give a warm German welcome to Mr George Davies!'

Well, George can keep the fame. But I have the satisfaction of knowing that under my stewardship NEXT's stock market value increased by over 120 times, from a low of £25 million to a high of £3.5 billion, and that NEXT today is one of the most respected and admired names in British retailing.

That is my reward, and it is also my incentive to put reticence aside at last and tell my story. Doing so is inevitably an egotistical exercise, but it is also an opportunity to write about many other characters besides myself. In one sense, the two biggest characters in this book are not the people but the companies, NEXT and Grattan, which have occupied the last 24 years of my working life.

Of the two, NEXT is clearly the star of the show, as an iconic brand name at the cutting edge of fashion retailing and the focus of an epic corporate drama. But Grattan deserves recognition too, for what I might call the best supporting role. As a long-established home shopping business, serving millions of customers well, it is perhaps a more workaday character – but when the critical moment came it was Grattan that saved NEXT, and for that I shall always be grateful.

But companies are made up of people, and this book is also an opportunity to pay tribute to all those who have helped, educated and inspired me along the way. First of these is the Wolfson dynasty. My career has been intertwined, for almost 45 years, with four members of this remarkable family, representing three generations. First there was Sir Isaac Wolfson, the builder of the Great Universal Stores empire and one of the greatest British entrepreneurs of the twentieth century. As a young man at Kays, one of GUS's mail-order subsidiaries, I fell under Sir Isaac's spell, listened to his stories and learned from his wisdom.

More importantly, in the 1960s and 1970s at Kays and its sister company British Mail Order Corporation, I worked alongside Isaac's nephew David – now Lord Wolfson of Sunningdale – who I can unequivocally describe as my business hero and the possessor of the best commercial brain I have ever encountered. In mid-career we went our separate ways: he went into politics as one of Margaret Thatcher's closest aides, I moved from GUS to Grattan. But we came together again as chairman and chief executive of NEXT in 1989, and I believe we made a formidable combination. And we were joined there by David's son Simon, an outstanding young man who followed me as chief executive and is now taking NEXT to new heights of success.

The fourth Wolfson in my story is Isaac's son Leonard – now Lord Wolfson of Marylebone – who was my ultimate boss at GUS. Leonard (as I shall call him here for simplicity, though I never called him less than 'Mr Leonard' or 'Sir Leonard' to his face) falls into a different category of career influences, along with George Davies a few years later. I had my differences with both of them, but I certainly do not bear either of them any ill-will. We had good times together as well as difficult times, and I learned important lessons from both – though some of the lessons were negative rather than positive.

There is one more person who has been a constant friend, partner and influence for good in my life: my wife Ann. We have been together since she came to work temporarily at Kays in the summer of 1967. One day a rumour went round that there was some 'new talent' in the post room and I made a detour on my way to the canteen to find out. There were several pretty girls there, but one in particular caught my eye, so I made sure I was behind her in the queue at tea-break time. She told me that she had just finished college and was working for pocket money before starting a teaching career in Bristol. I invited her to have dinner with me the next day, 24 August, and I picked her up from her parents' home in Worcester in my white Vauxhall Viva.

I remember every detail of that evening, including the vodka and tonic, the prawn cocktail and the steak and chips that she ordered. Six months later we were engaged, and a year to the day after our first date we got married at St Barnabas Church in Worcester. We had three fine children – Alison in 1970, Richard in 1973, Stuart in 1974 – and became a strong and close family unit. Ann had to give up teaching to look after the kids, but has always been tremendously supportive of my career.

She accepted that my job is desperately important to me, even when at times I put it ahead of the family. She shared the excitement of my successes, put up with my long working hours and absences, and upped sticks without complaint when my career took us first from Worcester to Manchester and then (with a bit of complaint) from Manchester to Yorkshire. When times were tough in our early years together, and at the lowest point of NEXT's fortunes when I was close to personal bankruptcy, she was a brilliant family finance director. And she has helped me every day for over 20 years to cope with Parkinson's.

I owe Ann everything. She and the children, and David and Simon Wolfson and the team of loyal colleagues who moved with me from GUS and Grattan, are (if you'll forgive the pun that provides the title of this book) the people who have been next to me all these years.

Finally – or almost finally – there are two people who inspired me to write a book about it all. The first was my father, though the book he made me want to write was not this one. Dad lived with us at Ilkley for the last 11 years of his life, and about two weeks before he died in March 1995 he asked if he could borrow my pocket tape recorder. In his last few days he recorded many stories about his own life.

When I plucked up the courage, months later, to listen to the tapes, I felt an intense sadness and shame because there were so many things I did not know about my parents: about their own childhoods, how they met, their struggle when Dad was unemployed and much more. I decided there and then to write my own story one day, so that at least my children and grandchildren would know a little more about my life. What I originally wrote was intended only for them; it was a very personal chronicle and there were only ever three copies of it, which I put in a safe place with the intention of presenting them to the children on some appropriate occasion.

But the person who inspired me to go public, and to write a different kind of book, was Michael J. Fox, the Hollywood actor. Ann and I were in Florida in 2002 for an Easter golfing holiday when I read his autobiography, *Lucky Man*. Like me, Michael was diagnosed with Parkinson's in his thirties and kept it a secret from all but his closest friends for several years. The frustrations, fears and shame he described, and the relief he felt when he finally told everyone that he had Parkinson's, uncannily mirrored my own experience.

The most important thing about his book was the simple fact of talking openly about the disease. The majority of sufferers do not want to admit they have it; they think of it as an embarrassment, a thing that makes you shuffle and shake and makes other people think you're drunk or incapable of controlling yourself.

Michael triumphed over all that. Like me, he had to battle with his symptoms every morning. But for as long as was physically possible for him, he maintained a screen persona that was smart, wisecracking and upbeat, and made him a role model for a generation of American youngsters. By telling his story he undoubtedly encouraged other Parkinson's sufferers to face the world with more confidence.

I thought perhaps, in a smaller way, I might be able to do the same. I decided to turn this book into an opportunity to raise money for Parkinson's charities, an activity to which I have devoted increasing amounts of my time in recent years. But I thought the best way to do that was to write about David Jones the Parkinson's sufferer only in this Introduction and again in Part III, where I will draw together all the important strands of my experience. In between those two bookends, I decided to write primarily about what the other David Jones – the one who refused to let Parkinson's ruin his life – has learned from a long career in business and entrepreneurship. By focusing my energy on business, I believe that I conquered a disease of which I may never be cured. That is where I want to focus the central energy of this book.

Before I move on to the meat of the story, let me introduce one more hero. I first saw him on television in September 1958, when I was a teenager with two O-levels, no prospects and no idea of what I wanted to do with my life. He was a young American singing sensation with big ears and dark glasses. Though I never met him, his voice entered my soul and he became my lifelong idol, so much so that my family and friends will always associate him with me.

Even my children, before they were 10, could sing all the words of his songs in the order that they were sung on his *Greatest Hits* album, from 'Only the Lonely' to 'Pretty Woman'.

He was, of course, Roy Orbison, and to me he was the greatest singer who ever lived. He had more than his fair share of ill-luck and tragedy to overcome in his own life, and he died of a heart attack, aged 52, after a concert in Nashville, Tennessee on Tuesday, 6 December 1988 – two days before I became chief executive of NEXT.

'Oh, DC, I've got bad news!' my secretary June greeted me as I got out of the lift on the fourth floor of the Grattan head office in Bradford on Wednesday, 7 December. DC was how she always addressed me. I had just returned from a tense meeting in London.

'I've lost my job?' I stammered.

'No!'

'Something's happened to my father?'

'No!'

'The dog's died?'

'No!'

'For Christ's sake, June – what's happened?'

'It's Roy Orbison. He's dead!'

It was a strange, sad distraction in the most crucial week of my life – a week of high tension that came to a climax the following evening when the board of NEXT, in a brief, formal meeting carefully orchestrated by lawyers, fired George Davies as chairman and chief executive and asked me to take charge in his place.

To understand why it made sense at that moment – why it was vital for NEXT's survival – to switch from George's charismatic, never-a-dull-moment style of leadership to my low profile and safe pair of hands, we need to trace the whole story of retailing, home shopping, consumer behaviour and City psychology during the 1980s. To set the scene, let me start by telling, for the first time, the full story of George's departure.

Part I

1986–1996

Rescuing NEXT

Chapter 1

'Gentlemen, we have a deal!'

George Davies and I got on very well for the first year or so after NEXT and Grattan merged in the summer of 1986. But by the beginning of December 1988 we were barely speaking to one another. In between those two dates, the whole British consumer economy turned from soaring boom to almost bust. What happened at NEXT was a part of that wider story and – thanks to some decisions that had more to do with ego than with economic trends – a particularly extreme example of it.

It was Roger Seelig who first suggested I should meet George. Roger was a star corporate financier at Morgan Grenfell, Grattan's merchant bankers. He and George Magan and their team had taken Morgan Grenfell to the top of the City league with deals such as Dixons' bid for Currys. They were very aggressive not only in taking potential deals to their corporate clients, but in pinching major clients from other, more traditional merchant banks. In the boom year of 1986 Morgan Grenfell acted in more than 100 takeovers, worth over £15 billion.

Roger was probably the cleverest deal maker in the City, but he was about to become notorious as one of the defendants in the series of criminal trials that resulted from Guinness's £2 billion bid for the Distillers Company, the Scotch whisky and gin makers. Roger was accused of fraud – alongside Patrick Spens, who comes into this story in a moment – for setting up a scheme to support Guinness's share price during the bid. When he came to trial in 1991 he conducted his own defence, but fell ill with depression and the judge decided the case could not continue.

Although Roger eventually cleared his name, his business career did not recover. As far as I was concerned, however, he was someone who never gave me any bad or dubious advice and who had a real grasp of business issues as well as a drive to do deals that made big fees for his firm. He understood what I meant when I told him in early 1986 that I felt I had taken Grattan as far as it could go as a traditional, big-catalogue home shopping business, and that I didn't know what we were going to do for our next trick.

By then Grattan was making profits of over £30 million and was valued on the stock market at around £200 million. As I will describe in more detail in Chapter 8, we had come a long way since I took over in January 1981, when the capital value was around £25 million. My personal reputation was quite high with institutional shareholders and retail-sector analysts. But what the City demanded in those go-go days was continuing excitement and growth. To keep up the momentum for Grattan, it was obvious that we either had to expand the mail-order business (for example, I tried in vain to persuade Empire Stores, also based in Bradford, to merge with us) or tie up with a high-street retailer to provide them and us with a new dimension – a truly sophisticated home shopping alternative.

The High Street, like the City, was a rapidly changing scene in the mid-1980s, but Marks & Spencer – then under the leadership of Derek Rayner, who was the first non-family chairman of M&S and was also Margaret Thatcher's adviser on efficiency – was still a great name. Even if with hindsight you could say that its store designs were beginning to look a bit dated alongside a new wave of retailers of which NEXT was one, M&S was still beloved by every British middle-class shopper from Margaret Thatcher downwards for its reliability and value for money. So my first move was to prepare a paper on why Marks & Spencer ought to buy Grattan.

Grattan was not a clothing brand: it was a 'delivery' brand. People shopped with Grattan because the catalogue was attractive and the prices were reasonable; it was easy to buy goods on credit and our very good stock and office systems ensured that most orders were despatched immediately. And the product – if not especially exciting – was acceptable. But in the new consumer mood of the 1980s – when everyone suddenly had credit cards and cash to spend, and vast new shopping centres were being built in every city – traditional mail order looked a bit dowdy. It was the beginning of the end of the era of the profitable 1000-page mail-order catalogue, although home shopping was destined to make a spectacular comeback in the twenty-first century thanks to the development of the internet; of which more later.

Even if the business model belonged to an earlier era, a well-run mail-order firm like Grattan still had tremendous operational advantages, and if we could put them together with a stronger product brand we would have an almost unique business opportunity. I put my case to Marks & Spencer, but unfortunately I could not secure an appointment with anyone important there. I had two meetings with its 'corporate strategy' department, but that was a complete waste of time. I don't believe the 'wet behind the ears' young graduates who listened impatiently to my carefully prepared proposal really understood what home shopping was.

I often wonder what might have happened to Grattan, NEXT and Marks & Spencer if I had been able to talk to one of the top M&S people – Derek Rayner or Rick Greenbury. I am certain that NEXT Directory would never have been launched, because it was Grattan that was going to provide the operational expertise that was so vital to its success. I am also certain that my career would have been very different, and less exciting. But the real loser was M&S: it tried several times after that to make home shopping work, but never really got out of the starting blocks.

So George Davies, at Roger Seelig's suggestion, was my second call. Before I actually approached him, I decided first to find out a little more about him. He had started out as a merchandiser at Littlewoods, the mail-order giant in his native Liverpool – where as a lad he had been given a trial by Bill Shankley to play for the great football club – and from his earliest days he had a fascination with clothing design. In the mid-1970s he had helped turn around Pippa Dee, a Burton-on-Trent-based lingerie 'party-plan' operator (which means that it sold its merchandise through home parties, like Tupperware) that had at one stage been close to bankruptcy.

George seems to have got into a power struggle at Pippa Dee in which he eventually lost out. When the company was bid for by another clothing business called Amber Day – which became better known a few years later after Philip Green took control of it – George was opposed to the bid, but a majority of Pippa Dee's share-holders accepted it, and the new owners pushed George out. By then, however, he was already talking to an old-established menswear chain – J. Hepworth & Sons – about setting up a womenswear business for them. This was the concept that blos-somed so spectacularly as NEXT.

Hepworths was a sleepy old menswear business; alongside Montague Burton it was one of several Leeds-based multiple tailors that had prospered on the huge growth of the off-the-peg suit mar-ket before the Second World War and demob suits afterwards, and at its peak it had 350 branches around the country. By the late 1970s it had started to fall well behind the times in fashion terms. Except that somewhere, someone in the business had the bright idea of recruiting George Davies to launch a womenswear range for it in a chain of stores called Kendalls – based in Leicester, and best known for rainwear under the slogan 'Kendalls keeps you dry' – that Hepworths was about to buy from Combined English Stores.

George said it was County Bank (the merchant banking arm of NatWest) that first suggested his name to Hepworths, having been impressed by the way he stood up to Amber Day. But he must also have had the support of a key member of the Hepworths board in Terence Conran, who has been a major influence on British retailing and design, and latterly the restaurant scene, for the past 30 years and was to play a big role in the early development of NEXT. Terence was chairman of Hepworths from shortly after George arrived in 1981 until 1983, when he handed over to Michael Stoddart and moved on to concentrate on his own Habitat–Mothercare business.

So George was given the opportunity to pitch to the Hepworths board members. He told them that the British High Street offered stylish clothes that were expensive, or unstylish clothes that were cheap, but not much in between. The gap was for a brand that was both stylish and affordable, which he famously described as being 'between Jaeger and Marks & Spencer'.

Hepworths bought George's idea, and he and his team from Pippa Dee (including Liz Devereaux-Batchelor, who four years later became George's second wife) moved over in March 1981. They set to work on creating the NEXT look, influenced by European brands such as Mondi from Germany, Hermès from Paris and most significantly Benetton from Italy, which in those days had only two small shops in Britain, in Knightsbridge and South Molton Street, but with long queues outside them every day.

Benetton's shop designs – with a relatively narrow range of clothes folded on shelves around the perimeter of the store, rather than on conventional racks in the middle, and striking window displays that did not use dummy models – were an important influence on the shop design that George developed for NEXT with a team from Conran Design. As for the name itself, it was suggested by one of the Conran people, John Stephenson, and George immediately recognised the brilliance of it: 'it represented both the immediacy of fashion and the sense of the future.' And it was not feminine, so it did not rule out a move into menswear in due course.

The first seven NEXT stores opened in February 1982 and were an immediate success. The chain began to grow at a phenomenal rate, and in the summer of 1983 George became group retail director, responsible for Hepworths' own stores as well as for NEXT. Within two years he had revamped them all as NEXT For Men, launched NEXT Interiors and started to look in all sorts of other new directions. He had commissioned a new headquarters complex for NEXT at Enderby near Leicester, had become group chief executive, and had been named *Guardian* Young Businessman of the Year for 1985. He had become a star – and he behaved like one, revelling in all the media attention.

Meanwhile NEXT, like Grattan, was under pressure from analysts and fund managers to keep up its amazing growth rate. George opened more and more stores – sometimes very close to each other. In 1985 he also made his first major acquisition, of 142 Lord John and Werff fashion shops for £11 million from the Raybeck Group, right under the nose of Stephen Marks of French Connection. Finally, in 1986, his triumph was complete when he changed the name of Hepworths to NEXT plc.

This whirlwind of the retail scene was the George Davies I met for the first time in a private room at Brown's Hotel in Albemarle Street on Thursday, 15 June 1986. My wife Ann and I had been to Ascot Races for Ladies' Day and we had left early so that I could attend the meeting. I was the only person there from Grattan; with George were Robert Cooper, his finance director, and John Roberts, his corporate director. Roger Seelig was there to introduce us.

We exchanged pleasantries about our respective careers, and I was impressed that George seemed to have done at least as much homework about me as I had about him. Basically, we got on very well. I explained the situation at Grattan and my idea of linking up with a high-street brand to start a new home shopping catalogue. George's mail-order background at Littlewoods meant that he immediately understood the importance of having the good back-up systems that Grattan clearly offered. We agreed to think it over and meet again the following week.

I found out over the weekend that George had been talking to Roger and to John Richards of County NatWest, who was considered to be the City's best retail analyst, about a possible tie-up between our two companies. Roger no doubt smelled a lucrative deal, and John Richards could see the advantages to be gained by merging two businesses with management teams that complemented each other so well.

Back at Grattan's headquarters in Bradford I discussed the meeting with my two closest friends and colleagues, John

Whitmarsh and Dick Swain. They both agreed that it was worth taking the discussions further, though John was not convinced that we should go for a full merger with NEXT. He was more attracted by the idea of launching a new catalogue as a joint venture. The following Tuesday John Whitmarsh, Peter Lomas (Grattan's finance director) and I went down to Leicester to meet George and his colleagues.

One reason that George had moved the head office of NEXT from Leeds to Enderby on the outskirts of Leicester was to break away from Hepworths' old culture. It was a good decision, and there was a real buzz around the place. At that stage the offices were in an old warehouse complex, but a dramatic new building was almost completed on an adjacent site.

We talked in broad terms about how a merger could be structured and agreed that – as NEXT was the bigger company in terms of market value and profile – it would have to be done by means of NEXT acquiring Grattan's shares. A price of around £5 a share was lobbed into the conversation, but I explained that we would need to talk to Roger Seelig before we went any further. This was the first problem, because Roger wanted to act for NEXT on the basis that it would be the dominant partner in the merger and he wanted to retain it as his client afterwards.

I understood his position, and asked him to suggest someone who could act for Grattan in his place. He suggested Lord (Patrick) Spens, the managing director of a smaller merchant bank called Ansbacher & Co. Patrick was a City maverick who had worked alongside Roger at Morgan Grenfell for many years until moving to Ansbacher, and had very recently been working with him on Guinness–Distillers. What they did in the Grattan–NEXT merger – though on a significantly smaller scale – was in fact not so very different from the machinations of the Guinness deal that got them into such hot water; but let me return to that in a moment.

First I had to persuade my own board that a merger was the right way forward. The Grattan board met at the end of June to discuss the proposal that we should open formal merger discussions with

NEXT, on the basis that the deal would be done by NEXT purchasing Grattan. As John Hann, the chairman, asked each director in turn for their opinion, my mind wandered back to that great 1957 Sidney Lumet film *Twelve Angry Men* – in which a murder jury is persuaded to acquit by one stubborn, doubting member – with myself in the role of Henry Fonda. By the time the chairman got round to me, the merger proposal was definitely looking like a lost cause.

Every director expressed reservations. Some of them were genuinely concerned about merging with a young company that, although incredibly successful, could turn out to be a nine-day wonder. I also sensed the inevitable concern about their individual positions. Whatever the underlying reasons, the consensus was pointing towards a joint venture to launch a new home shopping catalogue, but no merger. I said I favoured a merger, and set out to persuade them to my view.

I argued that the traditional mail-order catalogue had had its day, and that Grattan either had to link up with a high-street brand or get into the High Street on its own account. I said that we could create a new concept of home shopping in Britain that combined aspirational product with efficient systems. The High Street had moved out of the darkness of the 1970s, and this was our opportunity to do the same for home shopping.

I tried to calm their personal fears by saying that the City's main concern about NEXT was its lack of good senior managers, because it had expanded so rapidly. Our management, by contrast, was very strong, and a merger would create a lot of new openings for them. But it was my final argument that seemed to clinch it: I reminded them that our responsibility was to Grattan's shareholders, and did they believe that by our own efforts, without a merger, we could boost the share price to £5 in the foreseeable future?

A second round of voting produced a unanimous decision to continue the discussions, with a view to securing a deal that was in the best interests of our shareholders and staff. Peter Lomas and I were asked to consult Patrick Spens about how we should proceed and report back.

My first meeting with Patrick, the following day, was an interesting and unexpected experience. I thought he would go straight to the subject of the price we should ask for the Grattan shares. Instead he asked, 'Why do you want to do this deal?'

At first I was put out by the question – he wasn't there to interrogate me, he was there to represent us in the negotiations. But as it turned out, I was extremely grateful that he raised such a fundamental issue, because it forced me to explain – to a very intelligent financier who was unfamiliar with the home shopping industry – why it was better for Grattan to merge with NEXT rather than stay independent; and I think I convinced him.

He then advised us on the procedure for the deal, and finished by asking for our latest profit figures and forecast for the year to January 1987, so that he could work out overnight what price we should ask for our shares.

The Grattan board reconvened the following day, and Patrick recommended that the price we should seek was 21 NEXT shares for every 10 Grattan shares or a cash alternative of £5.40. The NEXT share price was standing at £2.50 and Grattan's was at around £3.50, before rumours that we were talking to someone about a merger started to push them upwards.

Immediately after the second board meeting, John Hann, Peter Lomas and myself went to a house that NEXT owned at Oakley Street in Chelsea to meet Michael Stoddart, George Davies, Robert Cooper, John Roberts and Roger Seelig. In the taxi on the way to the meeting John Hann said that, as I had had most of the dialogue with George, it should be my role to play the hard man this time. So far I had generally been the nice guy, given that I firmly believed that the merger was the best way forward for Grattan and that the £5 per share we had initially talked about was a good price. My playing the tough guy at this stage turned out to be a good tactic.

After the formalities we got down to business. I announced that after discussion with our merchant bankers we would be asking for a price of 21 NEXT shares for every 10 Grattan shares, with a cash alternative of £5.40. George stayed quiet. Roger Seelig said that the price was too rich and we would have to compromise. Robert Cooper said that he could not possibly advise the NEXT board to pay that price – it represented a price–earnings ratio of over 20 times historic post-tax profits. But I stuck firmly to my guns, and to my utter amazement George suddenly left the meeting saying that he had had enough. I was in no doubt that his tactics had been pre-arranged, just as mine had.

Michael Stoddart left soon after George and John Roberts took over, obviously working to instructions. Champagne was served, and we were treated to a pocket history of NEXT and its inspirational founder, the retail genius whom everyone in the company would willingly die for. After two hours of champagne and 'we love George', the meeting broke up with John telling us that he would be in touch. We heard nothing for a week and I honestly thought that George had changed his mind.

Meanwhile, news that NEXT and Grattan were talking leaked out and our share price went up to £4.50. The retail analysts and the financial press gave the idea a resounding thumbs-up. One paper called it 'a marriage made in heaven'; another said it was 'the combining of the two best talents in retail'; a third commented that 'NEXT will benefit from the expertise of the Grattan management' – this was a theme adopted by many of the analysts, who were concerned that NEXT was growing too quickly and lacked the depth of management and the infrastructure to cope with George's ambitions. Thankfully, it confirmed what I had said to the Grattan board about the merits of a merger.

At last a call came from George on Monday, 15 July to say that if we were still interested we should meet at Ansbacher's offices at 2 p.m. the following day. We were still interested, I replied, and we would be there. Before he put the phone down he added jovially: 'but don't think that you are going to get more than £5!'

At a pre-meeting with Patrick Spens we agreed our shopping list. We were holding out for our price of 21 NEXT shares for 10 Grattan shares with a £5.40 cash alternative, and we wanted all the share options granted to Grattan employees to be honoured either in NEXT shares or in cash, whichever the option holder preferred. We wanted the transaction to be presented as a merger, and were ready to insist that there should be equal numbers of NEXT and Grattan executives on the main board plus John Hann as a non-executive director.

The full teams from Grattan and NEXT faced each other across Ansbacher's table. A new addition to the NEXT team was David Mayhew, a partner of Cazenove & Co., the stockbrokers. Mayhew's views on what terms institutional investors would accept were highly respected. He had been another player in the Guinness affair and some time after this was briefly arrested, but no charges were ever brought against him and his career was unaffected.

Seelig and Spens did all the talking, though in practice there was not much to be said. Spens recited our price terms, and Seelig replied that the deal was not 'doable' at that level. Spens said that it had to be that or nothing, and Seelig referred to Mayhew, who said that with the NEXT share price at £2.60 the £5.40 cash alternative was not possible. I expected Spens to back off a little, but he would not budge.

Seelig then recommended a short break and the advisers all walked out, leaving the two company teams huddled in opposite corners of the room. About 30 minutes later, the advisers returned in a much more cheerful frame of mind. NEXT's share price had gone up to £2.65, so £5.40 was now possible after all, Seelig told us. 'Gentlemen, we have a deal!'

'That was lucky,' I thought at the time. But a little later, when I studied the intricacies of the Guinness affair, I realised that luck had probably played no part in our deal at all. What had happened was that Patrick Spens had asked an investment company called TWH to go into the market and buy NEXT shares, so that their price would go up to the level that made the deal possible for the underwriters.

Some time after the merger had been completed, I was told there would be an invoice coming to Grattan to reimburse the investment company for their loss on this transaction. I made it very clear that I would not accept the invoice or be party to any such arrangement – and that was the last I heard of it. In the Guinness case, a very similar arrangement was made with investors to support Guinness's shares. But in that instance it was Guinness itself that stood behind an indemnity against any losses the investors might make, which was tantamount to secretly buying its own shares and was considered illegal.

I guess that the purchase of NEXT shares, with the objective of increasing the share price marginally to a level that allowed the deal to be done, was also technically the wrong side of the line: at least an infringement of the spirit of the City Takeover Code, and possibly illegal.

But the best defence of the Grattan–NEXT deal was that it was actually good for everyone involved. Grattan's shareholders received 21 NEXT shares for every 10 Grattan shares they owned – and as the NEXT share price was £2.65 on the day we did the deal, that was equivalent to £5.56 per share. If the shareholders wanted cash, they got the £5.40 we had asked for, compared with a market price of £3.20 on the day I had my first meeting with George, and 54p on 1 January 1981 when I became the chief executive of Grattan. In five years we had multiplied the capital value of Grattan 14 times over, from £25 million to £350 million!

It was good for Grattan's management, because it was presented to the world as a merger of equals, with equal representation on the main board: the three directors from NEXT were George Davies, Robert Cooper and John Roberts, and the three from Grattan were John Whitmarsh, Peter Lomas and myself. Our employees were very happy too, because George had been very fair in agreeing to pay cash for all the share options they held. On the day the cheques were distributed, the manager of Barclays Bank in Bradford phoned me to ask what was going on, because his intake of cash that day had broken all known records.

As for me, I had been treated well too. I was appointed deputy chief executive at a salary fixed at 80 per cent of George's. And I had a pleasant surprise when a sparkling blue Bentley arrived as my new company car – enabling me to give my father the thrill of his life when I picked him up and drove him to the local pub in it.

I had given Michael Stoddart a commitment that I would not sell any of the NEXT shares that I received in exchange for my Grattan shares – so that when I received a tax bill on the transaction of £1 million, I arranged a bank loan secured against my shareholding, which was valued at £3 million. It was an arrangement that would come back to haunt me when NEXT was in very low water a few years later, but at the time it made me feel like a wealthy man.

The more immediate irony was that on the Friday before I met George for the first time I had sold 20,000 Grattan shares at around £3 each in order to pay for an apartment I had bought in Sotogrande, Southern Spain. If I had delayed the sale by four weeks I would have received £5.40 – but when the share sale appeared in the circular to shareholders it was evidence of the speed with which the deal was done, and the fact that I had not anticipated it to my own advantage.

Finally, the deal was good for George and his team too. Without Grattan's mail-order know-how, George could not have moved forward with the launch of NEXT Directory, an idea to which he had become passionately committed. And he said at the time that he was excited about working with me, because we seemed to get on so well and because I had disciplines that filled some of the gaps in his management skills.

Perhaps most of all, the deal kept George in the headlines, where he loved to be. He was hailed on all sides as a shining product of the free-enterprise Thatcher era. He was bracketed with Ralph Halpern of Burtons, Terence Conran and Gerald Ratner the jeweller, but he was probably more widely respected and admired than any of them because he was seen to be the local lad from the provinces who had taken on the retail establishment and beaten it, and had contributed to an epoch-making change in British shopping habits.

So we were all carried away with the euphoria of it all, and intoxicated by the ever-increasing share price. If you worked at NEXT you felt you were really somebody. Our product training events were an example of the mood. Every six months we would bring all the store managers to Enderby to show them the new season's ranges, which of course we all said were 'fantastic'. After three days of saying 'fantastic' to each other there would be a gala dinner and party, the main purpose of which was to pay homage to the god-like presence of George himself, who would present awards to the best-performing store managers.

I really enjoyed those first 12 months of the merger. Grattan was continuing to perform well, and I was given the responsibility for Club 24, a wholly owned subsidiary of NEXT that provided finance for a number of retailers, the main one being Dixons. The Grattan computer team was given the responsibility for all of the group's systems. We had begun planning for the launch of the first NEXT catalogue, and were well on target to have the operational side ready for the start date in 1988. We were a little concerned that the selection of product for the catalogue was behind schedule and the creative cost was escalating, but 'Don't worry, David', I was repeatedly told, 'George knows what he is doing.'

And there was no doubt that in his core business, George really did know what he was doing. He was a risk taker, but his feel for the clothes that NEXT customers wanted, and how to sell to them, was remarkable. At every opportunity I travelled with him to look at our stores – and our competitors – and listened and learned as much as I could about the art of retailing.

In fact I was enjoying myself so much that it did not really concern me that I never received a copy of the NEXT Retail monthly profit figures. Nor did it bother me to be continually told that NEXT had a unique culture, with everyone working 24 hours a day, seven days a week because they just loved working for George.

And George was eager to make the business even more exciting: there were deals going on all around us – Burtons had bought Debenhams and Habitat–Mothercare had got together with British

Home Stores – and George was anxious not to be shoved out of the spotlight. For a while he had House of Fraser in his sights, but when that came to nothing he turned his attention to another target. We were still in honeymoon mode in May 1987 when he decided to bid £340 million for Combined English Stores (CES) – which with hindsight, was the moment it all started to go wrong, for George and for NEXT.

CES consisted of a number of different businesses that had been thrust together with very little logic. It included a chain of chemist stores, a carpet wholesaler, two large chains of jewellery stores – Zales, which was a relatively upmarket brand, and Collingwood & Weir's, which was more downmarket – plus two camping holiday operators, a chain of accessory stores, a textile importer, a chain of ladies' fashion stores and a few sweetshops. Its attraction was that it had a large number of prime retail sites. The best ones traded as the Paiges fashion chain, which had once been owned by GUS but was now jointly owned by CES. But the main reason we became interested in actually bidding for it was because Gerald Ratner wanted it, and George did not want him to get it.

Ratner actually got as far as announcing that his bid for CES had been accepted, but George called a board meeting on Bank Holiday Monday to see whether we could offer a better price. Again George turned to Roger Seelig for advice, even though he was under the shadow of official enquiries into the Guinness affair and our merchant bankers were now Lazards. Roger advised him to try to buy a 17 per cent stake in CES held by Warburg Asset Management – and the famous Carol Galley of Warburg, at that time the City's most powerful woman, agreed to sell it to him.

It was a fascinating battle, which NEXT won because not only did we offer a higher price, but Gerald Ratner had the good sense not to overpay. In fact, the only winners were the shareholders of CES, who received £340 million for a company that made a profit after tax of £15 million – a price–earnings ratio of 22 times, which became more like 30 when you stripped out some of the creative accounting.

And in order to fund the acquisition, NEXT issued two convertible Eurobonds totalling £148 million. These carried a low rate of interest and could be converted into ordinary shares at a certain price after five years. If NEXT's shares did not reach that price, the bonds were repayable at par plus an additional cost equal to the underpayment of interest from the date of issue. Little did any of us realise in those euphoric times the impact these Eurobonds would eventually have on the future of the company.

But still, there were some amusing stories about the CES acquisition. My car was off the road being repaired – someone had driven into the back of it outside Grattan – so I borrowed a new Daimler that had recently been acquired by Murray Gordon, the chairman of CES. This car had every possible extra: when I switched on the ignition for the first time a very sexy voice said: 'I'm ready!'

And CES's portfolio of companies turned out to include a small importer called J. Teale & Co., run by a delightful old man of 92 called Leon Aelion, whom I had known in my days at Kays. When he was told that NEXT was taking his business over, he rang to greet me and tell me that he was very well but a little concerned about his future!

During the battle for CES, George and I presented a united front. The board backed his decision to go ahead with the bid, so I cannot put all the blame on him for what went wrong afterwards, but I think even at that stage our relationship had started to go sour, and I am not sure what it was that triggered the gradual collapse.

I can think of a number of possibilities, some of them remarkably trivial: there was a row about authorising new company cars for the Grattan directors, and another one about a woollen cardigan, which Ann had bought at NEXT in Leeds and which had literally fallen to pieces after one wash. I took it down to Leicester on my next visit and showed it to George, honestly thinking that I was doing the right thing. In GUS and Grattan we always encouraged staff to tell us of any problems they had with our own products and services, because we believed that it was better to hear it from them and put it right than to continue to upset customers. George obviously took a different view.

'How dare you criticise our merchandise?' he yelled at me. 'If the deputy chief executive is heard criticising, what will the City, the customers and the NEXT people think?'

All attempts to point out that I was telling only him about it were totally ignored.

Then I found a very serious problem at Club 24. It had originally been a 50–50 joint venture with Forward Trust, part of Midland Bank, but NEXT had recently exercised an option to buy out Forward Trust for a nominal £100,000. Club 24's main business was the funding and handling of all Dixons' credit business.

Thanks to my experience in mail order I was pretty knowledgeable about the consumer credit business, and perhaps I had a nose for hidden problems. I felt something was not quite right at Club 24, and my investigations revealed a huge underprovision for bad debts on Dixons' debtor book – for some reason the credit director did not believe in credit-scoring systems (computer-based statistical methods that assess borrowers according to personal data they are asked to supply) but preferred to rely on his own idiosyncratic judgements. It became very obvious that we were actually losing money on the Dixons account, and I had to advise the board that we would have to provide at least another £25 million to cover the potential bad debts.

George was very upset, because he genuinely believed that Club 24 was a good business. The management had let him down by entering into an agreement with Dixons that resulted in Club 24 having to provide credit to high-risk customers. I felt sorry for him on this because it was an additional problem he did not need. But unfortunately, it increased the antagonism between us.

And there were other changes that did not help matters. We had not been together long before Robert Cooper decided to return to the world of merchant banking; he had come to NEXT from Flemings. I got on well with Robert, and it was not his fault that

George had instructed him not to show me NEXT Retail's monthly accounts. The beginning of the end for Robert was at a board meeting held at Grattan early in 1988. He expressed concern at the rapid outflow of cash and implied that there was a lack of control. George took this as a direct personal criticism and subjected Robert to a long tirade, accusing him of disloyalty.

For the first time I formed the view that George did not like people questioning his authority or competence. I suppose none of us likes criticism, but one has to distinguish between open, constructive debate between boardroom colleagues and outright personal criticism. I am sure that Robert intended his comments to provoke a meaningful discussion, but unfortunately George seemed to take them very personally. The same thing was soon to happen to me when I tried to discuss the issues that NEXT faced in the latter half of 1988.

Soon after Robert Cooper realised that his future lay elsewhere and left to return to merchant banking, I was able to persuade George to appoint Peter Lomas as group finance director. Peter had joined me at Grattan in 1982, and like me he had been brought up to believe in conservative accounting.

In the 1980s many accounting devices were widely accepted that would not be accepted today. The most popular of these was 'acquisition accounting', whereby costs would be written off in the balance sheet of the acquired company before it was entered into the books of account of the acquiror company.

Another example was the absence of a provision on unsold stock at the end of a season because 'we always sold the stock for more than the cost price'. And there was the capitalisation of interest costs on property investments: interest costs were simply added to the balance sheet value of the investment, so that not surprisingly in a falling property market, the balance sheet value stood higher than the market value.

On the other hand, property trading profits were shown as retail profits: one property in London that was bought and sold within a four-month period produced a £5 million profit that somehow went into the retail profit figures. Then there was the use of sale-and-leaseback property deals to fill in the shortfall in NEXT Retail's forecast profits. As the year-end approached, the volume of freehold property sales and leasebacks would rise to reflect the extent of the shortfall. In the early 1980s Hepworths still had one of the best freehold property portfolios in the High Street, but that was certainly not true eight years later, because so much of it had been sold and leased back to create artificial profits.

In the early 1990s the accounting profession introduced measures that stopped this widespread massaging of figures. But in the glory days of the 1980s it was all accepted practice, and our auditors signed off the accounts without qualification, as did the auditors of many other public companies that used similar methods.

Nevertheless, I was beginning to get worried that the business was spinning out of control. I calculated that in an 18-month period, when the declared profits were around £100 million, the cash outflow had been over £250 million. In particular, our expenditure on shopfitting was horrendous. I knew that we had acquired a lot of good selling space when we bought CES; that was the one good thing about the deal. But I could not get my hands on any information about the cost per square foot of converting CES sites to NEXT stores.

There were two classic examples in London of very high shopfitting costs. The first was our 'flagship' store in High Street, Kensington, the largest in the NEXT chain. John Roberts refused to tell anyone the cost of the shopfit, but I found out that it was in excess of £8 million. We had a grand opening party for analysts, financial journalists and institutional shareholders. Among them I bumped into a very worried-looking John Richards of County NatWest. John, as I said, was one of the most respected analysts in the City and someone I would meet every six months to talk about the retail scene. I asked him why he looked so concerned.

He gestured around him at the opulently spacious store and said: 'It can't possibly work. It's going to lose money.'

Of course he was right, but I did not find out how right he was until much later.

Then there was the 'Department X' saga. We had acquired with CES a prime site on Oxford Street that was destined to be an entirely new shopfitting concept for NEXT. The store was heavily boarded up with 'Department X' written in large lettering on the front. Only George, the designer and the shopfitters were allowed inside. We naturally assumed that this was simply the code name for the new concept, so we were all amazed when the store actually opened under the name of Department X. Some of us had a quiet laugh when a small company in Liverpool got in touch to inform us that it had the rights to the name of our new store. The concept was based, incidentally, on the idea of having a store that looked like a warehouse, with a lot of carousels and metal racking: at the first opportunity after George had gone, we abandoned it.

Despite all the problems that were growing between George and me, we actually got on reasonably well when we were planning the NEXT catalogue. While there were many aspects of the catalogue project that I could never accept (the huge cost of design-ing the catalogue itself, for example), there were some features that I disagreed with at the time but that George was right to insist on. He was right about the name, NEXT Directory, he was right about having it printed in hard covers and bound like a book, and he was right to charge £3 for it. He was right to insist on 48-hour delivery – but not that if we failed to deliver within 48 hours, the customer had the item free!

We launched the Directory in a blaze of publicity in January 1988, and it was reasonably successful. On the plus side we recruited more customers than we had budgeted for. On the minus side, how-ever, we gave a poor service in the early weeks because we had not ordered enough stock and lead times for reordering were very long.

And we had a public disagreement at the launch. In reply to a question on the rate of returns, George said that because NEXT's merchandise was of a much better quality than you would find in a traditional home shopping catalogue, the returns rate would be no more than 10 per cent. Then I chimed in: 'Quality is not a significant reason for returns: 50 per cent of returns are because the garment is too small, 50 per cent because the garment is too big, and 50 per cent because they don't fit!'

I know that this adds up to 150 per cent, but the point I was making was that fit was by far the main cause for returns – many customers actually order two or more sizes of a garment, knowing that they will keep only the one that fits them the best. But whether my numbers added up or not, George certainly did not like being contradicted in public.

Incidentally, some years later we commissioned a research group from one of the local universities to study our womenswear sizing charts and compare them with the measurements of a large sample of our customers. It was no surprise to me when they reported that our patterns were accurate but that a majority of our customers were 'between sizes' – it follows, therefore, that the majority of ladies are wearing clothes that do not fit them! No wonder mail-order returns are high.

The acquisition of CES with its motley collection of store chains, plus the launch of the Directory, was already a huge strain on our resources of cash and management time. But we had also bought, in July 1987, a chain of 270 Dillons (mainly suburban) newsagents for £28.5 million. In April 1988 we added 140 Alfred Preedy confectioners and newsagents in the West Midlands, for another £21 million. There were simply not enough good people around in the group to run all these businesses efficiently, and the City was beginning to have serious doubts about the logic of our strategy.

In fact, George wanted to buy these chains on the whim that they could be used as delivery points for NEXT Directory customers – what he called developing NEXT's portfolio so that 'when the future came, we would be able to reach out to our customers' demands'. In practice, it was one more reason why, when the future came, it did not include George. But for the time being, he was unstoppable. We purchased a £20 million stake in British Satellite Broadcasting, when Richard Branson flew to the NEXT head office in his helicopter wearing a yellow sweater. There were two satellite channels at the time, BSB and Sky, but there was probably only room for one. We wrote off this investment in 1989, though we did get some money back when BSB and Sky eventually merged.

There was more nonsense to come. We launched NEXT the Jewellers in 50 stand-alone stores with very high shopfitting costs. Even more ridiculous, we launched a gardening catalogue, which necessitated the purchase of a garden supplies company called Suttons. At a meeting to discuss the gardening venture, I produced a budget that showed a huge loss for the first three years. But there was no discussion, just an instruction from George to increase the forecast sales figures to a level that would result in a profit!

Unfortunately, by now the relationship between George and me had deteriorated so much that we hardly spoke to each other, and it was becoming an open secret that we were not getting on. Others were beginning to suffer too. One who nearly lost his job was Peter Webber, the head of the NEXT legal department.

A report was issued that quoted NEXT as the company that had the most complaints made about it to the Advertising Standards Authority. I can understand why George was concerned, but he lashed out at John Roberts and Peter Webber without bothering to finding out first the reasons for us being named as the worst offender.

I did bother to find out. There were 15 complaints and they all related to Kaleidoscope and Scotcade, the 'direct-response' mail-order businesses (advertising products direct through the media, rather than by catalogue) run by Grattan. I called for details of all the complaints, and they turned out to be pretty bizarre. One related to a competition to win a sports car that, according to our advertising material, you could 'enjoy driving at 150 miles an hour!' So somebody had complained that we were encouraging people to break the speed limit. Another referred to a grandfather clock that was advertised as 'Made in England': some clever dick found a small part of the mechanism that was made in Germany, and protested that our advertisement was misleading.

I phoned Peter Webber at home over the weekend to tell him that the complaints were unimportant and certainly not a sacking offence. As a result we became good friends, and Peter proved to be a useful ally at Enderby.

All these issues contributed to the breakdown of relations, while out in the real world the great mid-1980s consumer boom, which had made so many of George's wilder initiatives look briefly as if they might actually pay off, was rapidly petering out. From a 1980s low point of 7.5 per cent in May 1988, Chancellor Nigel Lawson raised interest rates to 11 per cent by August and to 13 per cent in November. The rising property market, which had given people the illusion of wealth and enabled them to borrow against the value of their houses to spend in the shops, was also beginning to run out of steam.

Reflecting that trend, NEXT's results for the half-year to the end of July 1988 came as a serious disappointment to the stock market. The pre-tax profit we announced, £31 million, was only a fraction up on the previous year, and our shares fell to half of what they had been worth before the 1987 crash. Underlying the figures was a cautionary tale: we had opened too many stores and bought too many businesses – at George's instigation – and we had borrowed too much money to pay for them, on terms that were now coming back to haunt us. And the weakness in our sales figures that autumn was an indication of deeper troubles to come.

It was around this time that Liz gave birth to a baby daughter, Lucia. I remember that it was just before the British Open golf championship at which Grattan had a hospitality tent, principally for clients of Westscot, our credit referencing company. One of the well-established Grattan suppliers, anxious to make an impression on George and Liz, enquired when the baby was due, only to be told by a rather sour Liz that she had delivered three weeks earlier.

A little later, George and Liz went on holiday to a quiet hotel in the south of France and, to my surprise, I received a message from George's secretary inviting Ann and me to join them for a long weekend to 'sort out our differences' and have a few games of tennis. Despite the fact that I had not played tennis for nearly 20 years – and largely thanks to Ann, who had recently taken it up – we gave them a good game. George and I discussed NEXT's situation in a civilised way, but our views were totally opposed: George believed that we could trade our way through our problems, whereas I wanted to retrench in order to get the business under control.

Unfortunately, at the dinner table on the second evening I had 'the shakes', probably caused by taking extra drugs to enable me to run round the tennis court. I did everything I could to try to hide it, sitting on my hand, folding my arms and gripping the chair very tightly. But George noticed my discomfort and asked me what the problem was. I told him about my Parkinson's. He was the first person I told outside my close circle of friends and I am grateful that despite all the difficult times that followed, he never, to my knowledge, revealed my secret.

The weekend did not solve anything other than to confirm that we were on a collision course. The ousting of George and the rescue of NEXT were about to begin. The battle I fought to achieve that recovery – with the help of a loyal and very talented team – was the most challenging phase of my business life, and ultimately also the most satisfying.

Chapter 2

'Mr NEXT sensationally fired!'

The beginning of the final drama was signalled by a furious row between George and me over the future of the home shopping side of the group. This consisted of two distinct businesses: Grattan, which I had run for five years before the merger and which was very close to my heart, and NEXT Directory, which was very much George's new baby. Around October 1988, George announced that he proposed to bring Grattan's product range under the control of NEXT's buying team at Enderby.

The Enderby buying team was led by George's wife Liz, who had recently joined the main board. I recall Liz coming to a board meeting dressed in an off-white T-shirt, a long grey skirt and pumps, and Brian Marber, who had just joined the board as a non-executive, whispering to me: 'Is *that* our fashion director?' I was not against the concept of giving her responsibility for the Grattan product in principle, but I was very much against the timing of the move and the proposal to move all Grattan's buying departments at the same time.

I argued that NEXT's buyers at Enderby were already under pressure with the launch of the Directory and the introduction of a new retail concept – NEXT Originals – and would it not be more sensible to test the move with one small department before committing the entire business? Several hundred staff were involved, and it really was a big strategic change that required careful planning. I got nowhere, and George and Liz announced their intention to arrive in Bradford the following Monday morning to put the plan into operation.

The scene was set for a blazing argument. The week before there had already been a clash at a meeting in Enderby about progress on the Directory and Grattan catalogues. The Grattan people attending got together in the local pub beforehand and agreed to play it very low key, because it would be better to have the argument about the proposed transfer of the Grattan buying departments on our home ground in Bradford.

Unfortunately, one of the Grattan team, Dick Swain, forgot the plan. George had left the room to take a phone call when Liz raised the subject of the high returns rate on Grattan's womenswear. This was too much for Dick, who in an aggressive tone pointed out that the returns rate on womenswear in the Directory was in fact higher than the Grattan returns rate, 'because your merchandise is crap!'

When George returned, Liz was crying. She complained that Dick had called her product 'crap'. But George seemed to be preoccupied with his recent telephone conversation and just walked out of the room again. The meeting broke up in disarray and we returned to Bradford to plan our tactics for the following Monday. I held meetings with my team over the weekend to make certain that everyone knew the party line. More importantly from my point of view, we went through the pros and cons of transferring the buying function to Enderby to make sure that we really were right to resist the move. When we finished that analysis, I was even more convinced it would be a disaster.

On Sunday evening after dinner, I called an emergency board meeting of the Jones family. We had these meetings from time to time, usually to decide on where to go on holiday. I had not talked much to Ann about the growing problems at NEXT, because I did not want to worry her. But she knew me well enough to sense that I was not happy. I explained the problem to Ann and the children… and Jodie, our yellow labrador.

(Why, you might ask, was the dog present at the meeting? Well, Jodie was not just a dog, she was a very intelligent board member who had earned the right to a vote. If she raised her right front leg she was in favour of the motion, if she raised her left front leg she was against. If she raised both front legs it meant that she was hungry! Boom-boom!)

Anyway, I told them that I intended to fight George because I believed that his proposed action would do great damage to Grattan, and that I was increasingly alarmed at the general state of NEXT's profitability and cash flow. Recession was beginning to bite, interest rates were rising, our share price was drifting down and we had these two convertible Eurobonds hanging round our necks: I honestly believed that the company could go broke.

If that happened, or if I lost the argument about Grattan and lost my job, it could mean that we would have to sell Whinbrae, the home in Ilkley we all loved, and that private education for the children would have to go. My daughter Alison, as usual, assumed the role of family spokesperson: 'We understand the problem, Daddy, and we'll support you – but don't you dare lose!'

So, armed with the support of my family and the backing of my Grattan colleagues, I arrived at my office early on Monday morning to await the invaders. George and Liz arrived by helicopter at 9 a.m. and Peter, my loyal driver, picked them up from the helipad we had built in the grounds of Grattan's nearby Listerhills warehouse complex. He reported that George and Liz were in good spirits, having told him they were looking forward to 'sorting Grattan out'.

Liz went straight to the buying department. George went to the gents' washroom on the fourth floor. When he came out, he bumped into Dick Swain – which we had planned, so that George would know who and what he was up against.

'Ready for the big day?' George greeted him.

'You can't do it!' Dick responded.

'What do you mean?'

Dick then explained in no uncertain terms that Enderby was just not capable of handling the Grattan buying operation. George stormed into my office and demanded I give instructions for the move immediately. I tried to voice my concerns, but George told June, my secretary, to get the Grattan board together immediately. When they were assembled he told them bluntly that he intended to transfer the Grattan buying and merchandising functions to

Enderby, and that was that. But when he realised that without exception they supported me, his face was like thunder.

He turned his anger on Dick, criticising the marketing work he had been doing for the Directory. Dick moved towards George, and I actually thought he was going to hit him. But instead he shouted 'I don't have to put up with this shit!' and stormed out of the room. I don't know who was more surprised, George or me.

Realising that he was not going to win this battle, George too got up and stormed out, told Peter to take him to the helicopter and flew back to his home near Leicester. Unbelievably, he was so incensed by the morning's events that he actually left Liz behind.

In the excitement we all forgot about her and only realised that she had not gone back with George when she appeared in the directors' dining room at lunchtime. I could not help feeling sorry for her – but under the circumstances she declined lunch and we organised a car to take her back to Leicester. While George was still in the air, the jungle drums started working overtime. John Roberts, NEXT's group corporate director, phoned to say that George had called an urgent meeting of his closest colleagues at his house.

I related the sequence of events to John and to my amazement (at that stage, I thought of him as being very much in George's camp) he said that I was absolutely right. He did not believe that the NEXT buying team could take on Grattan's buying because they were struggling with both Retail and Directory, plus the NEXT Originals concept.

This was the very first time that John had expressed concern to me about the situation at Enderby. John was, or had been until very recently, one of George's closest friends: he had been NEXT's in-house lawyer before George employed him on a full-time basis and promoted him to the board. He had also been best man at George's wedding to Liz in December 1985.

One factor in John's change of heart may have been that his new girlfriend Anne Cunningham, who was a senior manager in the personnel department, had an insight into what was really happening and had told him that things were beginning to run out of control.

George later told an interviewer that his friendship with John and Anne had also become strained because Anne wanted to switch over to the buying side of the business, and George had resisted the move. Surprisingly, George's published diary recorded that he and Liz had been round to John and Anne's for coffee on a Sunday only ten days before this final crisis began, and that 'we all got along fine'. It seems the relationship really fell apart only in these last few days, when George began to suspect John (not without reason, it's fair to say) of disloyalty.

I had no further contact with George until later that week when all the directors attended a charity event in London – the annual swimming contest between the House of Commons and the House of Lords – which NEXT had sponsored. The format was that every swimmer was auctioned, and if you bought a winning swimmer you won 50 per cent of the total amount raised by the auction of all the swimmers in that race. George and I hardly spoke, but his temper was not helped by the fact that I won £5000 – which I quietly gave to the charity.

George, John Roberts and I flew back to Leicester in the helicopter and George invited me to stay the night at his home. He was not pleased when I said that I had already accepted a bed at John's house. That bed did not get used, because John and I stayed up all night emptying several bottles of excellent red wine talking about the situation. We agreed that I should have a frank discussion with George to try to persuade him to stand down as chairman so that we could appoint an independent non-executive chairman. I would also suggest that I should take clear responsibility for the operations and financial side of the business, and that he should concentrate on what he did best – product selection, marketing and selling.

I delivered this carefully composed speech to a very sullen George in his office the following Monday morning. But I achieved nothing in return other than the suggestion from George that we

should undo the merger between NEXT and Grattan and go our separate ways, with NEXT Directory remaining to be run as a joint venture. This threw me, because I had never even considered it a
possibility. I argued that a demerger was not possible because NEXT
was now so dependent on Grattan to run all its computer systems;
in practice, NEXT could no longer function without Grattan.

At the time this seemed absolutely right, but later when we
had to sell Grattan to fund the repayment of the Eurobonds, we
were able to solve the problem by a relatively simple agreement
with the new owners of Grattan to continue providing services to
NEXT. As it was, I believe this was the first time that George
realised how much control the Grattan contingent had of 'his'
business. I went on to say that I thought the group's financial situation was close to desperation and I felt so strongly about the
p roblems that if he did not accept we had to take urgent action, I
would have to talk to the non-executive directors – about him.
His short reply was that he believed he could trade out of the
financial crisis, and that he too would be speaking to the non-
executives – about me.

It was all becoming very messy. I knew I was right about the
problems, and what I really wanted was to find a solution that
might avoid a final showdown. I always prided myself on my ability
to find solutions to any problem, but I was kidding myself that,
when I did so, George would see the wisdom of any plan from me
to save the company.

I decided to seek outside advice, and arranged to meet the wis-
est person I could think of: my former boss Sir David Wolfson (as
he then was, before he became a life peer in 1991). I had only seen
David twice since he left GUS: once when he accompanied Mrs
Thatcher when she opened the new office at Enderby, and again
when he visited Grattan with David Sieff (one of the family directors
of Marks & Spencer) and a broken shoulder, an injury acquired
falling off a horse. We met in his office in London. He listened carefully to my story before saying, 'You'll never get away with it. He's
the darling of the City.'

After a board meeting the following week, George and I had our separate private audiences with the non-executive directors – and were both firmly told to sit down and sort out our differences. I was willing to try, but George interpreted their instruction as an endorsement of his own position and rejected my attempts to start a new dialogue. Three weeks went by and things got no better; in fact they got worse. Trade in NEXT Retail and Grattan was sluggish, and George's most recent brainwaves, NEXT the Jewellers and the Gardening Directory, were both proving to be disasters.

We did, however, have one late bit of good fortune. We were able to sell the jewellery chains that we had acquired with CES – Zales and Collingwood & Weir's – to Gerald Ratner, along with the Salisbury's accessories business, though we retained some of their best sites for either NEXT Retail or NEXT the Jewellers. We were very pleased to receive a good price for these businesses, because while Zales was a good brand, we had struggled to make Salisbury's work for us.

As the peak Christmas trading period approached, sales continued to be poor. I sat down with John Roberts, whose relationship with George had continued to deteriorate since the night I stayed at his house. We agreed that something had to be done quickly, and we decided to ask for a private meeting with Michael Stoddart, NEXT's senior non-executive director and George's predecessor as chairman. In Michael's office at Electra, I explained why I thought the problems had become so serious and my reservations about whether we could survive under George's leadership. Michael listened, asked a few questions, then asked me to leave so that he could talk to John on his own.

I left and caught the train back to Bradford. When I arrived back at my office at Grattan, June met me at the lift with the news about Roy Orbison. Then John rang to tell me that Michael was calling the board together the next day, without George and Liz, to discuss the future strategy of the company and in particular whether George had a future as its leader.

John also told me he had heard that George had organised an impromptu get-together the previous evening for the senior people below board level at Enderby. John had not been invited to the party – which George, incidentally, described in his autobiography as 'a special surprise reception for me' laid on by colleagues who 'wanted to show that in spite of our flat results, they were totally behind me'.

Evidently to make sure that was so, George had spoken privately to everyone present during the course of the evening to explain that there was a power struggle going on between him and me, and to ask them to pledge their loyalty to him. That must have put many of them in a very awkward position as to how to respond; what I did not understand until afterwards was that the majority of senior people at Enderby already believed, by this stage, that George's days were numbered. The events of the next 24 hours were by no means as unexpected to them as to the outside world.

The board duly met at 10 a.m. the next day, Thursday, at the rather anonymous offices of our legal advisers, Slaughter & May, in Basinghall Avenue in the City of London. When we convened – with representatives from Slaughters and Lazards, our merchant bankers, to guide us – the only absentee apart from George and Liz Davies was Brian Marber, who was in Hong Kong on business. Brian was a friend of George's and had made it clear that he wanted to be kept in the picture and was against any drastic action. We agreed at the start of the meeting that any decision to replace George would have to be unanimous, so Brian's absence represented a procedural problem to be dealt with when the time came.

Besides Michael Stoddart, the other non-exec present was Jeff Rowlay, who as managing director of J. Hepworth & Son, NEXT's original parent company, had been partly responsible for giving George the opportunity to create the business back in 1981.

And in addition to John Roberts, the other executive directors present were my loyal Grattan colleagues Peter Lomas and John Whitmarsh. It was one of George's beefs afterwards that by agree-ing to have three of us from Grattan on a board of nine he was playing against loaded dice, but it was not really so. We were not indulging in office politics and the three of us had not got together to put any pressure on John Roberts or the non-executives. We were all just genuinely trying to steer the company away from the disaster that we believed was inevitable if we did not make drastic changes to the way it was being run.

We debated the situation all day. By five o'clock we had agreed that George and Liz should go. The next question was how to tell them. George was in fact spending the afternoon in the City making a series of presentations to institutions – and in normal circumstances I would have been with him. Against all the odds, he was still trying to sell them the idea that it would be possible to trade out of NEXT's current difficulties, and that he was the only man who could do it.

John Roberts was asked to ring George and Liz and ask them to attend a board meeting that evening at Slaughter and May's offices. He left a message for George at the National Provident Institution, his last call of the day. George evidently recognised what the message implied as soon as it was handed to him, and thought twice about whether he should obey the summons.

But he decided to do so, and he and Liz arrived at about 8 p.m., accompanied by D. J. Freeman, a solicitor who specialised in high-level dismissal disputes, and two consultants from Price Waterhouse, who had recently been asked by George to undertake an appraisal of the NEXT business, and in particular to study the merits or demerits of keeping NEXT and Grattan together. As one journalist put it later: 'It was obvious that Davies had allowed himself to become isolated among the very top management: the people he turned to in his hour of need were outsiders.'

George's group were shown into a separate room, and we did not see them until the formal board meeting was convened around 11 p.m. Instead, Michael Stoddart – a tough City veteran whose main job was as chairman of the very successful Electra Investment Trust and who never shied away from a fight – moved between the two rooms, carrying proposals and counter-proposals back and forth.

At one stage Mr Freeman made the suggestion of a 14-day cooling-off period. Jeff Rowlay, who was becoming tired and a little irritable as the evening wore on, pounced on the suggestion as a way of getting home for the night. But this was the moment when John Roberts made his most significant contribution. He argued passionately that George had to be forced out immediately, because NEXT's situation was critical and it had to be rescued at once.

What John also meant was that if George stayed then he, John Roberts – probably more than me or John Whitmarsh or Peter Lomas – was certain to lose his job, because he was the executive director who had switched sides and given me the majority I needed to confront the non-executive directors. A week earlier, according to the diary George later published, John had actually said to him, 'I'm frightened of you. You scare me George... and I've come to a decision: if I have to go, I'll go.'

But his speech brought the consensus of the group back into line: it was George who had to go. All that remained was to obtain Brian Marber's vote, but we were unable to make contact with him in Hong Kong. It was well into the early hours of the morning there. I believe I must have taken down the phone number he gave me incorrectly, because when we dialled it to try to contact him, it turned out to be the celebrated Bottoms Up nightclub in Kowloon – providing the only moment of light relief in a very depressing day.

Anyway, it was resolved that Michael Stoddart could be appointed as Brian's alternate for the meeting, and matters proceeded towards their inevitable conclusion.

At 11 p.m. the board finally met. George was calm throughout but looked grey and uneasy, far from his usual ebullient self. Liz disguised whatever she was really feeling behind a tense smile, from time to time showing her contempt for what was happening by laughing. They both registered a formal protest that issues of such magnitude were to be dealt with at this late hour, and indicated that if they were dismissed they would immediately sue for breach of contract.

That was a threat we knew had to be faced, but a relatively minor one in the circumstances. There were seven motions to be voted on – the seventh, and the only one that was uncontroversial, being a request from Brian Marber that a further meeting should be convened as soon as he returned to London to discuss the respective roles of all the remaining directors. George and Liz asked it to be recorded that they were strongly opposed to all the other six motions, for which they felt there was 'no justification'.

The first motion was to remove George as chairman. In modern corporate governance – which I will talk more about in Chapter 10 – it is no longer acceptable for the same person to hold both top jobs as chairman and chief executive of a public company. Giving George so much power (he had succeeded Michael Stoddart as chairman in October 1987) had certainly contributed to NEXT's difficulties. If he had had a strong chairman to restrain him during that crucial year, who knows, he might not have been facing the sack.

But the more immediate tactical problem was that we needed a chairman to conduct the rest of this meeting in an orderly way and to break the news to the City afterwards. Hence the second motion, to reappoint Michael Stoddart as chairman in George's place.

Third – and without any further discussion – we voted to terminate George's employment contract with NEXT; fourth, to terminate Liz's contract; fifth, to remove George as chief executive; and sixth – the most important moment of my business career – to appoint me as chief executive in his place.

However, it was not a moment for congratulations, or recriminations. It was all very clinical. It was over in as short a time as it took to read out the motions and take a show of hands from the directors – although of course George and Liz could not actually vote on the motions that dealt with their own situations, and I could not vote for myself to become chief executive. George described the whole evening as a 'macabre' experience, and I understand what he meant. For a man who had achieved something so bold and original in the NEXT concept, and who had been fêted every day of the past five years by the retail trade, the business media and the City, it must have been absolutely sickening.

Nevertheless, the fact that we made it happen tells you how deep NEXT's problems had become. Some of those problems were to do with the state of the economy and the stock market in that winter of 1988, which saw the first signs of one of the bitterest recessions in living memory, in which many high-flying companies came to grief. But it is my firm belief that a lot of the problems were also of George's own making. There was no doubt in my mind that he had to go.

I stayed at the Royal Lancaster Hotel in London that night after the board meeting, but I did not go to bed. I made telephone calls to everyone who needed to know. John Roberts and Peter Lomas were delegated to return to Enderby to make certain there was no trouble there, while John Whitmarsh went to Grattan in Bradford, where they would probably be dancing in the streets at dawn!

In the morning Michael Stoddart and I organised a press conference, to be followed by a series of one-to-one meetings with the top retail analysts. When I was in a taxi on my way to the press conference, I noticed the headline on a newsstand placard: 'MR NEXT SENSATIONALLY FIRED'.

I had been so absorbed in the battle that I had not even thought about the publicity that would inevitably follow. At the press conference there were television cameras and radio reporters as well as the usual financial journalists, all anxious to interview me. Ann telephoned about midday to tell me that there were reporters camped outside the house. I asked Peter, my driver, to collect the family and drive them to Ann's brother's house near St Albans, where we could hide for the weekend. It was rather ironic that the editor of a daily newspaper lived next door to our hideaway and never realised the story he had missed!

I remember one question at the press conference from Michael Walters, financial editor of the *Daily Mail*: 'Who will select the product now that George has left?'

My reply probably surprised both of us: 'The same people who selected the product when he was there.' But it turned out to be largely correct: George took some of his people with him, but the senior ones whom we hoped to keep all stayed with NEXT.

After the meetings with the analysts I flew to Enderby in the helicopter with Steve the pilot. I asked him if he knew what had happened; he obviously did. I asked him if he had any problem with it. He said that he didn't. He then asked me if I wanted to learn to fly the helicopter – apparently George had nagged Steve continuously to let him have a go at the controls, and Steve had been fearful that if he did not, he would eventually be sacked. I remember his relief when I said: 'Steve, you stick to your job, and I'll stick to mine.'

Back in Enderby, one of the subsidiary board directors had attempted to organise a revolt, but got no support whatsoever. I called all the senior executives together and explained why we had taken this drastic action. Amazingly, no one seemed to be surprised by what had happened. Even more amazingly, most people seemed to be relieved.

The newspapers on Saturday and Sunday were full of the sensational news that George had been fired. In the *Sunday Telegraph*, Matthew Bond, to whom I had spoken at some length, gave a fair account of the story under the headline 'Why Davies had to go': 'Quite simply, it appears, Davies had over-ruled too many decisions, changed his mind far more than once too often and sacked too many people. He had even perhaps had too many bright ideas.'

However, the balance of opinion was that the sacking was a bad move for NEXT. The fashion press, which loved George because, almost single-handed, he had dragged clothing out of the dark days of the 1970s, was firmly on his side. Many other editors loved him just because he would always express an opinion on almost any subject. Kathryn Samuel in the *Daily Telegraph* wrote of 'shock waves' reverberating through the fashion industry: 'Davies *is* NEXT. For good or ill, it cannot be the same without him.' And Nick Bubb of Morgan Stanley, one of the top retail analysts (and still in the business today, at Evolution Securities) described it as 'throwing the baby out with the bathwater'. It was not going to be easy to convince people otherwise.

As for George himself, I have never seen him or spoken to him since that evening at Slaughter & May – though I did try to contact him, six months or so later, about an odd but in the end amusing turn of events. I was in my office at Enderby when my secretary June came in to tell me that there was a man on the telephone who would not give a name, but who said that he had some very important information for me.

I told June to put him through. The mysterious caller said that he was in Jersey, and that what he had to say was so sensitive I should ring him back on a more 'secure' telephone. I rang the number he gave me and he told me an incredible story. He had been in Germany the previous week and had been at a meeting with 'some rather dubious people', who told him that they had been hired by George Davies to investigate me using whatever methods necessary so that I could be 'disgraced'.

He went on to name some of George's close friends, who he said had been at the meeting. He added that my office, telephone and boardroom were being bugged, and that I was being followed day and night. He sounded plausible, particularly when he described my office, my car and the house that I lived in at Leicester during the week. I was inclined to believe him. I thanked him for the information, and he replied that he would ring again shortly when he had more.

I immediately hired a security firm to 'sweep' my office and boardroom, the Leicester house and, to be on the safe side, the family house in Yorkshire. Nothing was found.

The following week the man phoned me again, and went through the same procedure of asking me to call him on a secure line. This time he said that he had attended another meeting and had taken photographs of the 'conspirators', which he would let me have if I could meet him in Madrid the following week. When he mentioned that I should bring £5000 with me in cash, I began to get very suspicious. He then named some more conspirators: they were all people who were genuinely connected to George, except one – he named Marcus Agius of Lazards.

I knew immediately it had to be a 'sting': Marcus was one of the most genuine professionals I have ever met and the last one in the world who would become involved in anything like this. I thanked the caller for the information and said that I would be contacting the police. I never heard from him again.

Two months later I was having lunch with a group of businessmen at the invitation of Jeff Randall, who is now the BBC's business editor but at that time was City editor of the *Sunday Telegraph*. He related a story of how he had been set up by a mysterious man who asked him to travel to Madrid to collect some photographs.

I briefly outlined my story. Jeff started to laugh and said that George Davies had told him that he had received a call two months ago to the effect that I was carrying out an investigation on him and that if he would travel to Madrid with £5000 he could have photographs of the conspirators! I am happy to say that George did not fall for it either. I was so amused by the whole scenario that I decided to use it as an excuse to make contact with George, but he did not return my call.

I am told that even to this day he feels very bitter about what happened. In his book *What Next?*, which appeared a few months later, he said (perhaps on lawyers' advice) very little about my role, or Michael Stoddart's, in the sacking. Instead, he expressed his sadness about what he saw as John Roberts's betrayal of him, and his 'all-encompassing anger' towards the City – which throughout the golden years from 1982 to 1987 had urged him to go for flat-out growth, to open more stores, to make more acquisitions. The City had made bundles of money out of George in fees on his deals and out of the rise in NEXT's shares, but stood back and watched when the board turned against him. In the weeks after the sacking, he wrote, he and Liz received 2500 'letters of support' from customers, suppliers, members of staff and total strangers, 'but not a single one issued from the institutional investors for whom I had made so much money in the past'.

Perhaps it was the genuine shock of this rejection by the City that made him adopt such a restrained tone about me in the book. Certainly he was much less restrained when Amanda Cochrane interviewed him for *Management Week* in July 1991, two and a half years later. There he said that I 'lacked flair' and 'didn't understand the rationale of high street retailing'; that I would never 'go down to the merchandise floor' to keep in touch with the product the way he did, partly because so much of my time was taken up with internal politics.

That wasn't true, by the way: I did just as much 'management by walking about' as he did, but I tended to talk to people about stock control, pricing strategy and so on – and to get the buyers to talk to me about the product, which was their area of expertise, not mine.

In the end, George and his supporters were convinced it was all a plot. Although George himself never said so explicitly, there were even some who believed that the 'coup' against him had been planned right from the time when I first met him to talk about merging Grattan and NEXT. As Amanda Cochrane wrote, 'it was fear for their jobs which caused David Jones and others to conspire against him… That George Davies is a genius is not in doubt. The NEXT directors who fired him were spurred on by anything but the good of the company. In losing him, they despatched NEXT to the wastebin, as events are now proving.'

But that was the very opposite of the truth. As it happened, by the time the article appeared, NEXT's fortunes had already turned around – and have never looked back since. That turnaround was in large part a financial exercise, but it was also a matter of changing the culture of the business, and that meant exorcising the ghost of George.

Kathryn Samuel had been right to say that George in his heyday *was* NEXT: everything about it reflected his personality; it was a cult as much as it was a company. I told an interviewer from the *Times* that those days were definitely over: 'We recognise that NEXT is known as George Davies's NEXT. I hope and pray it will never become known as David Jones's NEXT.'

When I first worked with George, one of the things that started to get up my nose was his talk about the specialness of the NEXT culture, in which people worked 24 hours a day, 7 days a week for the good of the cause. What he did not realise was that when he was away, the car park was empty at 5 p.m. If George was in you stayed at your desk, because if he wanted you at 8.30 p.m. and you weren't there, he would accuse you of losing interest in your job. In contrast, I have never wanted people to work late into the evening or at weekends, because a happy family life means a happy employee. I know that if there is something that has to be done then people will put themselves out for me to do it on time.

The new head office at Enderby was another example of the excesses of George's regime. Margaret Thatcher herself had per-formed the opening ceremony, but the building was unbelievably expensive to complete; we had to write off many millions to bring the book cost down to a realistic figure. The avant-garde design was very light and airy but it created a huge amount of wasted space – and incidentally, only the directors' suite had air condition-ing, which in a heat wave was fine for the directors, and very uncomfortable for everyone else.

But this was NEXT, and in George's time NEXT was proud to be different. Now the profits were falling faster than the share price, although initially everyone in the company carried on in the same extravagant way. 'Crisis? What crisis?' was the mood at Enderby, until suddenly people realised that the fashion guru of the century had been replaced by a middle-aged, grey Yorkshire accountant (me) who was talking about cutting cost, selling the helicopter and downgrading the company cars. I had to spend a great deal of time bringing them into the real world.

As I have said, I liked George from the start and fully recognised that he had talents I never had and could never expect to acquire. He said in his book that when we first met he could see that I had the sort of management disciplines he knew he lacked, and that was what made us such a good fit; but as time went on he forgot about that. If he had gone on accepting it, I think that we would have been an unbeatable long-term partnership. I still regret the fact that what seemed at first to be such a promising alliance between us ended so bitterly.

Anyway, I hope George feels better about it all now, and perhaps even a little grateful, because I am certain he has made more money having left NEXT than he would have made if he had stayed – or if, as he seemed to be hoping at the time of that interview, I had been chucked out in the depths of the recession and he had been called back to 'rescue' NEXT.

In fact, what happened to George was that he and Liz set up a new design company, George Davies Partnership, with some of the people who had been closest to them at NEXT. After an ill-fated attempt to launch a direct catalogue called Xtend, they teamed up with the Asda supermarket chain to launch the incredibly successful GEORGE range of clothing. The proposition was that shoppers could be persuaded to buy their basic clothing at the same time as they bought their weekly groceries in out-of-town superstores, and George came up with a low-priced but stylish range for men, women and children.

Over a decade this venture built up annual sales of more than £600 million, at one time representing 2.5 per cent of the entire UK clothing market. But when Asda was acquired by the giant American retailer Wal-Mart in 1999, George was reported to be less comfortable with the new management, and moved on to form a new alliance with his old enemy in the High Street, Marks & Spencer.

Until then he had been one of M&S's most outspoken critics, for its frumpy designs and its failure to respond to customers. But he was asked to create a new range for M&S that would bring back the fashion-conscious women customers it had lost, and the result, called Per Una and launched in autumn 2001, was another big success. It briefly boosted the flagging fortunes of M&S, which bought the concept from George for £125 million!

So his luck stayed good in the end. He has had a remarkable career that places him among the most successful entrepreneurs and style makers of his generation, whereas if he had remained in charge at NEXT he would have been known as the founder of a great concept that did not survive. At NEXT, it is fair to say that he had one outstandingly good idea, the original NEXT clothing brand. All the things that followed – the Gardening Directory, NEXT the Jewellers and all the rest – were bad ideas. In my view, George suffered from two flawed beliefs: because he had one very good idea, all his ideas must be good; and because he was able to run one business well, he could run any number of businesses equally well.

Neither of these beliefs was true. This highlights my theory that there are three breeds of entrepreneurs: those who can create new concepts; those who can acquire new concepts and take them forward; and those who can create new concepts and take them forward. I think I fit into the second category, able to take new concepts forward and manage them reasonably well. There are very few people in the third category, able to create new concepts and drive them forward – Stanley Kalms of Dixons is one example; my friend Philip Green, about whom I shall say more later, is another. As for George, he has always been in the first category: a brilliant creative thinker, but not temperamentally suited to running a public company for the long haul under pressure from shareholders and the City.

This analysis also brings to mind another question: what talents should chief executives of fashion retailers have? I believe the answer is that their talents can vary from person to person. Despite the sentiment expressed about me when George left NEXT, I think I have proved that a chief executive does not need to have fashion skills, but he or she does need the ability to select and motivate a team, the awareness of the importance of financial discipline, and the precious gift of common sense.

So I have been happy to watch George's brilliant successes as a designer in recent years, but I have never regretted my role in his departure from NEXT.

Chapter 3

'If the worst comes to the worst...'

I have always referred to 1989 and 1990 as 'the wasted years', because I had to spend so much of my time just keeping the company afloat and not enough time developing the business.

Fortunately, I had alongside me my trusted colleagues from my GUS days who had joined me at Grattan – Dick Swain, John Whitmarsh, John Cutts and John Williams – and we soon had the cooperation of some of the NEXT people who had realised long ago that time was running out for the George Davies era. But in those early days after the historic board meeting, I had to spend so much of my time and energy on the problems George had left behind that I still had no idea what I was going to do about saving NEXT.

I decided to take a week's holiday at Christmas to think, and I returned to the office in the New Year full of optimism. The plan was simple enough: we had to restore the balance sheet to health by selling all the businesses except NEXT Retail, the Directory and Grattan; we had to close down Club 24 as soon as possible; we needed a couple more non-executive directors to add weight to the board; and I had to pray that the City would give me enough time to see the plan through.

I started by asking Marcus Agius of Lazards for his suggestions for non-executive directors and he came up with one outstanding candidate, Alistair Mitchell-Innes, who had been the UK chief executive of Nabisco, the biscuit makers, until its American parent, RJR Nabisco, was taken over by some Wall Street 'raiders' called Kohlberg Kravis Roberts in one of the most famous corporate battles of that era.

For the second vacancy I decided to approach my old boss, David Wolfson. He had by this time given up his Downing Street job as Margaret Thatcher's chief of staff – in her memoirs she described him as one of the few people who could get away with telling her to shut up – although he was still involved in policy discussions from time to time. Apart from a couple of small company directorships, he seemed to be spending the rest of his time playing golf – at which he was very competitive, a 'bandit' playing off a handicap of 15 – and bridge, at which I believe he was and probably still is of international standard.

We had lunch in London and I asked him if he would consider becoming a non-executive director, with a view to becoming chairman within 12 months since Michael Stoddart had agreed to take the chair for the second time around only on condition that it would be a stop-gap appointment. David replied laconically 'I don't have too much on at the moment', and accepted the offer.

My two new non-executive directors proved to be winners. I never had any doubt that David would be a good addition, but Alistair was a big bonus, and for 15 years played a very important part in the turnaround and subsequent success of NEXT.

My second decision was that I had to spend most of my time securing the financial future of the business and so I could not be hands-on running NEXT Retail, the Directory or Grattan. To give myself space, I appointed John Roberts as managing director of NEXT Retail, Andrew Varley to run the Directory and Mike Bottomley at Grattan. To be frank, none of these appointments was entirely successful; my only excuse is that I did not have a lot of choice.

Then I identified the businesses that we had to sell. The list included clothing manufacturing subsidiaries at Ashington in Northumberland, and in Belgium and Mauritius, and the two chains of convenience stores, Preedy's and Dillons, which George had bought as pick-up points for Directory customers. From the Combined English Stores portfolio, we wanted to sell off the two camping holiday firms, Eurocamp and Sun Sites, as well as Mercado's, the carpet wholesaler, and a ragbag of smaller businesses. Also up for sale were Westscot Data and Scorex, which had been set up by Grattan to challenge GUS's credit-referencing and credit-scoring businesses.

In addition, we had an investment property portfolio valued at £150 million, though we knew – in a rapidly deteriorating property market – that most of it would have to be sold at a loss if we wanted to realise the cash as quickly as possible. At the same time, we gave notice to all Club 24's customers that we would be closing the business down as soon as we had collected the outstanding debts.

But the most immediate task was to get through the announcement of NEXT's annual results for the year to 31 January 1989. I instructed Peter Lomas to clean up as much of the debris as he could. The results were pretty horrendous: although we were still in profit to the tune of £62 million pre-tax, the figure was far below brokers' expectations, which back in November had still been in the £85–90 million range.

In the circumstances, the meeting with analysts after the results went pretty well. Most of them were prepared to give me the benefit of the doubt. Michael Stoddart made a passionate speech about his confidence in the management team and told analysts that there was no hope of a quick fix: the recovery of NEXT would take time.

There was trouble outside the building, however. Journalists and television crews who had turned up for the meeting were unhappy that they had been refused entry, and hung around all morning to try to catch me as I left. In an effort to draw them off, Justin Downes, our PR man, put on my overcoat and with the collar turned up to hide his face ran to my Bentley, to be driven away in a cloud of smoke and screeching tyres. While this was happening I made a dignified escape through the back door, but unfortunately a reporter positioned on that side of the building spotted me and raised the alarm. I ran down the street pursued by a horde of cameramen and journalists, as well as passers-by who wanted to see what all the fun was about.

I was not famous for my athletic ability and they were catching me up. In desperation I ran into what seemed to be a derelict building, and hid in a cubicle in the ground-floor ladies' toilet. I locked the door and listened. To my horror, I heard them come into the toilet and start kicking the cubicle doors open. But I was in luck – the cubicle had a window. I opened it and started to climb through, but got stuck halfway – with an awful vision flashing before my eyes of a picture of my head protruding from a toilet window on the front page of the *Daily Telegraph*, and another of my backside dangling from a toilet window on the front page of the *Sun*.

It is amazing what the human body can achieve when under that sort of stress. Somehow I squeezed through the window, clambered over a fence, hailed a taxi, and rejoined my anxious but now relieved colleagues at the Regent Crest Hotel.

The reasonable reception of the January 1989 results was only a momentary respite. Taking everything into account, NEXT's debts amounted to over £750 million. With interest rates cripplingly high – from November 1988, base rate stood at 13 per cent for six months, before Nigel Lawson raised it to 14 per cent in May 1989 – it was imperative that we started to reduce this burden. We disposed of the Preedy's and Dillons businesses to T & S Stores for £54 million, and Mercado's to its management team for £11 million; we also sold Eurocamp to its managers.

Most of the investment property portfolio went too, and I remember one property transaction in particular: Headrow House in Leeds. Our advisers put a value of £5 million on it and we had a buyer at that price. But two or three weeks later the purchaser sold it on for £6.5 million, and everyone got upset about the fact that we had 'lost' £1.5 million. I did not see it that way: we asked for £5 million, we got our asking price, we should be satisfied. The fact that someone else was clever enough to make £1.5 million within three weeks was his good fortune. I was reminded of the bookmaker I used to work for on Saturdays as a teenager in Worcester. He told me: 'Worry about the downside before you try to maximise the upside.' And he was absolutely right.

We got out of manufacturing, and I was particularly pleased to be rid of the Belgian subsidiary, Van Over Dyke. Willy Van Over Dyke, its founder and a great pal of George's, was a difficult man. I went over to fire him with Peter Lomas, and we were treated within the space of 30 minutes to the whole range of his moods: pleading with us to let him keep his job, then getting aggressive, then crying and pleading again, then back to extreme aggression. If Peter had not been with me I would have been quite scared, particularly when Willy took a swing at me. Fortunately, he missed!

I was much sadder about selling our factory at Ashington. I had visited it numerous times and I really liked the local people – when I could understand their Geordie accents! Ashington was an old coalmining town, so it had already suffered in the changing economy of the 1980s. Our factory, which employed 500 at its peak, was a survivor from the earlier Hepworths days when it had thrived on making up 'made-to-measure' suits; when that trade declined Hepworths wanted to close it, but George had been very proud of the fact that he persuaded it not to. For a while the factory had become very successful again. But I could not afford to be sentimental: there were thousands more NEXT jobs at stake if I did not do my job properly.

The fate of Club 24 was better news: in fact, it turned out to be a bonus that I never expected. We stopped writing any new credit agreements, discontinued our arrangements with Dixons, and set about closing the business. The team under Arnie Iverson and then Steve Fairbank did a great job of collecting the outstanding debtors. In the end we got back more cash than we expected, which helped us to start buying back the troublesome Eurobonds. This team also laid the foundations for a new lease of life for Club 24 as a service bureau and call centre business that did not include the funding of debt – it was either funded by the client or by the client's banks. We found a new generation of clients, including retail group Kingfisher and mobile phone providers such as Cellnet, and eventually changed Club 24's name to Ventura. It is now a profitable and trouble-free part of the group.

Overall, I was quite pleased with the progress we were making to reduce NEXT's mountain of debts. But we were still not out of the mire. NEXT's share price was continuing to fall. We were taking the right action to control costs – the helicopter had been sold, the Bentley had been replaced by a Vauxhall, and the number of store staff had been reduced to reflect the footfall of customers from day to day by employing more part-time staff. But we simply had not had time to look at our product ranges to make sure we were offering what customers wanted. At the same time, customers were feeling the recession biting in a number of ways: high mortgage costs, tighter credit, job losses. Sales were not increasing at a rate that would improve our profitability.

Around the middle of 1990 Peter Lomas, the finance director, sat me down and quietly advised me that we had a very serious problem. The Eurobonds we had used to finance the CES deal would have to be redeemed in the 1991/2 financial year, and the amount we required, including the extra interest payable because they could not be converted into shares, was £200 million. Not only did we not have the funds in hand, there was very little likelihood of us being able to borrow on that scale, with the obvious result that our auditors, Ernst & Young, would have to qualify our 1990/1 accounts or even refuse to sign them off.

I told Peter I thought he was being excessively pessimistic. But he returned two weeks later with conclusive proof that we would be 'hitting a brick wall' around the middle of March 1991, because the indications were that the auditors would not be prepared to sign off our accounts as a 'going concern'.

What could we do? Around this time I had informal discussions with several institutions about the possibility of leading a management buy-out, which would have taken NEXT private and refinanced as much of it as we could salvage, with the management and staff owning a substantial part of the ordinary shares and institutions providing a second layer of capital in various forms. I was advised that this would be possible but not easy, because I had not yet proved that I could manage a high-street retailer successfully.

Even if it had been relatively easy to raise the institutional funding, I simply did not have the necessary funds available myself, or indeed the courage, to lead a buy-out. So – much to my later regret, because I think it would have made all our fortunes – I left the idea aside.

By this time David Wolfson had taken over as chairman from Michael Stoddart. Peter and I arranged to see him to tell him about the brick wall. He listened carefully to Peter's assessment of our problem, then turned to me and asked in a matter-of-fact tone: 'Did you forget to tell me about the Eurobonds, David?' No one was laughing.

The following week Peter and I met Marcus Agius of Lazards and Paul Hamilton of Warburgs. We showed them our three-year profit and cash-flow forecasts. We also gave them our best estimate of the 1990/1 results. This showed a huge loss – mainly due to the write-off of fixed assets following store closures, the loss on the disposal of the investment properties, and an additional bad-debt write-off in Club 24.

Marcus and Paul agreed to come back to us the following week with their thoughts. As I left the meeting, I said: 'If the worst comes to the worst we could always sell Grattan.'

I thought I was joking. But when we reconvened the following week Marcus and Paul were both deadly serious. We had to have an influx of cash. A rights issue was not possible. The share price had fallen below 40p. The only way out of the mess we were in was to sell Grattan. If that was not possible, then NEXT plc did not have a future and would go broke, leaving the corporate vultures to pick up the pieces. The thought of selling Grattan, the baby that I had nursed back to health with tender loving care, was at first unbearable. But I soon admitted to myself that it was the only way we could raise any significant amount of cash. In simple terms, to secure the survival of NEXT we needed to sell Grattan at a satisfactory price before the financial year-end on 31 January 1991.

It was then the middle of December 1990. I had been chief executive of NEXT for two years and I felt a complete failure. I had failed the business – and I had failed my family. Personally, I was all but flat broke. The £1 million overdraft I had taken out to pay the tax bill on my NEXT shares after Grattan was taken over in 1986 was secured against shares that were once valued at £4 million but were now – with the share price down again to 35p – worth less than £40,000.

Then the share price dropped even further, to a low of 7p. It was a Friday, and there had been a rumour in the City that the banks were pulling the rug out from under us. The night before there had been a very heavy snowstorm in Leicester and the NEXT office at Enderby had been cut off from the rest of the world. Nobody could get to work, so that when analysts and journalists rang the office to ask if the rumours were true they got no response. At least one junior analyst interpreted that as meaning that we must already have gone bust!

When a business is as close to the edge as we were at that moment, bad rumours can all too easily become self-fulfilling. The only way forward was to find a buyer for Grattan as soon as we possibly could.

The sale of Grattan was in many ways the most crucial event in my career, and the most exciting three months of my 45 years in business. It is not a story I would recommend for readers with a nervous disposition or a weak heart. It was achieved against all odds at a price that we never dreamed of reaching when we first embarked on the process, and it saved NEXT from going bust. Almost as important, it gave us a platform – financially, operationally and psychologically – that enabled us to make NEXT plc the success that it is today.

Our advisers, Marcus Agius and Paul Hamilton, told us that we had to sell Grattan for a minimum of £140 million. We forecast that Grattan's profit for the year to 31 January 1991 would be around £10 million, so on a full tax charge the price that we had to achieve represented a price–earnings ratio of 20. Who would buy at that sort of price?

The obvious choice was Sears, a substantial retail group born out of the British Shoe Corporation and once controlled by the great wheeler-dealer of the 1950s and 1960s, Sir Charles Clore. Sears owned several fashion retail brands, including Selfridges, Miss Selfridge, Richard Shops, Wallis and Warehouse, and in 1985 had bought Freemans of London, a home shopping competitor of Grattans, for the heady cash price of £400 million.

Michael Pickard, who in a previous incarnation as chairman of Grattan had headhunted me to be chief executive there, was now the chief executive of Sears – and it was he who had instigated the Freemans acquisition. Michael would clearly have a very good idea of the potential savings to be made by putting Grattan and Freemans together. I telephoned him and explained that I was lumbered with the onerous repayment of the two Eurobond issues, and had reluctantly decided to seek offers for Grattan because I needed all my available cash flow to expand NEXT Retail and NEXT Directory.

The downside of the proposal to sell Grattan to Sears was that, because Grattan's computers did all the processing for NEXT Retail and NEXT Directory, and the Grattan delivery operation handled Directory customer deliveries as well as merchandise deliveries to NEXT Retail stores, these vital services to NEXT would have to be supplied by a competitor for the foreseeable future. But, as they say, 'beggars can't be choosers'. I arranged to meet Michael Pickard at his London flat on the following Wednesday evening.

David Wolfson and Peter Lomas came with me. Michael had his finance director, John Lovering, at his side. We agreed that we would dispense with the usual ritual of signed confidentiality letters. I knew Michael well, and his word was good enough for me. I outlined the profit forecast for the current year and Michael said that subject to the forecast figures being confirmed, Sears would be prepared to offer a figure 'in the range of £125 million to £140 million'.

David replied that provided the offer figure was at the top end of that range, we would recommend to the NEXT board – which was due to meet at Michael Stoddart's office at Electra House later that evening – that negotiations should begin. We parted amicably and agreed to meet for breakfast at Michael Pickard's flat the following morning to start the ball rolling and agree the necessary press releases.

The NEXT board meeting went well. We discussed the proposal to sell Grattan to Sears in every detail and reached the unanimous decision to open talks with Michael Pickard and his team. It was a less straightforward decision for Mike Bottomley and John Wallis because they were the only two members of the board who would be 'sold' with Grattan, but afterwards I talked privately to them both and gave them my commitment that if they were not happy with the situation after the acquisition by Sears, then I would honour their three-year contracts in full.

When we reconvened at Michael's flat early the next morning, I could tell something was wrong. I tried to make eye contact with Michael but he would not look at me. David Wolfson confirmed that the NEXT board had agreed to enter into discussions with Sears at the price range agreed the previous evening, and I handed over copies of the draft Stock Exchange announcement that would also serve as a press statement.

We waited for Michael's response – and waited. He cleared his throat, but it was actually John Lovering who spoke. In a carefully matter-of-fact tone, he told us that they too had debated the issue at a board meeting last night and that they had revised the range of their offer to between £100 million and £115 million.

I was astonished. I looked across at Michael Pickard, who gravely nodded his agreement. I could tell that David was livid, but he kept his cool and said if that was the case we would have to progress down a different route. He looked to me for confirmation, and I said that we were grateful they had been upfront with us, because it had saved us all a considerable amount of work.

I could not believe the change of heart, and was convinced that it was not of Michael Pickard's own volition. He was a man of the highest principles and he must have been instructed by his chairman – Geoffrey Maitland Smith – to reduce the price. Many years later Michael told me that I was precisely right, and that for a while he had considered resigning over it.

We shook hands and parted still on good terms. In the same conversation years later, he told me he had warned his board that we had another party to talk to. He was pretty taken aback when I said that we actually had no one, and nothing else, up our sleeve.

'Well, young Jones,' David Wolfson said in his characteristic half-serious-half-joking way, in the taxi that was taking him to his office and me to King's Cross station, 'we're up the creek without any paddles in a ship that is sinking fast. What do we do now?'

'I have an alternative,' I said. 'But you must never ask me about it.'

He seemed convinced that I did in fact have an alternative. I was glad that I had convinced him. There was only one problem: I actually had no idea what I was going to do next. It was my old stubbornness coming out again. I genuinely believe that there is always an answer to every problem – it's just a matter of finding it.

On the train back to Leeds I racked my brains. I listed every British company that might be remotely interested. GUS and Littlewoods would almost certainly be barred by the Monopolies Commission, because a merger with Grattan would give either of them too dominant a market share. My old friend David Alliance – the Manchester-based textile entrepreneur who controlled another home shopping competitor, N. Brown – would certainly not pay the price we needed.

So I went through the names of every major UK retailer, but none of them looked an obvious bet. I then listed all the big retailers in the US – and dismissed them on the basis that no one from over here ever made any profit over there, which seemed to put off retailers over there from coming over here.

I turned to the continent of Europe. La Redoute in Paris was a possibility. So were two German names, Quelle and Otto Versand. Wait a minute, I thought, didn't I meet someone on a train to

Leicester a few months ago who was a senior man in Salomon Bros, the US investment bank, and who said he was very friendly with Dr Michael Otto, the chairman and controlling shareholder of Otto Versand – which was based in Hamburg and was one of the biggest mail-order businesses in the world? What was the banker's name?

Instead of going straight home, I went to my office in Bradford and searched through the piles of business cards I had accumulated in my desk drawers. One of them was Ron Freeman's, of Salomon Bros. That was him. I dialled his number, praying that he was still there (in fact he subsequently left to become vice-chairman of the new European Bank for Reconstruction and Development). Luckily, he was.

'Ron, I'm about to give you some price-sensitive information, but first I have to ask you if you're prepared to be made an insider.'

I have never known anyone reply that they did not want to be made an insider. When he confirmed that he was happy to speak on that understanding, I said, 'Out of the blue I have received an offer for Grattan…' – well, I had received a price range from Sears, so that wasn't entirely a bluff – '…but some time ago I promised Michael Otto that if Grattan was ever for sale, he would have first refusal.'

My assumption was that Ron would speak to Michael Otto on the basis that he had information from an undisclosed source that Grattan might be for sale. I sat back to see if the bait would land the big fish.

It did.

The following morning I received a call from Keith Chapman, the chairman of Fine Art Developments plc, a Bradford-based mail-order house. He explained that his company had a joint venture with Otto Versand, and that he had been asked by Dr Otto to see if Grattan was up for sale. He seemed to think that the call was a waste of time, obviously expecting me to say that it was not for sale at all. I was very cagey, as though surprised by the approach, but I did agree to meet Keith at his house, which was not far from mine, on the Saturday morning.

I went to Keith's home with Peter Lomas for an exploratory conversation. The only negative seemed to be that Dr Otto wanted NEXT Directory to be part of the deal. I had to explain that Retail and Directory were like Siamese twins and could not be parted. Keith agreed to come back to me the following week.

Days went by without a response; by Friday I was getting anxious. Then at about 5 p.m., just as I was about to leave the office for the weekend, Keith telephoned to say that a team of senior executives from Otto Versand would be flying over on Monday to have preliminary discussions with us.

My spirits began to lift. I didn't mind having my weekend plans ruined. That evening I exchanged confidentiality letters with Dr Otto, and rooms were booked in the unglamorous setting of a hotel off the M62 near Halifax for the first high-level meeting. Then I called David Wolfson and told him what had happened. He was relieved, but at that stage he did not ask any detailed questions: he was happy to let me get on with it.

The Otto contingent were very efficient and well prepared – very German, you might say. After the initial short meeting of both teams (all the Grattan directors were there), we split into working parties to discuss the entire business by each individual function.

Their team seemed to be very pro Grattan – and very pro me, so much so that they asked me directly whether I would stick around to manage the business if they bought it. It was a question I had not considered, but I said yes – because if that was a condition of getting the deal done, I did not want them to go back with any doubts. When they left after a very long, exhausting day, Horst Hansen, their team leader, promised to come back to me the following week.

So once again I sat staring at the phone, willing it to ring. It did – at 5 p.m. on Friday. Tactics as usual, I said to myself. Horst told me that Michael Otto himself would come to Bradford on the following Monday morning to 'negotiate a deal'. I rang David Wolfson with the news: he told me he had an appointment he could not break in London on Monday morning, but that he could be in Bradford by lunchtime if we could arrange a helicopter.

I talked to my colleagues over the weekend to finalise our tactics to squeeze a minimum of £140 million out of Dr Otto. By Sunday night I was exhausted, but I could not sleep. I had done my research on Michael Otto and had found out, among other things, that he preferred to be addressed as 'Herr Doktor'. In my nervous state, I was gripped by the thought that this could be the most important meeting of my career, and that the outcome would decide the future of NEXT, or whether it had a future at all. I fell into a restless sleep, only to wake in a cold sweat having dreamed that I had called Herr Doktor 'Herr Hitler'. Oh dear; as Basil Fawlty used to say, 'Don't talk about the war!'

I arrived at the office early on Monday and had a final rehearsal with Peter Lomas, who was a great chap to have on my side. I told him about my nightmare; he laughed and promised to kick me at any sign of a slip of the tongue. I decided to have the meeting at the Listerhills warehouse, which is separate from Grattan's main offices, because it was unlikely that anyone would take any notice of a group of visitors there and I did not want rumours floating around the offices.

Michael Otto arrived just before 10 a.m. with his team. I had met him once before many years ago, and he had not changed. He was tall and distinguished looking – women would certainly call him handsome – and his manner was very friendly. I liked him. We exchanged pleasantries over coffee and I offered David Wolfson's apologies and said that he would be arriving at 1 p.m. We started the negotiation, and I felt we were making good progress. I had not said anything out of place and the gremlins from the night before had disappeared. Otto's offer was creeping up towards the magical figure, and had reached £137.5 million when Herr Doktor asked for an adjournment to consult with his colleagues.

We broke up into separate rooms. I felt buoyant: I told Peter I sensed that the adjournment was requested so that Otto could agree with his team to go to the £140 million. There would be nothing for David to do when he arrived except open those two very expensive bottles of Gevry Chambertin that I had been keeping for a suitable occasion.

Or so I thought. When we reconvened, Herr Doktor announced that £137.5 million was his final offer. I kept cool and said that we should wait for my chairman to arrive. I took Dr Otto and his colleagues on a conducted tour of the warehouse, and he seemed suitably impressed. Keith Chapman, who was with him, whispered to me that Dr Otto did not want to give me his final figure, only to have to increase it when David Wolfson arrived. But still I felt very uneasy.

During the trip round the warehouse Dr Otto asked me if I would stay with Grattan, just as his people had asked me during the first meeting. 'I'll do whatever you want me to do,' I mumbled. We returned to our separate rooms to await David's arrival. I could do no more than pace up and down, waiting for the sound of the helicopter.

At about 12.40 I heard it and was so relieved that I walked into the room where Michael Otto was waiting – more patiently than me – and said without pausing to think, 'The eagle has landed!'

Oh my God! What had I said – and where was Peter Lomas when I needed him to kick me? But Herr Doktor just turned and smiled and remarked that the chairman was early. What a diplomat, I thought.

David Wolfson joined the fray, and it soon became apparent that Herr Doktor had indeed not reached his final offer, but had been waiting to meet David face to face, chairman to chairman, to finalise the deal. David played his part superbly, and we came to a total price of £142.5 million. We quickly agreed a joint press release, and parted company in good spirits for the Christmas holiday.

I mentioned to David that Dr Otto had asked if I would stay at Grattan, and that I had definitely given the impression that I would in order not to jeopardise the deal. That clearly was not part of our own plan, so he promised to have a word with Dr Otto at the appropriate time.

When I returned to my office, I phoned Michael Pickard at Sears and told him that a Stock Exchange statement was about to go out. To this day I am not sure why I made that call. Was it to make him aware that we really did have an alternative, or was it to say 'You had it in your hand and lost it'? Either way, it dramatically changed the course of the deal.

Peter Lomas and I worked for most of the Christmas holiday on Grattan's year-end forecasted profit and loss account and balance sheet. It was vital that we achieved the profit figure we had indicated to Dr Otto. The last thing we wanted was to fall seriously below forecast and to have to renegotiate the sale with a much weaker hand.

On the first working day of the New Year, Peter and I were working on the figures at Grattan when I received a startling telephone call from Marcus Agius. He told me that Sears' advisers had just contacted him with an offer of £150 million for Grattan. I got in touch with Michael Otto immediately. Keith Chapman arranged to see David Wolfson and me at Grattan that afternoon. Once again, we hired a helicopter to get David Wolfson to Bradford on time.

By the end of the day we had a revised offer of £151 million from Otto Versand – but only on the basis that we would recommend this offer to our shareholders even if Sears increased its offer to 5 per cent above the £151 million; that is, to not more than £158.5 million.

We were happy to give this undertaking, not only because we had already got more than the price we wanted, but also because we preferred Otto Versand as a prospective buyer. Why? Because Grattan would be continuing to provide computer, warehousing and delivery services to NEXT, and with Otto Versand these services would be in the hands of a non-competitor, whereas Sears was competing with us head-on in the High Street with its various brands. Not only that, the customer profile of Sears' Freemans home shopping catalogue was dangerously close to the NEXT Directory customer profile.

Before he left, Keith Chapman insisted that David sign a letter pledging the NEXT board's support for Otto's increased offer, even if Sears went above it by 5 per cent. David glared at him, and pointed out that he had given his word. But Keith insisted that we signed something, because 'all you have to do is go to Sears and get them to up their offer marginally above ours'.

David looked at him sternly. 'Do you really think that I am going to risk my personal reputation by double-crossing you?'

For a horrible moment I thought Keith was going to say 'yes'. But he backed down. We left him holding an unsigned piece of paper, and David and I caught a train to London for an emergency NEXT board meeting, at which we confirmed that we would continue to support the Otto Versand offer unless Sears increased its offer to £160 million. We all felt comfortable with this figure because haggling over small differences in the price was pointless: as David put it, one hiccup on an important computer processing run could swallow up the extra cash that we might get from Sears.

Sure enough, Sears increased its offer to £155 million. But we kept to our bargain and continued to support the Otto Versand deal. Although we had good support from institutional shareholders, some journalists failed to understand our stance and came close to implying that something improper was afoot. I had to work very hard to stop David Wolfson from suing them.

We moved on to an extraordinary general meeting at which the shareholders confirmed the company's resolution to go with the £151 million offer from Otto Versand. There was a lovely moment when David allowed the chairman of Sears, Geoffrey Maitland Smith, to address the meeting, introducing him to the audience as 'a very nice chap'. Geoffrey did his best to persuade the investors present that Sears' higher offer also made good commercial sense for the future of the businesses, but the motion favouring Dr Otto's offer carried the day.

It seemed to be all over bar the signatures, but it wasn't. First, there was a social break: England versus France at Twickenham, the decider for the Grand Slam. It was a cracking game, from which

England emerged as very worthy winners. After the game, as usual on these occasions, we went to celebrate with Michael Pickard and his friends, who always park together in the West Car Park. Despite pouring rain we were all in good spirits, and it was particularly enjoyable because my two sons were with me.

Michael beckoned me to one side and whispered: 'Today we have stuffed the French, tomorrow we will stuff the Germans.' Then he asked me what price it would take to win an acceptance from the NEXT board. 'It would have to be in the mid-160s,' was my guarded reply.

I arrived home well after midnight, a little the worse for wear. It had been a welcome relief from the worries of the business, and I was not exactly bright-eyed and bushy-tailed the next morning when both telephones in the bedroom rang almost simultaneously. Ann answered the house phone and took a message from Michael Pickard, while I picked up the private line. It was David Wolfson, and the message on both sides of the bed was the same: 'Sears has increased its offer to £167.5 million.'

David asked me to contact Peter Lomas; the two of us were to meet him at Lazards at 4 p.m. to discuss our next move. As my brain started to clear, it dawned on me that we had started this saga looking for £140 million for Grattan, and that after a false start we were now sitting comfortably with an offer of £167.5 million. How much further could the game run? I said to Ann, 'We could get £200 million.'

I decided to tell Keith Chapman what had happened. He was in the shower, but called me back ten minutes later. All he said was 'Give me 20 minutes', but he did not need that long. Within five minutes he was back: 'You now have two offers of 167 and a half.'

Keith had tracked Michael Otto down on a boat somewhere in the Greek Islands. Dr Otto had immediately agreed to match the price, knowing that we would recommend his offer. But what if we could get Sears to go to 175?

We had a cheerful meeting at Lazards that afternoon. Sears' increased offer would be issued to the Stock Exchange at 7.30 a.m., to be followed at 8 a.m. by notification that Otto Versand had matched that offer, and that this had been recommended by the board of NEXT.

We were all back at Lazards early the following morning to witness the next episode of the saga. The Sears statement came up on screen, then the Otto statement, closely followed by the recommendation by the board of NEXT. We waited impatiently for further developments – and even started to debate what price Sears would offer before 9 a.m. It was a big anticlimax when the door opened and a clean white handkerchief came into the room, waving frantically, followed by a smiling Marcus Agius: 'Sears has thrown in the towel.'

Now I was deflated, because we were not going to get £200 million after all. Memories can be remarkably short: two months previously, we would have snatched the hand off anyone offering £140 million.The moral of this story – and it is a very fortunate one for NEXT – is that Sears totally messed up the unique opportunity we offered. If it had confirmed its original price range at that first breakfast meeting, I would never have approached Dr Otto – and I do not believe that Otto Versand, being a traditional German company unfamiliar with the Anglo-Saxon world of contested takeover bids, would have joined the fight unless it had been invited.

Sears also missed an opportunity to buy the entire NEXT group. For 50p a share – around £200 million – it could have bought us lock, stock and barrel. Otto Versand would never have engaged in that particular battle, because it had no interest at all in high-street retailing.

Some time later, I was told that Sears did not want to bid for the whole of NEXT because it was worried about the £400 million of debts in Club 24. It did not realise that after the restructuring of Club 24 over the previous two years, NEXT could walk away from that debt without any liability.

Regrettably, Michael Pickard and Geoffrey Maitland Smith left Sears soon after these events. This retail empire built up by one of the great entrepreneurs of the twentieth century, Charles Clore, eventually went to the brink of collapse. A decade later Philip Green bought the ailing business and made a small fortune selling off the component parts – great for Philip, but a sad end to a once splendid company.

Interestingly, Philip Green sold the ladies' fashion chains within Sears to Arcadia for £150 million, and John Hoerner, the chief executive of Arcadia, was reported in the press to have been boasting that for a small sum of money he had bought a business the size of NEXT. It never fails to amaze me that so many people boast about what they are going to achieve, not what they actually have achieved. Hoerner was sacked not long afterwards and replaced by Stuart Rose.

But that is another story altogether. Back at NEXT, we had two weeks to finalise the Grattan sale before our year-end.

The corporate priorities were to renegotiate our bank facilities, to complete all the documentation for our shareholders, and to organise an agreement between NEXT and Otto Versand for the continuation of the services that Grattan provided for the NEXT brand businesses. My own first priority was to escape from any moral obligation to stay with Grattan. This was achieved by David Wolfson, who simply told Michael Otto that he had expressly asked me to remain with NEXT – and would Michael therefore release me from any commitment I might have made? There was no legal obligation involved, and Michael courteously agreed to let me go – but asked me to be a consultant for a year for a fee of £100,000, payable to NEXT.

Peter Lomas and I spent many days talking to banks, and eventually we were able to put the necessary funding in place. With two very honourable exceptions – Derek Arden of Barclays and Bernard Paine of HSBC – most of the bankers were totally unhelpful, as bankers too often are. I remember on one occasion threatening to abandon Club 24 because of the difficult stance taken by some banks in the syndicate that now provided its funding. We were quick to point out that if NEXT abandoned Club 24 the cost to us would be less than £8 million, whereas the loss to the syndicate would be anything up to £400 million. That helped to concentrate their minds.

It was around this time that my younger son read NEXT's annual report and asked me how I managed to sleep at night knowing that we owed the banks almost £1 billion. I told him that I slept very soundly; it was the bankers who had to lie awake worrying whether we would ever be able to pay them back.

The paperwork that had to go to the shareholders was a big job, handled for us by the solicitors Simmons & Simmons – who provided the best commercial lawyer I have come across, Anthony Dove. He is one of the few lawyers I have met who will give you a straight answer to a straight question. Most of them give you pages of alternatives, leaving you to decide which one to take, but Tony always gave me a clear account of the legal options followed by a commercial recommendation. Not only that, he had amazing stamina. He could keep going long into the night, but when he was tired he would stop, go back to a makeshift bed in his office, sleep for two hours, then return to the mountain of paper in front of us and get on with the job.

Meanwhile, progress on the agreement for NEXT to continue to be serviced by Grattan was getting bogged down. Time was running out: we had one week to go before the year-end when I walked into the room where the NEXT and Grattan operations team were laboriously going through every item in minute detail. I listened for a while, then announced that I would be taking personal charge of the agreement. I sent everyone home except Peter Webber, who was head of our internal legal department and another good, common-sense commercial lawyer. We sat down together and I wrote out my version of the agreement on one sheet of paper:

'Otto Versand guarantee that they will for a period of 5 years from 1 February 1991 provide all services to the NEXT group that Grattan presently provides, at the same cost structure and service levels as provided over the last two years.'

Some of the Grattan people thought that this abbreviated approach carried unacceptable risks; someone even told me it was 'utter madness'. But I knew that unless we short-circuited the overelaborate agreement they had all been working on, we would never complete in time.

We nearly did not make it for another reason. We had reached 30 January 1991, and we were getting close to signing the closing documents. The Grattan team were in a room idly chatting and waiting for the Otto Versand team to tell us that they were ready to sign. We were enjoying a Chinese takeaway (this and the cuisine of McDonald's in High Holborn had kept us going during the all-night sessions) laid out for us in hot tin-foil containers on a beautiful antique table.

I was busy worrying about the damage this might do to the table, when suddenly the door opened with a bang that made me think it had come off its hinges. Horst Hansen marched in with a face like thunder, followed by his team who were having some difficulty in keeping up with him. He slammed a folder of documents on the table close to David Wolfson's chicken chow mein, and exploded: 'I thought we were dealing with gentlemen!'

David was brilliant. He unfolded himself very slowly – he is a tall man – looked down at Horst and put an arm round his shoulders. 'Now then, Horst,' he said very calmly: 'What seems to be the problem?'

Apparently there was an existing agreement between all the companies in the NEXT group, excluding Club 24, that each subsidiary was responsible for the debts of any or all of the other subsidiaries. Due to an oversight, this guarantee had not been cancelled by the sale document. If Otto had signed without spotting it, then technically Grattan – and its new owner, Otto Versand – would still have been liable for all NEXT's debts if we were unable to meet them.

David explained that this was a genuine oversight. He apologised to poor Horst, shook his hand and invited him to join our Chinese banquet. Horst accepted that it was not intentional, but nevertheless instructed his team to go back over the agreement line by line in case there were any other 'oversights'. In consequence, the documents were not signed until the early hours of Saturday, 2 February – which happened to be my 48th birthday – though they were backdated to 31 January.

For the ten weeks that followed, Peter Lomas and his crew worked around the clock preparing Grattan's year-end accounts so that the deal could be completed and the annual accounts of the NEXT group for the year to 31 January 1991 could be finalised.

That set of accounts gave me the last opportunity to clean up the balance sheet once and for all. We threw everything in – not just the kitchen sink, but the kitchen, most of the house, the double garage and the cars! We wrote off the assets in stores closed or scheduled to be closed, we wrote off all the set-up costs of the Directory, we made yet more provisions for Club 24 debtors, we wrote off property losses and losses incurred with the sale of various businesses, and we wrote off a £6 million 'cloth mountain' that we had found in a locked warehouse in Belgium.

On 16 April 1991, we actually received £167.5 million, plus £3 million of accrued interest from 1 February, from Otto Versand. On the same day, we announced our results for the full year: a pre-tax loss that in its final form (after the extraordinary items were restated the following year) amounted to £445 million after tax.

It was a huge day for me. Some City journalists had been predicting my downfall. Jeff Randall in the *Sunday Telegraph* made his headline 'JONES MUST GO'. There was even speculation – perhaps encouraged by George, whose media contacts were still as good as ever – that George Davies was coming back.

Incidentally, I should add that Jeff was the first journalist to ring me when our fortunes began to improve and admit that he had got the story all wrong. I cannot criticise his headline because at that point – early in 1991 – it really was still touch and go. As he said to me very recently, who would have imagined that NEXT would recover to reach a stock market valuation of £4 billion and sales of £3 billion?

At 10 a.m. we were due to have a meeting at Lazards with retail analysts, the financial press and selected large shareholders. Just before we were going to start, David Wolfson put his arm round my shoulders, guided me to a quiet corner and said: 'I'll run the meeting, David, you keep a low profile.'

In David's language, that loosely translated as: 'Look chum, they all think you're an idiot, so don't open your mouth and prove it.'

I did as he suggested. There were over 100 people in the room when David, Peter Lomas and myself took our places behind a long table on a platform. The chairman was in the middle with Peter on his left. Peter, incidentally, had opted to stay with Grattan, partly because his roots were in West Yorkshire but also, I suspected, because he was not confident that NEXT could be turned around.

I took my place on David's right, trying to appear inconspicuously confident, my chair about a foot further back than the others. Several of my analyst friends – if that is the right word – were in the front two rows, but would not make eye contact. I'm sure they all thought I was going.

At precisely 10 a.m., David slowly stood up and was about to start the meeting when the door opened again and a little old lady came into the room. She walked slowly towards the platform. Nobody made a sound as she approached. She looked up at David, who must have towered over her by five feet.

'Is this where they're presenting the life-saving awards?' she asked.

Quick as a flash, David replied, 'We'll let you know in a minute.'

Everyone burst out laughing, and no one noticed the old lady leave. The atmosphere was transformed by this strange interruption. There were no questions. I survived. The rest, as they say, is history.

Before I left Lazards I asked a security man where the life-saving awards were being presented. He gave me a funny look and said that there was no such function; it would be an odd event to hold in a busy merchant bank. He also said that no one had seen an elderly lady walk into the building that morning.

I certainly saw her walk into the room, and I'm sure everyone heard her ask the question and laughed at David's witty reply. But who was she and why was she there? Later that day I related this strange story to Ann, describing the little old lady as 'a bit like my mother'!

Chapter 4

'This is the day when life begins again!'

U p until the day we sold Grattan, we were so occupied with the priorities of staying alive that we never seemed to have time to work on the detail of improving the product range, the stores and the internal organisation. But we did make some important decisions.

The most significant was to close and sell over 100 of our stores and reduce the size of another 70 – once we found out that they were contributing nothing, or less than nothing, to our profits. Finding that out was far from easy.

At Enderby we had a number of 'mock shops' that we used for deciding on our window and in-store product displays. Once they were agreed, they were photographed and the pictures sent out to the stores. This was how we ensured that the look of the stores was consistent. One day, on my way to the restaurant (in most companies, the place where the staff ate would be referred to as the canteen, but at NEXT it had to be 'the restaurant'), I noticed that there was a six-foot-long green fish in one of the mock windows. At my first meeting with the retail directors, I asked what the fish was for. I was treated to a lesson in retailing: 'You have to have something in the window that makes the passing shopper stop and want to enter the store.'

'Fine. But we sell clothes, not fish,' I responded, and the look I received from the assembled experts said it all – what did this grey Yorkshire accountant know about the art of retail? My next question was treated with similar looks of disbelief.

'How many of our stores make a profit?' I asked innocently.

'Every one of them does,' came the condescending answer.

'How do you know?'

The truth was that they assumed every store was making a profit, because every store had been opened by George and he would not open a store unless it was going to be profitable. That was not my kind of logic, so I asked for a detailed store profitability report. When the report was completed two months later, it showed that out of 428 stores, more than 150 did not make any profit, even before charging out the cost of our central overheads. In fact, I was staggered to find that we made more profit in Barrow-in-Furness than we did in Regent Street, London.

I insisted that each store manager should know what profit or loss their store actually made, a proposal that was greeted with universal horror:

'We can't do that!'

'Why not?'

'What happens if a store manager leaves and joins Burtons?'

'Look, if we don't know what to do with the information, what do you think Burtons is going to do with it?'

This rather surreal discussion resulted – probably more by luck than judgement – in one of the best and most important decisions that I ever made at NEXT. Mainly as a result of the large amount of high-street selling space that we acquired when we bought CES, we had duplicated our presence in a large number of High Streets. It was such a stupid decision that I cannot believe George actually made it.

For example, we might have a store in a High Street with a turnover of £500,000, making a contribution before central overheads of, say, £75,000. That was good – until we opened another store in the same street that was budgeted to turn over £500,000, and also make £75,000. It was an attractive theory, but in practice it did not happen. What did happen was that the combined turnover of the two stores would increase to, say, £600,000. But because the operating costs were almost double, the profit disappeared.

There was only one thing we could do – close down all loss-making and duplicated stores. Once again, I was told that it could not be done. Why not? Because of the cost of writing off the capital value of the shopfitting, they said. This had all too often been the excuse for not taking necessary action: the accounts could not stand the cost of writing off unprofitable assets. In my view the opposite was the real truth: the accounts simply could not afford to continue making losses on unprofitable stores. If you ever find yourself in a similar position and you need convincing, forget the intricacies of profit and loss accounting, just look at the cash flow.

It was to the great credit of our property director, Andrew Varley, that we were able to sell the leases on over 100 of these loss-making stores in less than 12 months. We were extremely fortunate that there were many other retailers that did not have the problems we had and were yet to be seriously hit by the advancing recession. There were still plenty that were expanding and willing to buy our surplus stores.

This strategy of shedding underperforming stores was not popular, but there was no time to debate it: it just had to be done. Apart from the asset write-off argument, some retailers will claim that they cannot close stores because the reduced level of sales will not cover the central overheads. This is also a flawed argument – you have to work hard to get the costs in line with the level of sales. All this was part of a larger process in which we squeezed the cost base in every possible way. The team worked well and everyone played their part. Bob Harrison, the operations director of NEXT Retail who also had responsibility for the financial accounts (and later joined the main board as operations director), was an important member of the recovery team. He had wanted to resign when I first took over, but I persuaded him to stay. He was tough and uncompromising, with a vital ability to 'lose the cheque book' at the right moment. Every item of expenditure had to be authorised by a director. Deals were done with hotels and airlines to reduce our travelling expenses.

And we cut even deeper by using consultants to monitor the efficiency of every job at head office and in the stores and in the warehouses, which led us to cut staffing levels across the company quite dramatically: between January 1989 and January 1991, the number of full-time-equivalent staff fell from 16,835 to 10,624.

I have never relied on consultants before or since, because my view is that consultants come into your business, pick the brains of management and staff, produce verbose reports summarising what you have just told them, charge a small fortune in fees and leave you to get on with it. That is still my general view, but in this instance our consultants, Proudfoot, did a very good job. In particular, they introduced the concept of using part-time staff to cover busy shopping times, which is much more economical than maintaining the same number of full-time staff throughout the week from Monday to Saturday.

The second major decision during the wasted years was to consolidate the retail offer into one. George had launched NEXT Too as a second high-street brand to attract younger customers with a different range of merchandise; an idea I always assumed he had adopted from The Limited, the big US retail group, which introduced Limited Too around the same time. But it was never a success, and George in due course abandoned it – only to replace it with NEXT Originals.

So when I took over we had NEXT Collection stores and NEXT Originals stores. An easy way of describing the difference between the two product ranges was that Collection was more fashionable and Originals was more basic. An analysis of the relative performance of these chains revealed that the larger Collection stores did well in the main shopping centres, but in the smaller locations Originals outperformed Collection. For the time being I endorsed the earlier decision to continue with the dual concept.

But David Wolfson had a bee in his bonnet about it: he saw the analysis and accepted that the figures were correct, but he would not accept the conclusions we had drawn from them. When he kept coming back to the subject, I started to worry about it. I worried even more when, in a meeting intended to nail the issue once and for all, our womenswear director managed to get the pictures mixed up: when she was describing the typical Collection customer she pointed to Originals merchandise, and vice versa. I fear she heard the chairman's comment as she went out of the door: 'If the director in charge can't tell the difference, what chance do the customers have?' She left the company soon afterwards.

I decided the only thing to do was to go out and talk to the store managers – not exactly an earth-shattering idea, but better late than never. I started at our biggest store, in the huge Meadowhall shopping centre in Sheffield. Here they had both Collection and Originals; in theory, one range was to be displayed on one side of the store, and the other on the other side. Except this particular store manager had done it her own way: she had decided that the ranges looked better mixed up and displayed in different 'stories'. Who was I to say she was wrong when she was 30 per cent ahead of her sales targets?

Chastened, I sought support from managers of some of the smaller Collection and Originals stores. At this level, Originals was definitely doing better. Then I had a stroke of luck: I found a store manager who had been transferred to a Collections store from an Originals store. I asked her a question: 'What was the stock value in the two stores?'

'I don't know what the value was. But the deliveries were always bigger at Originals.'

How could I have been so stupid? I had wrongly assumed that the reason the Originals stores were outperforming similar-sized Collection stores was that the customers preferred the Originals range. But it wasn't the range that made the difference, it was the stock levels. The Collection merchandiser looked after the larger stores first so that the smaller Collection stores got the dregs of the stock, whereas the Originals merchandiser only had small stores to worry about and they were always better stocked with winners.

When we went ahead and amalgamated Collection and Originals into one offer, there were a number of beneficial outcomes. There was obviously a saving on the cost of buying and merchandising staff, and the reduction in the total number of options, in the one range rather than two, certainly helped the warehouses to cope more efficiently. Life was so much simpler. We had one format of store design that was simply called NEXT. Stockholding in the stores benefited from the redesign of the entire ordering and store allocation system. When we got down to the detail we found, for example, that we never ordered enough size 8 garments to allow every store to stock at least one of them, because the initial order quantity was based on the number of size 8 garments we had sold in the previous season – when only the larger stores stocked them.

Having found the answer to one major problem by talking to the store managers, I embarked on a series of trips around the country to meet more store managers and find out what else they thought was going wrong. These were very enjoyable and productive meetings. The managers were absolutely great in the way they responded to my challenge to help get NEXT moving forward again. I remember several store managers complaining about the overblown training manuals: when I eventually found these documents, I could not understand the five thick folders that a new sales consultant had to study. In consequence, the training procedure was changed so that new starters were 'adopted' by experienced store staff who taught them how to do their job. This was basic common sense!

I also found it strange that NEXT was almost divided into two separate companies – the head office and the stores – and they hardly ever communicated. 'We can never get an answer from head office' was a frequent comment. It resulted in a letter to all store managers, copied to all head office departmental managers, giving them the right number to call for particular types of query – and giving them a second number to call if they had not had a satisfactory answer within 24 hours. The second number was my own direct line at Enderby. It worked: after the first week I got no more calls from store managers who could not get an answer from their initial call.

And they also prompted me to introduce a priority system in the warehouses to deliver out-of-stock bestsellers to the stores direct from the Goods Inwards department, because the store managers told me quite simply that if their stores have stock of the top ten sellers then they will have a good sales week. More basic common sense!

These chats with the store managers were so useful to me that I started to hold similar meetings with small groups of head office staff, about 30 at a time. They were just as rewarding. I told them what our plans were, and asked them how they thought they could contribute. When they realised that their comments could lead to change, they were encouraged to say more. People like to be part of a team; they like to know that the management really cares what they think. They told me what was wrong, and I did my best to put it right.

That was how I heard about the watch problem. What watch problem? Well, it turned out that about 80 per cent of the watches we sold were being returned to us because they did not work! By chance I had heard that the watch buyer from Kays, Brian Fell, had been made redundant and was very unhappy with the way he had been treated. Brian and I went back a long way: to the very first morning of my career on 31 October 1960, in fact, when he had jumped ahead of me in the queue at Kays' personnel office. But I had long ago forgiven him for that. I made contact, we met, and he joined NEXT to create a successful high-quality watch business.

People who worked at NEXT tended to care deeply about the company, so once they realised I was willing to listen they queued up to tell me what was wrong. At an evening meeting at head office the area managers let loose: on the subject of bonus schemes, a long-serving manager from the South West area called Peter Thomas said in desperation, 'I've had a bonus of £55 for the spring/summer season and I've no idea what it was for.'

The sales director, Stuart Soloway, started to read out from the operating manual the basis for calculating area managers' bonuses, only to be told by the HR director that it was three years out of date. On another occasion, David Wolfson rang one morning to tell me that the store windows in the central London area had not been changed for six weeks. When I challenged Stuart about this, he referred to the confounded manual again and told me that the windows were changed every three weeks. That was what was supposed to happen – but the trouble was that it just was not happening.

Stuart did not stay with us for very long, which was a pity, because he had some very good ideas, one of which was to introduce 'centre floor' fixtures. In George's day the product was all displayed on fixtures around the walls, with great open spaces in the centre of the store. We designed new fixtures for the floors, which transformed our sales per square foot.

Yet another important discovery was the relationship between the number of options in a range and the space allocated to them in the stores. We had 96 styles and colours of men's formal shirts, but only enough space even in the larger stores to display 35 of them. Likewise, we had 120 different styles of ladies' shoes and could probably only display 50. One by one we began to identify these weaknesses and eradicate them. Perhaps the most famous decision we made in the wasted years was to do with end-of-season sales. Previously, like every other high-street retailer, NEXT held sales at the end of each season lasting for several weeks, in which gradual price reductions were implemented on a weekly and sometimes daily basis – what I always referred to as 'death by a thousand cuts'. I really don't understand why so many retailers follow this misguided practice.

Every buyer has 'dogs', items that simply do not sell. Some retailers try to turn dogs into good sellers by giving them prime display positions or discounting them by, say, 10 per cent within what is still supposedly the full-price selling season. Some stores have special '20 per cent off' days to shift the dogs, but these generally have the opposite of the desired effect: they produce higher sales of good-selling items at significantly lower gross margins, but no increase in the sales of the dogs, because the discount is not big enough to shift them. A dog is a dog whichever way you look at it, and in my view the only way to shift a really poor seller is to slash the price dramatically in the end-of-season sale.

But the problem with extended reduced-price end-of-season sales is that the retailer's overheads remain constant, so the longer the sale lasts, the more you lose. It follows logically that the most important rule for a successful sale is to mark the selling price right down from the start – the first markdown is always the best – and sell as much as you can in the shortest period possible. NEXT's end-of-season sales have become a legend: 50 per cent off, but for no more than 10 days. Customers start queuing in the early hours of the morning and the first day is chaotic, but the whole exercise is very successful. The customers are happy, and so are we.

One spin-off from these aggressive end-of-season sales was that we had much less unsold stock to transfer to the NEXT to Nothing discount stores. In some cases George had allowed NEXT to Nothing to be opened in High Streets close to our mainstream stores. In my view this made no commercial sense. I was glad to be able to close them down and prevent any long-term harm to the NEXT brand.

So maybe the two years were not so wasted after all.

One more decision during that period was to appoint myself as managing director of the NEXT brand – that is, of NEXT Retail and NEXT Directory. When I first took over as chief executive, I had appointed John Roberts as managing director of NEXT Retail, and Andrew Varley as managing director of NEXT Directory. Both John and Andrew had admirable personal qualities and their appointments worked well enough in the short term, because they gave me the time I needed to address the group's overwhelming financial problems.

John was a lawyer rather than a retailer by instinct and training, but he did a good job holding the retail ship steady. Andrew also tried very hard, but much of his energy was taken up by his main role as property director, getting rid of all our surplus stores – a task he did very well. In due course both of them stood down from the managing director roles. John opted for early retirement, having recognised that the company no longer needed his legal skills for the immediate future – in the earlier phase of NEXT, he had become very expert in the process of buying other companies, but all our effort now was on consolidation rather than expansion. Andrew, having shed his responsibility for the Directory, had more time to run the property side, which was vital when we were disposing of loss-making stores, and became even more important when we started to increase the size of our stores again in the mid-1990s.

My intention was to take on the managing directors' roles myself, so I was quite upset when David Wolfson (who had succeeded Michael Stoddart as chairman in June 1990) suggested that we 'bring in a retailer' from outside. I am not sure what would have happened to me if we had. I was present when one candidate was interviewed, and rejected for good reasons. I never knew how many others were interviewed without my involvement, but there was evidently no one suitable, and after a while the idea disappeared.

But David also had another idea that might have taken NEXT, and my career, in very different directions – a takeover by Alexon plc, a retail group that had previously been called Steinberg. David Wolfson had at one time been chairman of Steinberg, which I believe had been founded by one of his uncles. He knew the management team well and we had one meeting with them at which they were full of talk about how well their business was going and how what NEXT needed was a 'retail genius' to pull it through. I was totally against the idea of a link-up with Alexon. I did not rate the business or the people, and although David pursued it for a while, this idea too went away. Within a year, Alexon issued a series of profit warnings and its entire management team was replaced.

One thing a sale of NEXT to Alexon would have achieved, however, was a significant easing of my personal finances, which were in dire straits. As I have described, I had a £1 million overdraft which I had originally used to pay the tax bill on the value of the NEXT shares I received after Grattan was taken over in 1986. That was not a worry when the shares were worth £3 million and my salary was £400,000 a year. Now, however, the shares were worth only £25,000 and I had volunteered to halve my salary to reflect the reduced size of the business. Interest rates were sky-high and I could not even afford to pay the interest.

Fortunately, I had a very understanding bank manager who agreed to roll up the interest for 12 months and then review the situation. When that review came round I still was not quite out of the woods, but the NEXT share price had reach £1 and the bank manager was a little more relaxed. I never told Ann quite how critical our financial situation was. Fortunately she has a natural tendency to be careful with money anyway, and somehow we survived.

The bank was Barclays and the manager who saved my bacon was John Clapham, who had taken over as the local director in Bradford from an equally understanding man called Freddie Walker. This was when the local managers knew their customers personally and had the authority to make decisions. Regrettably that system has been replaced by unfeeling centralised controllers – and I now bank at HSBC!

Incidentally, I managed to make matters worse through a desire to help a friend who had nothing to do with NEXT. About two years before I had accepted an invitation to become a non-executive director of Sharp & Law plc, a long-established Bradford company that was involved in shopfitting, painting and decorating. I intended to resign at the board meeting after I became chief executive of NEXT, but at that meeting a 'black hole' was reported that threw the company into severe financial difficulty. I could not abandon a sinking ship, and agreed to stay and help find a solution. I was furious with myself because I felt I should have spotted the problem from the monthly reports I received.

The fact that none of the executives on the board spotted it either did not ease my feeling of guilt. I am very hard on myself if something goes wrong that I think I should have seen coming. I do not like letting people down, and I may sometimes be inclined to be a bit too generous when people ask me for help. I tried hard to find a white knight to save the business, but it went into liquidation.

And I am also a gambler – not on horses or dogs or casino tables, and not for high stakes, but I take chances from time to time. When Brian Considine, the managing director of Sharp & Law, put together a group of investors to help him buy the shopfitting subsidiary for £150,000, I was happy to chip in with a stake of £30,000. Soon after we agreed on this, I was in a NEXT board meeting when June came in and handed me a note saying that Brian wanted to speak to me urgently. He was distraught: he was within minutes of completing the deal and his other four backers had just pulled out. Without hesitation I told him that I would put up all the cash he was short of. I made a quick call to the long-suffering bank manager, who thankfully agreed to lend me the money to put into Brian's business – which survived and flourished, and in the end I made a good return on my investment.

I took a lot of other gambles during my corporate career, and I have taken more in recent years, since I started to get involved with backing individuals and small businesses; but more of that in Chapter 11. Back in April 1991, my overwhelming priority was to find a strategy for the recovery of NEXT. While the fact that I was close to personal ruin added another dimension to the problem, it was also a powerful incentive to finding a solution. And at last I was able to get on with the job properly.

One of my most enjoyable tasks as chief executive of NEXT was to hold informal chats with the staff on the afternoons after we announced our half-yearly and annual results to the institutional shareholders, retail analysts and financial journalists. I always referred to this as 'going back to the real world'.

I never rehearsed for the staff meetings. I just used to stand in front of people and try to explain our accounts in language that everyone could understand. They were usually happy to listen, particularly when our fortunes improved, because this was also the occasion when the aggregate amount of the annual head office bonus was announced.

The meeting in the staff restaurant at Enderby on 16 April 1991 was special – we had come within a whisker of going under, but we had survived. We had set ourselves a target of £140 million from the sale of Grattan, and in the end we had managed to get more than £170 million. Most importantly, everyone remotely connected with the retail trade had been expecting NEXT to fail. Now I had to make NEXT's own people believe that this was not going to happen.

I was in full flow, talking from the heart, without notes, when suddenly I stopped and said: 'Remember this day – 16 April 1991 – because this is the day when life begins again for NEXT!'

I don't know why I used that phrase, 'life begins again'. Travelling up to Leicester after the meeting with the analysts, press and shareholders, I had worked out in the car roughly what I was going to say. I wanted to explain that the sale of Grattan had raised enough cash to repay the Eurobonds on the due date and keep the business going; and that we had also taken the opportunity to write off or provide for every known contingency – what became known as the 'kitchen sink' job.

I went on to say that I still felt that much of the last two years had been wasted in terms of progress in the stores, but that it had been imperative to sort out the finances first. The sale of Grattan, for example, enabled us to start buying back the Eurobonds in the market below par, which not only saved on the capital repayments but also the extra interest we would have had to pay on maturity. Without the sale we would, quite simply, have gone bust. Grattan had been very dear to my heart because it was the company I had nursed back to health in the early 1980s, but it had to be the sacrificial lamb to save NEXT. Now, however, 'life begins again...' I told the employees that in the year to January 1992 I wanted to make over £10 million profit, in 1992/3 over £20 million, and in 1993/4 over £30 million.

At the time those targets seemed wildly out of reach, but when the time came we beat them. In fact we beat them by a mile, hitting £73.5 million for the year to January 1994 – by which point the recession in the High Street was effectively over, we were free of our debt problems, and NEXT was moving confidently forward again on all fronts.

How did we do it? As I said in the Introduction, for a long time I was reluctant to talk about our strategy in public. Now that time has passed, however, I can do so, and I want to start with the people of NEXT. At every level, people in the company worked incredibly hard to keep NEXT alive and turn it into a success again.

When I took over from George and moved my office to Leicester, I soon realised that in one sense he was right: there really was a special culture at NEXT, but not in the rather egocentric sense that he had implied. It was not a George Davies culture, and it never became a David Jones culture. At bottom it was and is an immense pride in the NEXT brand. People who work for NEXT passionately want it to be the best. Maybe there are many companies that have this important quality, but in my career I have come across many that do not.

The people of NEXT were in fact the only real advantage I had in the challenge that was still to come. Before I tackled it in earnest, I took the family to our apartment in Sotogrande for an Easter holiday. While I was there I listed all the things I had to do to restore NEXT's fortunes. The list ran to ten pages, and was simply too much to think about. I tore it up and wrote on a single sheet:

Stores – make them look inviting
Staff – motivate them
Product – go back to the original concept of good-quality,
*   affordable clothes*

There was an enormous amount still to be done to achieve these simple-sounding objectives. The period from 1991 to 1996 was by far the most enjoyable, exciting, productive and challenging of my career.

We started with the product: having abandoned the Originals concept, we also abandoned George's philosophy that we should not sell more than 1500 of any item in case our customers bumped into other people wearing the same garment. We also concluded that small stores selling just womenswear or menswear were uneconomic and took every opportunity to put both in the same shops – womenswear on the ground floor and menswear in the basement or on the first floor. We started to place more emphasis on quality, and we started to find out who our customers really were.

Fortunately, whoever they were, they had not completely lost faith in NEXT – they still visited our stores, but too often they could not find what they wanted. We knew we were targeting the mass-market C1 and C2 social categories aged from 17 to 70, and that our main competition was Marks & Spencer. But beyond that, our targeting seemed to be very poorly thought through. I remember asking the product director for menswear to describe our ideal male customer. I was told that he was 25 years old, drove a Porsche and earned £50,000 a year – not a very large group, you might think. I was also told that we did not sell men's jeans because NEXT man did not wear them – which he quite obviously did, but not bought from us.

I came to the conclusion that many of the buyers never visited the stores to see what our customers actually looked like and I began to change the buying team, bringing in new buyers, appointing new buying directors, and strengthening the sourcing office in Hong Kong by appointing Jim Brown, who I knew from my Kays days, as managing director of NEXT Far East. Looking back, I can see that I should have replaced many of the underperformers six to twelve months before I eventually did. But it is one of my weaknesses as a manager that I instinctively dislike sacking people, especially if I put them into the job in the first place. If they fail, how much of that failure is my own responsibility?

Once the changes in the womenswear and menswear offers began to make an impact, we started to look at childrenswear. George's decision to go into this sector was a good one, but the implementation was flawed in two ways. The clothes were too fashionable, the sort of outfits that little Jamie or Samantha might wear to their baby sister's christening, but not for every day. And the concept could never work in expensively rented, small, stand-alone stores.

Having decided that we wanted to develop childrenswear as a core product, I persuaded a very competent merchandise manager called Julie Heath to take charge of this product area. She did an outstanding job and fully deserved her promotion to director before leaving us to pursue a different career. We changed the product range to include all the 'basics' and located the product, where space allowed, close to womenswear on the ground floor of our stores. It took off and soon became an important third arm of our business.

Later on, it also illustrated another important doctrine. A survey of the competition indicated that although our childrenswear sales were growing at the rate of 30 per cent per annum, our prices were higher than the competition. We would argue that our quality was better, but still I took the decision to reduce the gross margin over three seasons by 5 per cent. When asked why I decided to do this when our higher prices were apparently not harming sales, I said: 'The time to reduce the gross margin is when we can afford to reduce it, not when the business starts to suffer – because by then it'll be too late.'

This highlights an important part of the NEXT philosophy that I started and my successor has carried on – and to which I shall return in more depth in Chapter 9. We manage NEXT for medium- or long-term benefits; we are not interested in one-off, short-term, unsustainable successes.

Having sorted out childrenswear, I turned my attention to NEXT Interiors. This product range had been introduced in the NEXT Directory, and if it had not been a natural area for home shopping I don't think we would have persevered with it. In the early days of the NEXT Directory the Interiors range was selected by the Grattan buying team, but the range selected did not match the style and quality of the NEXT brand. I decided that we either had to do it better or forget about it.

Julie Heath was my main ally in the discussions that followed. We decided to headhunt a specialist, and identified a young man called

Mark Culbert from our biggest competitor, Marks & Spencer. When we approached him he was keen to join NEXT, but as our total business in 'home products' was less than £20 million for both Retail and Directory combined, a mere fraction of M&S's sales in that sector, it took a lot of talking before he finally agreed to come to us. Mark turned out to be one of my best senior appointments from outside the business, and 'home products' continues to be a strong growth area for NEXT.

I made another decision in 1993 that had an amazing effect on the future of NEXT: to merge the product offer of Retail and Directory. Directory had been launched with its own range of product selected and merchandised by a dedicated team. Of course there were some common lines, but these were a small percentage of the total offer.

By 1992 the Directory had established a good customer base and annual sales were approaching £100 million, but the net profit was minimal, and I could not see how it was ever going to improve if the Directory remained as a stand-alone product offer. The order quantities were small and the lead times were long, which often meant that the amount of merchandise actually in stock was pathetically low. The selling prices were higher than the equivalent garments in retail, and because for some unknown reason the preview catalogue (an important method of identifying the winners and losers before the main catalogue is distributed) did not give sufficiently reliable information, the amount of drop stock at the end of the season was very high and very difficult to get rid of.

In order to differentiate the two offers, the best items inevitably finished up in Retail rather than Directory, because Retail was the bigger business. Added to that, having two competing offers encouraged internal 'us and them' attitudes that were increasingly disruptive. The stores did not like recruiting customers for Directory because they thought they were helping a 'competitor'.

In my mind there was only one solution. There must be one product for both retail formats.

On the upside, this would mean one buying team, better initial order quantities, better pricing and better quality control. It would give us flexibility to switch product between the two methods of shopping, thereby maximising sales.

On the downside, I had to ask myself whether Directory customers genuinely wanted a different range so that they had more choice. I also had to take into consideration the fact that making one combined buying team would result in redundancy for a lot of people through no fault of their own. These redundancies were very regrettable, but I concluded that they were absolutely necessary. And there would also have to be a massive retraining programme to ensure that buyers and merchandisers were competent in both Retail and Directory systems, including the different time frames for product selection driven by printing deadlines for the Directory preview and main catalogue.

As an aside, in my opinion it was easier for home shopping merchandisers to learn retail disciplines than the other way round.

There was a very strong camp against the idea of common product, far outnumbering the pro camp – which consisted of me, the chairman and my young personal assistant, who I shall introduce properly a little later in the story. But I held the casting vote, because if the Directory customer did in fact want an alternative choice of product then NEXT Directory was dead in the water anyway, because it would never make an acceptable profit with a unique product range.

There was no way of testing the new concept, and no point. I did not trust the Directory marketing team to carry out any market research, because it is the easiest thing in the world to fix the answer you want. I have always maintained that if market research confirms your view you complain about the cost, and if it goes against your view you claim that the sample was too small!

Fortunately, this controversial decision proved to be the making of the Directory. In the two years that followed, Directory sales increased by 60 per cent and profit by 150 per cent, and although it took much longer than I had originally thought to merge the two teams into one team skilled in both selling disciplines, it is now where we wanted it to be. The product offer is the same, with four phases during the year. The main Directory catalogue is distributed in January and August in line with the launch of the new seasons in Retail. We distribute a smaller hard-cover catalogue in March covering the summer retail phase and in October for the Christmas retail offer.

This may all sound simple and logical, but it represented a giant step forward. 'One brand, two methods of shopping' became our new theme, followed by 'We don't mind if the customers buy from Retail or Directory as long as they buy from NEXT!'

Since that important decision we have purposely moved the two methods of shopping closer together, to make it as easy as possible for the customer to shop with us. There is now only one credit offer, so that you can buy on credit from Retail or Directory on the same account – whereas previously there was a NEXT gold card for Retail purchases and a Directory 'easy credit' account. You can order goods from the Directory in the store or by telephone or email, and the goods can be delivered to the store for collection or direct to your home. Returns can be handed in at the store or sent back by courier.

Some of those who were against the change were motivated by fear of losing their own jobs; some genuinely believed that Directory customers wanted a different product. But it turned out to be one of the best decisions I ever made, because from autumn 1993 onwards NEXT Directory went from strength to strength.

NEXT Directory is a unique home shopping business and I have already paid tribute to George Davies's part in its conception. Its long-term success, however, was entirely due to the combination of Grattan's mail-order expertise and NEXT's product expertise – the original rationale for the NEXT–Grattan merger. Directory is the only successful new large-scale catalogue launch in the past 20 years, though many others have tried – not only the traditional mail-order companies, but also Marks & Spencer, Debenhams and Arcadia, to name a few.

By the mid-1990s the retail sector had sailed into more favourable economic conditions and NEXT's business had stabilised. The product had improved, the operations were performing well, the Directory was profitable and we had a good portfolio of retail sites. NEXT staff were well motivated by good bonuses and good growth in the share price. We were not under pressure from the City because we were beating its forecasts time and time again.

And the low profile was working: we were no longer much of a story for the media. In the retail sector, it was Rick Greenbury at Marks & Spencer who was now attracting negative coverage and would continue to do so as the performance of M&S – still at that stage very much the market leader and one of Britain's most iconic brands – continued to suffer from internal controversy.

So at last we were in a position to go on the front foot again. We decided to take the NEXT business to another level by increasing our retail selling space, but in a very controlled way. During the recovery phase we said that the ideal size of store was 3500 to 5000 square feet. But as conditions improved, stores in good locations were achieving in excess of £1000 sales per square foot per year, which was a sure sign that the store was too small and that we needed more selling space.

I remember a conversation with one director (he has since moved on) who said that our objective should be to get sales per square foot in below-average stores up to the average. I told him I was not really interested in below-average stores, but that the ones to concentrate on were the high-performing ones with potential to go even higher if we could add more selling space. So we started, selectively and slowly, to increase the size of stores, not opening too many larger stores until we had proved that the formula actually worked. We maintained our very strict criteria for capital expenditure, and moved carefully forward – having been close to the brink of disaster once, we had no intention of going there again.

When we did open a store that proved to be too big, the downside was limited because it was only one store. We are still experimenting with store sizes today and, although there have been a few that have underperformed against the original targets, I believe that we have yet to find our optimum size.

There was still one more piece of the jigsaw to put the whole NEXT business in better shape. Getting the product right was one thing, but getting it to the stores at the right time was another. Fortunately, my ex-Grattan team were well able to improve our warehousing and distribution by the introduction of new systems and procedures, and better management.

It never fails to amaze me how inefficient the warehousing and distribution systems of some high-street retailers can be: it is as if they spend all their time and experience on the product, and expect it to find its own way to the store. What happens if a bestseller goes out of stock? How do you make sure it is identified at the receiving bay and fast-tracked through the system? These are the sort of issues that retailers too often fail to address.

In our case we were thinking about the right issues, but the rapid growth of sales in both Retail and Directory was putting heavy pressure on our warehousing capacity, and it became obvious that we needed new facilities. Having been thrust into the deep end at BMOC when the Martland distribution centre turned out to be such a shambles, and having been responsible for the successful Listerhills warehouse development at Grattan – episodes that I shall come back to in detail in Part II – I felt confident I had the experience to find a solution. And I still had some of my team with me from Martland and Listerhills. The question was what we should build and where.

We went through the options: should we duplicate our present warehouse structure in Yorkshire in another location in the south of England? Should we increase capacity by increasing the number of warehouses? Or should we acquire a greenfield site and move everything to a brand new facility?

We had gone through the same thought processes at Grattan before we built Listerhills. A southern warehouse would have meant splitting the stock, for example, creating costs that would outweigh the savings on transportation. It was probably not surprising that we again opted for one new, centralised site, as we had at Grattan. After trekking around Yorkshire looking for suitable places with good access to the motorway network and an available workforce, we purchased a large piece of land at South Elmsall – a former mining area – and created two monster distribution centres. One of these housed merchandise that was delivered on hangers; the second was for merchandise delivered in boxes. Both units included mechanised high-bay storage that supplied merchandise to the adjoining 'picking and packing' units.

Two years and £120 million later, both warehouses were fully operational. When they opened I took great pride in showing off the high-bay storage units to the non-executive directors, with 26 automatic cranes starting up one after the other and bringing boxes out of the storage unit. The implementation was almost perfect – which came as a surprise to many commentators, who normally associated new distribution centres for large retailers with logistical disaster, swiftly to be followed by profit warnings. I reckon that during my career I have been responsible for building more retail warehouses than anyone else in the trade: it is a part of the job that I shall miss!

I did not always get everything right, however. When we had spare cash in the bank in 1993 – some of it clawed back from Club 24's debtors – we made an excursion into the USA, which was one of the worst business decisions I ever made. I am not the only British chief executive to have made this mistake, but since almost no one had made the trip to the US successfully, I really ought to have known better.

I received a letter from a gentleman called Wasim Kabara, who proposed a trial opening of NEXT stores in Boston and Washington. We discussed the idea and decided to give it a go, on the basis that the downside was minimal and if it turned out to be successful we would have a good additional arm to our business. We gave it our best shot, but it just did not work: we closed down again after three years at a loss of around £10 million. This upset me enormously, but it gave us a lot of valuable information about trading overseas. One day NEXT is going to have to consider overseas expansion and the lessons learned from this failure will help us to get it right.

We were also invited – and foolishly accepted the invitation – to become the British end of an American venture called Bath & Body Works, a version of The Body Shop launched by The Limited, the huge US retail group founded by Les Wexner. David Wolfson and I visited The Limited's headquarters in Columbus, Ohio, several times, and on one occasion we stayed at the Wexner mansion. Buckingham Palace is the only residence I have set foot in that compares for size – the drive from the gate to the huge double-front doors seemed to take ten minutes. When the door finally swung open, we were greeted by the actor Michael Gough's double dressed as Batman's butler: 'Welcome my Lord, good evening Mister Jones,' with heavy emphasis on the Mister.

We opened five Bath & Body Works stores in the UK in the autumn of 1994, but the whole experiment was doomed to failure. We had to overprice the product because of import duty, and the sales per square foot were not high enough to cover the much higher rent charged in the UK compared with US stores. The market was already very competitive in this type of product: Boots, Marks & Spencer and The Body Shop itself offered very good products at better prices, and the supermarkets were beginning to get into the sector too.

We struggled to make it work and Mr Wexner began to get irritated with us. When The Limited decided to float Bath & Body Works as a separate company, we took the opportunity to come out of the joint venture without loss. Though 'lifestyle' cosmetics brands are all the rage again today, it was not an exercise I would rush to repeat.

There was one other venture in the United States that had a far more satisfactory result. Early in 1993 I was introduced to Gilbert Harrison. He was a New York-based financial adviser who specialised in the retail sector, and was making his annual pilgrimage to the UK to see what was new. Gilbert prided himself that he knew everyone in the retail trade, and by this time NEXT had recovered sufficiently to gain the status of being a company that he needed to know.

I liked Gilbert and we got on well – the only problem was that he always wanted me to buy other businesses. He wasn't particularly bothered what I should buy, and suggested some rather odd targets. But one day he telephoned me to say that J. Crew was for sale, and I suggested to David Wolfson that we spend some time looking at the idea. J. Crew was a private company, owned and managed by Arthur Cinader, which had established a strong brand in the US by targeting the 'campus' market. It started as a catalogue retailer but had recently opened stores in shopping malls.

We visited J. Crew in New York and loosely talked about acquiring the business, but Arthur could not make up his mind whether he wanted to sell and in the end – rather thankfully – we gave up. We did, however, get two benefits from the exercise. The first was that we copied one of J. Crew's catalogues and successfully launched a NEXT 'basics' leaflet, which became the forerunner of the mid-season catalogue that we now distribute at summer and Christmas.

Far more importantly, the connection led to two rounds of golf at Augusta, the home of the Masters and one of the greatest courses in the world. During one of our 'we don't want to buy' conversations with Gilbert Harrison, David Wolfson said in his usual joking style that it was about time Gilbert did something really useful, 'like arranging for us to play golf at Augusta!'

This was just David's way of diverting a boring conversation, but Gilbert took it seriously and three weeks later we were on a plane to Atlanta. David and I were close business colleagues but our social lives rarely coincided, and I regard this trip – on which he was in tremendous form throughout – as one of the highlights of our long relationship.

Our host was John Belk, whose family owned a chain of stores mainly in the southern states. We arrived on the first tee at 2 p.m.

on Sunday. I was feeling pretty nervous and it didn't help when David invited me to go first. My nervousness was partly due to the fact that my golf could be very erratic, but primarily due to the fact that, as David and I would be in each other's company from early morning to late in the evening, somehow I had to keep my Parkinson's symptoms under control for a very long period of time.

I almost made it. I was 'normal' right up until we were on the plane home, when I suddenly had the dreaded 'shakes'. Fortunately David was sitting on my left, and it was my right arm and shoulder that were shaking. I think I managed to hide it by sitting on my right hand, even though it made my arm totally numb. David made no comment – thankfully, because I certainly could not have lied to him if he had asked me what was wrong.

Anyway, back to the more enjoyable subject of golf. I was quite pleased with my first drive, about 180 yards slightly to the right but not in any trouble, so I was mildly irritated when I was invited by our 73-year-old host to 'have a mulligan'. Apparently the custom in the US is for each player to hit two balls off the first tee and choose the best ball to play, without incurring a penalty.

I declined the offer rather sourly and walked off the tee towards the four waiting caddies, who were standing next to four new golf carts. As one of the caddies walked towards me I shook hands with him and asked him his name.

'Leon, sir.'

'Right, Leon, put the clubs on the buggy, you can drive.'

'No sir, I have to walk.'

'Ok, Leon, put the clubs on the buggy and I'll drive.'

'No sir, I carry the clubs!'

So I was going to drive my new golf cart round Augusta, while my five-foot-three caddie was going to carry my big golf bag and 14 Callaway Big Bertha clubs.

There was a hold-up on the first fairway because one of the Americans had hooked both his drives into the bushes. To pass the time I had a friendly conversation with Leon – he was married, had three children and his wife worked on the night shift at a supermarket. When we eventually got to the first green I was very politely but firmly told that it was not done to talk to the caddies – all of whom, as you may have guessed, were black.

I was taken aback, but accepted that as a privileged guest I should abide by the customs of the course, and Leon and I did not exchange another word for the whole of the round. David and I both played badly and I could not get off the course quickly enough!

That evening we enjoyed the unique atmosphere of the club-house at Augusta, including a visit to the wine cellar, where David accepted the invitation to choose a red wine and selected a very nice – and I imagine very expensive – claret.

The conversation over dinner was amusing. David asked if they allowed lady members at Augusta.

'Yes, we do allow lady members,' came the answer, 'but there aren't any.'

When our hosts referred to the various problems of the British royal family, notably in relation to the Prince and Princess of Wales, David rather defensively referred to 'problems in your own royal family', meaning the Kennedys. The reply was entirely unprintable!

The next morning we were on the first tee again at 10 a.m., with the four golf carts and the same four caddies. Once again I was invited to tee off first and as I was addressing the ball, our host invited us to play for $500 a corner. My chairman and captain for the day accepted the invitation, much to my surprise, and the shock must have influenced the poor drive that followed – but fortunately the mulligan that followed was a good one.

When Leon joined me 195 yards up the fairway, he spoke to me for the first time since we had been at almost the same spot the previous afternoon.

'Seven wood!'

'Pardon?'

'I know exactly how you play. I'll guide you round this golf course.'

He proceeded to tell me what club to use, where to aim for and how to line up my putts. I had a par three on the short hole at Amen Corner, a par five on the 15th and a par three on the 16th, where Greg Norman drove into the water during that famous final round when Nick Faldo fought back from a seven-shot deficit to win his third Masters title.

David and I won the match three holes up with two to play, and I succeeded in going round this most famous course in 92 strokes, including an unfortunate eight on the final hole.

Our hosts were not entirely happy, but handed us $500 each. Out of sight of the defeated pair I gave my $500 to Leon and thanked him for his superb coaching. He flashed a huge grin full of gleaming white teeth and said: 'We sure stuffed them, man!'

It was a moment I'll never forget.

But these American adventures were minor diversions. The overall story of those years was one of step-by-step progress towards rebuilding NEXT as a market leader and a highly profitable business. By January 1996 we could show five years of continuous and remarkable growth in pre-tax profits, from £12 million in 1991/2 to £142 million in 1995/6. Not surprisingly, NEXT was seen by the stock market to be an increasingly attractive investment and the share price rocketed.

This was good news for many NEXT employees who had Save-as-you-earn share options paid for out of their monthly salary, or share options granted to middle and senior managers each year at current prices, to be purchased at that price three years later. Many public companies at that time granted options only to senior directors – and eventually ran into flak for doing so – but I adopted a policy of spreading the available options across a wide range of executives, including store and warehouse managers. Over six years a store manager could accumulate up to 10,000 shares at an average price of £2 and sell them at anything over £6, making a profit before tax of more than £30,000.

That was a tremendous motivating factor. It was also well deserved because – I can't say this often enough, so forgive me if I repeat myself – it was the people of NEXT that created its success.

Part II

1943–1986

Learning the trade

Chapter 5

'The most important decision is the next one'

My father was a gentle, considerate man, one of those old-fashioned people who always addressed anyone he considered to be above his station as 'sir' or 'madam', which in reality meant virtually everyone. He rarely lost his temper; on the odd occasion that he did – usually provoked by my brother – it was quite frightening.

My mother was a formidable lady who ruled the household, albeit with my father's blessing. She was the strength that supported the family through the bad times, particularly when my father was out of work. She was clever and I am sure she would have had a successful business career if that had been possible in those days. I can see so much of my mother in my daughter Alison, whereas my sons have slightly different combinations of Ann and me.

I have always tried to be respectful to people whatever their position in life, and I have never quite got used to being a captain of industry – traits that must come from my father. My mother gave me the ability to be tough with myself and sometimes with other people when it is necessary.

Looking back at an ordinary but happy upbringing and a rather modest school record in the 1940s and 1950s, it would be false to say that I can see precisely how the attributes that have helped me in business, and in coping with Parkinson's Disease, developed from an early age. Even less can I claim that I knew as a boy that I wanted to grow up to run a great company. In fact I had no career ambitions at all, and no idea of my own potential, until I was in my twenties and had a foot on the first rung of the ladder at Kays of Worcester.

But there are still some memories of childhood worth recalling here, because perhaps they do illustrate the boy who became the man, and sometimes because they taught me specific lessons that I have never forgotten.

I was born and brought up at Malvern Link in Worcestershire, where my paternal grandfather had a tobacconist and confectionery shop that also did watch and umbrella repairs and sold grandfather clocks. Many years later my father would watch grandfather clocks being valued on the *Antiques Road Show* and bemoan the fact that as a lad he used to chop old ones up for firewood.

Dad never talked about his early life, but odd comments that he made to Ann indicated that his childhood was not a happy one. He left school at 15 and did an engineering apprenticeship at the Morgan Motor Company in Malvern Link. His sense of loyalty to his mother resulted in him wasting many years in the backwater of the small shop started by his father when he could have been developing his engineering career. When he did return to engineering after his mother died, it was too late to achieve very much – though he did get promotion to foreman.

With a little more luck in his early life, I believe he might have been a very successful man, maybe with the Morgan Motor Company. The Morgan was and still is a unique sports car that gained a very good reputation by, among other things, maintaining a waiting list of buyers of up to five years.

Many years later I introduced Dad to Sir John Harvey-Jones at Bradford University, where I was receiving an honorary doctorate from Sir John, who was Chancellor of the University. Having finished my education with three rather modest A-levels and no prospect of going on to take a degree, this recognition of my achievements in later life was a very proud moment for me. As for Sir John, he had recently completed one of his celebrated *Troubleshooter* television programmes on Morgan, where he had very firmly told the Morgan family management that the way forward was for them to increase production and reduce the waiting list for new cars.

Dad believed that this was absolute nonsense and that the waiting list was an important factor in the appeal of the car – a theory I confirmed years later when I invested in my own specialist car company! He took Sir John into a quiet corner and proceeded to lecture him for ten minutes on why he had got his strategy for Morgan completely wrong, ending with a phrase that deserves a place in any good business studies lecture: 'It's just common sense.'

Sir John – who was well known for his infectious chuckle as well as his gaudy ties – took this in good grace, and told the amused crowd around him that he had been well and truly put in his place. I think I was more proud of Dad that day than he was of me.

Anyway, at the time of my birth in February 1943 – nine years after that of my only sibling, my brother, Fred – Dad was an engineer in the Royal Air Force, repairing fighter planes at an airfield somewhere on the south coast. After the war he returned to the shop to do watch repairs. Sometimes he took me to work with him on his old bicycle, pushing it up the steep hill to Link Top where the shop was, with me in the little seat behind the saddle.

I enjoyed watching him repairing watches and clocks, while his elder brother Bob mended umbrellas. Just possibly this was the birth of my interest in retailing – but if it was, it was hardly very inspiring because we had so few customers. When the trips to Link Top eventually stopped, I assumed the reason was that I had got far too big for Dad to push me up the hill. But eventually he told me that the shop was closing down and the creditors were chasing him for their money. It had been failing for a long time, but Dad kept it going as long as he could for the sake of his widowed mother, who lived in a little flat behind the shop. Soon after she died, the shop shut for the last time, and Dad became unemployed.

My mother, as I said, was the tough one. The closure of the business forced her to find full-time work to try to make up for the drop in family income, so she became head cook at one of the boys' houses at Malvern College, her speciality being baked ice cream.

She was a stout lady, reaching 18 stone in her prime. Her mother, who died before I was born, was apparently even heavier. This hereditary characteristic was to become a convenient excuse for my own excess weight, rather than blaming a lack of exercise or too much red wine.

I remember an incident that illustrated how tough my mother was. I was queuing with her at Towndrow's, the grocers in Malvern Link. In those days of rationing – which lasted until I was 11 – we would spend hours in this queue every week. I think it left me with a permanent phobia about queuing. It was depressing enough in itself, but it was made worse by young mothers crying and begging for coupons to buy food. I used to feel sorry for them, but Mum had no sympathy – she said that it was their own fault because they had traded their coupons for cigarettes.

Having waited for over an hour one day, we were about to be served when Lady Beauchamp – the Countess Beauchamp, no less, who lived in a grand house called Madresfield Court near Malvern – marched in, straight past the queue. Old Mr Towndrow turned away from my mother to ask what 'your ladyship' required this morning.

'This ladyship has been queuing for ages and is next to be served,' my mother interrupted, in a tone which was not going to take no for an answer. 'That ladyship can queue up like the rest of us!'

This one-woman revolution against the privileged aristocracy provoked strong vocal support from the rest of the queue, and Lady Beauchamp duly took her place at the back. Mum was fair to those who were fair to her, and her manner was always calm – if there was a difficult problem to face she would often say 'let's sleep on it and decide in the morning'. This was not a way of putting off the decision, but her way of making sure that everything was considered before that final decision was made – a practice I certainly inherited from her.

Our home in Goodson Road, Malvern Link was called Cwm, after the village near Ebbw Vale in South Wales where my mother was born. It was a semi-detached cottage with an old-fashioned open cooking range in the kitchen, an outside lavatory and – until a council grant came along later on – no bathroom. A tin bath once a week in front of the range had to suffice. My parents rented the house for many years until I was able to buy it for them in 1971. Shortly after that it saved me from my first major financial crisis, but I'll come to that story later.

One of my best memories of Cwm is of playing snooker in the front room. Dad was a very accomplished player – the only amateur I ever saw who, nine times out of ten, could place the white ball in the D on a full-sized table and pot the black off its spot into a top pocket. I remember the excitement at home when he installed a one-third-sized snooker table, complete with slate bed, rubber cushions, ivory balls and a green baize cloth that had to be brushed and ironed with tender loving care before each family tournament. I spent many happy hours in that room; the addiction to snooker has stayed with me all my life, and passed to the next generation of Joneses. The snooker room is still the heart of our family house in Ilkley.

The miniature snooker table was the only luxury we had in those lean, austere post-war years. But my parents gave me a stable, care-free childhood, and when I talk about the importance of a support-ive family life during the most difficult moments of my business life, I'm sure the happy days at Cwm are in my subconscious.

And even at that early age, I was the leader of the gang. It may not have been much of a gang – half a dozen other little boys from Goodson Road, one honorary member from round the corner, and a girl called Rosamund who was only allowed to join us in emer-gencies when we were short of lookouts to keep watch for small invaders from neighbouring streets.

Our territory – a cul-de-sac of nine houses and a dirt track through a wood to a farm – had to be defended at all costs. The road became Lords, Wembley, Twickenham or Wimbledon, depending on the time of year. The wood substituted for Sherwood Forest, the American prairies or the African jungle, depending on the latest popular film.

The only people allowed on our patch were the nuns from the convent set behind a 10-foot wall opposite our house. Over the years I saw many young girls coming to the convent as novices. They used to walk through the woods reading religious books as they went, oblivious to our efforts to talk to them. Mum said it was their calling, which baffled me, because I never heard anyone calling them!

Our biggest enemy was Frank Wilesmith, the farmer at the top of the road behind the woods. He used to roar past in his big car, looking smug, disrupting our cricket and football games in the street. But we all had to be polite to him because he gave everyone in the road – including my parents, particularly when Dad was unemployed – seasonal work picking peas and hops on the farm. I used to help them and I can remember that it became a matter of pride that the Jones family picked more than anyone else – maybe this was the start of my competitive nature!

So although we were hard up and my parents must have had worries, life was good. I had my own gang with the best territory in the neighbourhood, and a real treat on Sundays – a ride on Dad's Ariel Square Four motorbike and sidecar to a pub somewhere for a packet of crisps and a Vimto. The revelation that at the age of four I had to go to school came as an unpleasant surprise. I assumed that Dad could teach me everything I would ever need to know, including the difference between the engine noises of all the great motorcycle marques, on which he was an expert. But no, in September 1947 I was dragged, literally, to my first day at St Mathias's Church of England Primary School.

I enjoyed my six years there, and I owe a great deal to two teachers, Miss Andrews and Mr Lindsey. Miss Andrews took me under her wing and encouraged me to read everything I could get my hands on, even the carefully ripped-up pages of the *Daily Mirror* that sometimes had to substitute for a toilet roll in the outside loo. Not that this favouritism allowed me to escape from her terrible cane, an ancient weapon held together by multicoloured strands of wool; many times I went home with long red wheals on my left hand or my backside.

Miss Andrews, like Dad only more so, seemed to know everything. I cannot remember her ever referring to a textbook. Whether she was teaching history, geography or English, she just stood in front of us and the facts flowed out. Many years later I went back to attend her retirement party and asked her how she was able to remember so much. She smiled and said that we were all given a brain, but it was what we did with it that really mattered.

Mr Lindsey was the headmaster, and it is to him I owe my sharp eye for numbers. He taught us arithmetic on Tuesday and Thursday afternoons, and the format was always the same. He would write six mathematical problems on the blackboard, which I remember as being usually either LCMs (lowest common multiple) or HCFs (highest common factor). When you had completed the six calculations you rushed to the front of the class with your answers. When ten of us had come forward, he would go through the answers on the blackboard.

If you were one of the ten you received a red tick for every correct answer and five bonus ticks if you got them all right; thirty red ticks and you were allowed to go home! It was a nightmare for those who could not master simple arithmetic – their worried mothers were constantly ringing the school late in the afternoon to find out where they were. But these sessions helped me develop an aptitude for figures that would remain with me for life. Even now I rarely use a calculator, and I am always amazed to see young, qualified accountants using one to add two figures together.

Lessons with the headmaster also helped me to improve my memory. I developed my own method of remembering things, writing down names and facts and repeating them to myself over and over again. As a result (although it proved only moderately useful to my career in the clothing trade, since so much of the British textile industry had gone forever by the time I got there) I can recite even today the cotton towns of Lancashire – Manchester, Oldham, Bolton, Bury, Stockport, Preston, Wigan – and the woollen towns of Yorkshire – Leeds, Bradford, Halifax, Huddersfield, Wakefield, Barnsley, Morley, Dewsbury and Ripon.

Because St Mathias's was a Church of England school, I also had a strong religious education. I took part in religious plays and went to Sunday School. I became a 'boat boy', carrying incense in a silver container, and graduated to being a candle bearer at Sunday morning service at St Leonard's Church, where I had been christened (and which explains my third Christian name, Leonard, which I never use). But I did not keep up my church going, I suppose because I did not feel I was learning anything from it. I gradually drifted into the spiritual doubt that comes to us all: how can there be a God when so many terrible things happen to so many innocent people? At some stage I gave up trying to find the answer and concluded that we all start from the same place and finish in a similar way, and what really matters is what happens in between. To the extent that I have a creed, it is that I try to lead a good life and hope that if there is something hereafter, maybe I will qualify for it.

But long before I wrestled with tests of faith, I had to wrestle with the 11-plus, which would decide where I went to school next. It would be a local secondary modern school if I failed, or one of two grammar schools, Worcester Royal or Hanley Castle, if I passed. My parents – in fact, as in many families, it was my mother who took charge of this sort of decision – had to fill in a form saying which school they would prefer me to go to. There was also a line marked 'Other' to name another choice of school.

When the day of the exam came, I felt I had done badly. 'As long as you've done your best, you can do no better than that,' Mum said. It was no comfort at the time, because I knew that I could have done much better, but this simple phrase has stayed in my mind all my life. Winning is always the objective, but improving your performance is the real test. Ever since the day of that examination I have always assessed my performance each day before going to bed. Whether it was a presentation to retail analysts or chairing a board meeting, or even drafting out a chapter of this book, I have always asked myself if I could have done it better. I believe that just as you never stop learning, you should never stop trying to improve your own performance.

Four weeks later, after assembly and morning prayers, the headmaster came into the classroom and announced that he had just received the 11-plus results. He paused for a few seconds then smiled, as if he was enjoying the fact that he knew something we didn't. He started to read out the list of successful candidates. Some of the boys had passed into Hanley Castle Grammar, some of the girls were going to Worcester Girls' Grammar. But where was my name?

Mr Lindsey put down the list of results. I did not know where to look. My name had not been called out. My friends looked at me in a surprised but sympathetic way, while the ones I imagined to be my enemies, the ones who did not like the fact that I collected so many red ticks for arithmetic, started to sneer.

I was about to start crying when the headmaster began to beam. He said he was proud to announce that for the first time in the history of the school a pupil had passed to go to the Worcester Cathedral King's School – the premier public school in the county. That pupil was me.

I rushed home to Mum and Dad, and when all the hugging had stopped, I asked Mum why she had chosen the King's School. She told me she had decided to put it on the 'Other' line because she was unhappy with the way Worcester Royal Grammar School had, in her view, ruined my brother's education.

My brother had made a promising start to his academic career at the grammar school, but unfortunately became ill with scarlet fever and was in and out of hospital for many months. When he eventually went back to school he had missed a complete year. The sensible thing would have been to keep him in the same year and allow him the opportunity to catch up. But he was automatically put up to the next year, where he was so out of his depth that he struggled to keep up and lost all interest in studying. He left school at 16, joined the Royal Navy and was discharged on medical grounds ten years later. Fortunately he had completed his apprenticeship as an electrician, and he had his own one-man business until he retired. We have very little in common, although I think he is proud of what I have achieved. If I have had all the good luck in life, then he has certainly had more than his share of the bad.

In contrast to my time at St Mathias's, which I thoroughly enjoyed, my seven years at public school were a good deal less memorable. I had some fun, but it was always about beating the system and being a bit of a rebel. I had a couple of good friends, but none of us kept in touch after we left. I never felt at ease at the King's School, probably due to the fact that after a bright start, I struggled academically around the middle to bottom of the class. Nor was I a talented sportsman, so I had little opportunity to sparkle.

It was when Mum and I went to buy my new uniform from the school shop that I realised for the first time in my life that money was tight in the Jones household, because Mum had to agree to pay for the clothes at so much a month over six months. It was a big, open shop and everyone else there could see that she did not have enough money to pay in full. On the bus going home, I plucked up courage to ask her if they could really afford to send me to the school, because although I was on a free scholarship there were compulsory uniforms and sports clothes that had to be paid for. She said they could, but she obviously mentioned the conversation to my father when we got home, because he offered me a game of snooker – he beat me, as usual – and as we played he explained at last about the closure of the business and how he hoped he would find more work soon and everything would be fine.

For the next three months Dad studied the *Malvern Gazette* for jobs, and spent most of his days on the allotment that he rented from the Convent. 'Job or no job, we still have to eat,' he used to say.

I was ashamed at being a burden on them, and became deter-mined to make my own contribution to the family budget. Without telling my parents I successfully applied to WH Smith for a paper round. I used to get up at 5.30 a.m., cycle to Smith's, prepare my round – which I could do from memory – deliver the papers, be home for breakfast at ten to eight, then catch the bus to Worcester to be at school by five to nine for morning assembly. I earned 12s 6d per week, of which I gave Mum 10s. I found out years later (when one of the numbers came up and I won £50) that she used it to buy Premium Bonds for me.

The paper round taught me a lot about life. I worked hard, and had to get used to the discipline of getting up at 5.30 a.m. six days a week. I did not miss a single day, and the longer I continued with the round the more important this record became to me. I battled through blizzards and fevers to deliver the *Times* and the *Listener* to the posh houses, the *Mirror* and the *TV Times* to the prefabs and flats, and the *Daily Mail* and the *Radio Times* to the new middle-class housing estate that sprang up almost overnight in our midst.

My routine was so regular that people used to tell the time by where they saw me and know if they were early or late for work. At Christmas the people in the prefabs and flats were generous with tips, whereas the posh people in the large houses used to go out of their way to avoid me. When I stopped doing the round I typed out two cards. The one for the posh houses was a formal farewell:

'You don't know me, but I have been your personal paper boy for the last three years – never missing a day's delivery and ensuring that you had your newspaper to read at the breakfast table. I now move on to better things.'

The card for the prefabs and flats was jauntier and more personal:

'It has been my pleasure to deliver your newspaper every day for the last three years – I do not know your name and I doubt if you know mine, yet we know each other well. I now move on to better things. David Jones.'

The houses on the new estate got the friendly card if they had tipped me at Christmas, the less friendly one if not.

During school holidays I delivered other rounds as well, if there was a vacancy or someone failed to turn up, and regularly did four or five rounds in the morning. This meant that I got a lot of stick from people who received their morning paper at lunchtime, so I typed out yet another card politely telling them to complain to the manager at WH Smith and not to me, because I was just a paid employee!

I had been doing the paper round for three years when the lovely old chap who supervised us all died suddenly and I was asked to do his job. This was my first wage negotiation – I knew the old man got £5 per week and was more than a little miffed when I was only offered £2. After ten minutes' haggling I settled for £3. Not bad, I thought: 50 per cent more than I was first offered, even if it was 40 per cent less than they paid my predecessor.

The new job – from 5.30 a.m. to 7.30 a.m. each day – was fun, but I had to give it up when I reached my A-level year to concentrate on my school work. On my last day at Smith's the manager offered me a job as a management trainee. I turned him down; but I have often wondered what would have happened if I had said yes.

Funnily enough, many years later in 1997, after Bill Cockburn had resigned from the chief executive's job at WH Smith, I was approached by a headhunter to find out whether I would be interested in it. The headhunter was put out when I immediately declined. He telephoned again the following day to repeat the invitation and when he received the same reply he said, rather sourly, that he was surprised I had not even asked what salary was being offered. I told him there was no amount of money that could persuade me to take the job. This was not because I bore any ill feeling from my teenage years – quite the contrary – but because NEXT was my life and there was no way I would turn my back on the company or the people.

I started at the King's School in September 1953, and I recall from my first morning assembly the slow, impressive entrance of the headmaster, F. R. Kittermaster, an elderly, silver-haired figure who had been in the post since the late 1930s and was credited as the architect of what had become a very successful school. Everyone thought the world of him, and when he finally hung up his gown four years later we bade him a very emotional farewell. The other teachers, however, were a motley crew.

The master who helped me the most was 'Oily' Farrar, the deputy headmaster, who taught me French and German for my first two years. I made good progress in both, to the extent that I conceived an ambition to find a career that would involve languages. But this prospect was ruined by Len Aldridge, a new language master straight from university, whose lack of experience of class control allowed us to play him up unmercifully, with the outcome that I made no further progress and failed O-level French and German by the widest possible margin.

One of my fellow pupils, incidentally, was Geoff Mulcahy, who went on to become a big name in the retailing world of the 1980s and 1990s as chief executive and chairman of Woolworths, which became Kingfisher. Geoff was a year older than me and a bit of a loner at school. But he achieved far greater academic success than I did, and went on not only to Manchester University but – very unusually for our generation of British managers – to do an MBA at Harvard. I later found out that Leonard Wolfson was also at the King's School, from 1942 to 1945. I wonder how many schools can boast three prominent retail chiefs as old boys?

If my own academic achievements were undistinguished, my sporting achievements were non-existent. But there was one bright spot – I had a talent for chess. Dad had taught me to play when I was about eight, and having studied books by Alekhine and Keres, I could play pretty well. In my second year I entered the school chess championship and made rapid progress to reach the quarter-finals. I was drawn against an older boy called Graham, whose twin brother was the best player in the school.

The match was played in the sixth-form library in front of a size-able audience; my classmates turned out in force to support me, even though they had no idea how the game was played. Even 'Bertie' Balance, the master in charge of the school chess team, turned up. I was nervous, but I won – and the following week in the semi-final I beat a very good player who must have been having a bad day. I then played the defending champion, Steve Graham, in the final: I put up a good fight but lost to a better player. Nevertheless, I was immediately selected for the school first team.

I shall never forget my first match for the school – it was against the Worcester Blind College, and I played a young blind boy called Crombie. I watched his fingers feeling the chess pieces on his specially made pocket set: the white squares were depressed and the black squares raised, the white pieces had smooth tops and the black pieces pointed tops. I thought I had a good memory, but this fellow was truly remarkable. He had an irritating habit of smiling when I told him my move, as if he knew exactly what I was going to do. I lost, but it was a good game that lasted for three hours. Over the years I played Crombie many times and I think the honours finished up more or less even. In my final two years I captained the school team – and that was my only claim to fame in the seven years I was there.

I do not want to sound too critical of the King's School, but looking back I have two complaints. The first was that after the second year we were asked to choose between arts and sciences. It was an easy decision for me to choose arts, but for the wrong reasons – in the first two years we had one general science lesson a week that barely scratched the surface of the subject, so we really could not make an informed choice. The second complaint was that, while the general standard of teachers was good, some of them were lousy. How did they ever get the job?

Meanwhile, life was improving for my parents. Dad was not out of work for long, and found a good new job as an engineer at the Royal Radar Establishment (RRE) at Malvern – for which he was qualified by virtue of his apprenticeship at Morgan before the war. He loved it, and stayed there until he retired.

His Ariel motorcycle had been sold when he was out of work, but one Saturday soon after he started at RRE, Dad asked me to go to Bromsgrove with him for a mysterious purpose. We went on the bus, but we came back in a second-hand Ford Anglia – the Jones family's first car. Dad's new job also transformed the house: the old range came out and a less exciting modern fireplace took its place, and we got a brand new 21" screen television. Finally, we achieved the ultimate comfort: a bathroom with a hot water boiler and an inside toilet. It is amazing how today we take such luxuries for granted.

The most important outcome of Dad's secure job was that Mum was able to give up hers. She had worked hard for too many years and her legs were beginning to play her up, but now she could take life easier – and give a lot of her time to working for charity. She spent hours knitting cats and poodles and even kangaroos complete with a baby in their pouch. They sold like hot cakes at the school bazaar.

Back at the King's School, my work during the year was reasonable but I never performed well in year-end exams. I just seemed to freeze up. In the summer of 1958 I sat eight O-levels: English Language, English Literature, Mathematics, Latin, French, German, History and Geography. I worked hard for six of them – I had given up on French and German – and was devastated when the letter arrived two months later advising me that I had failed six and passed only two, Maths and Latin. I told my parents the sad news – and again Mum said, 'Well, as long as you did your best.'

But it was no comfort, because I knew I should have and could have done much better. I spent many unhappy hours thinking about how much I had let myself down, telling myself that it should never happen again. This increased my resolve to be self-critical about my performance and always strive to do better. It is a principle that has even applied to the writing of this book: every time I looked at the 'final' draft, I changed it again.

There were some bright spots to take my mind off the failure. I worked in the vegetable garden of the convent opposite the house for £3 a week plus an ample supply of fruit and vegetables every Saturday; I played snooker with my father on a full-sized table at the local working men's club at Madresfield. After snooker I watched him play three-card brag for small stakes with his friends. This was the start of my passion for playing cards, whatever the game. I had my first regular girlfriend, whose father used to enjoy playing chess with me on a Sunday afternoon, followed by tea and then a four hand of solo in the evening. And, as I said in the Introduction, I had discovered the joy of listening to Roy Orbison.

All these pleasures helped take my mind off my exam results. But I was not looking forward to going back to school. I rationalised the situation: I had two O-levels, I was not afraid of hard work. I had an open offer from WH Smith to become a trainee manager. If I left the King's School now I would never again have to go on parade with the Combined Cadet Force – which was compulsory unless your parents wrote to say it was against your religion, and I doubted that anyone would believe my sudden conversion to being a Quaker. I absolutely detested the CCF. I hated the uniform with its horrible itchy shirt, I hated having to blanco my belt and spats, polish my boots and clean the barrel of my rifle. I hated the parades and the marching, and I hated the Regimental Sergeant Major. Thank God they abolished National Service for those born after 1940!

I was getting nowhere trying to decide what to do with my life, when out of the blue I received a letter from Bertie Balance, the chess master who had taken over the responsibility for my day-boy house at the King's School. He gave me a ticking off for my O-level failures – particularly History, which he taught me – but said that all was not lost and that I could move on to the A-level course provided I passed two more O-levels in December. To my parents' great relief I went back to school, and succeeded in passing three more O-levels, in English Literature, English Language and History.

So I started on the last and best two years of my time at King's. We had very few formal lessons, I suppose because it was assumed that we were motivated to study hard for our A-levels so that we could go on to good universities. But I was as unambitious in that respect as I was about possible careers. I worked quite hard, but I also found time to improve my chess, read crime novels and take a new interest in sport – though not of a kind the school encouraged. I spent every Wednesday and Saturday afternoon in a betting office.

My girlfriend's father had a bookmaking business that operated from a small office in Worcester. This was before betting shops as we know them today were permitted: business was transacted by telephone or by 'bookie's runners', who would collect betting slips and cash from punters in pubs and elsewhere, then carry them to the bookmakers in pouches that had time-locks on them. These pouches had to be locked before the day's racing started and therefore could be delivered to the office at any time.

One Saturday there was a pouch that was handed in at the end of the afternoon but had been locked at 11.30 that morning. It contained a bet written on a rolled-up piece of paper that had a remarkably high number of winners. The bets were small, but the combinations of doubles, trebles, foursomes and so on added up to a substantial return. The following Saturday it happened again, and again the next. I mentioned it to the 'guv'nor' not because I thought that there was anything wrong, but more to point out what a shrewd punter this must be.

No one else in the office shared my admiration. When the guv'nor inspected the pouch he found a tiny hole in the seam, where the bookie's runner had been able to insert his own tightly rolled betting slip after the day's racing was over. It never happened again, and the runner turned up the next Saturday with a suspiciously swollen face.

In the office there was a ticker-tape machine that would continuously tap out pre-race betting odds and results. Small bookmakers played the percentages: large bets would come in by telephone from account holders, and as each one was recorded in the ledger one of the clerks would tell the guv'nor if there was a large liability building up on a certain horse. He would then make a decision whether or not to lay off part or all of the bet with a bigger bookmaker. I have always remembered his words of wisdom: 'Worry about the possible loss before you try to maximise the profit.'

I was fascinated, and found a new way of improving my skill in mental arithmetic. I used to try to anticipate the risks before they were pointed out to the guv'nor and work out what action I would take, then compare it with his ultimate decision. On balance I found I was more inclined to take risks than he was, but then it wasn't my money.

I even managed, by chance, to solve the problem of the Combined Cadet Force. One Saturday morning early in the autumn term, the bus was late and I missed the morning roll call. When we went on parade for CCF, the RSM took the roll call again. But he did not call out my name. Why not? It was obvious: he used the attendance list from the roll call in College Hall in the morning for the roll call for CCF in the afternoon. So, I thought, if I miss the morning roll call, I won't be missed on parade. It was perfect – for an entire year, I missed the morning roll call but attended the lessons, then slipped away to work at the bookies. And I even got promoted to corporal in my absence!

But still I had to face up to my A-level exams in History, English Literature and Geography. I carefully planned which parts of each syllabus to swot up. For English, I learned by heart great chunks of *Gulliver's Travels*, *Coriolanus*, *Julius Caesar* and the Prologue to the *Canterbury Tales*. For Geography I put a lot of effort into a field study on the history of Malvern's most famous export, its water. I was fortunate that a friend's father was the superintendent of the Malvern Water Supply Company and he let me follow him around for three weeks taking dozens of photographs with an old, borrowed Box Brownie. I have to say that this was one of my finest pieces of work – my father found it many years later and wanted me to publish it. I never did, but it was borrowed and copied by a number of the next generation's A-level students.

After the exams were over I did not agonise over reviewing my own performance because I really did think I had done my best this time. When the results letter arrived on the fateful day I was actually asleep, but Dad brought it up to my bedroom and lingered while I opened it. I had passed in all three subjects just above the pass mark – no distinctions, nothing that would get my name on the boards on the walls of College Hall, but at least they were passes. Bertie Balance, who had helped me through the O-level crisis, wanted me to stay on in the Upper VI and study for scholarship grades, which would have opened an easier path to university, but I had had enough of school. I was 17 and ready to take on the outside world – without having a clue of what I wanted to do.

I therefore started to think about a career. I knew that as a last resort I could get a job at WH Smith, but finishing up as the timid, brow-beaten manager of the Malvern Link branch was not appealing. Anyway, I thought, I had to find new horizons, not go back to a place where I had already worked for four years.

What I really fancied was the bookmaking business – I enjoyed the excitement of the build-up to a race and the need to make quick decisions about laying off the high risks. On many Saturdays there were eight race meetings around the country and decisions to lay off bets had to be taken every five minutes or so over a four-hour session. I was fascinated by the boss, a remarkable character who in his early life had set up a potato crisp business in New Zealand. Bookmaking had made him rich by anyone's standards, but he was also chairman of the local Communist Party branch and was often out canvassing for election candidates.

Besides his advice about protecting yourself against high losses, he taught me another important lesson. If he made a bad decision, he would sigh but forget it in a second; he used to say that the most important decision was the next one, not the last one. He never congratulated himself when he made the right decision and he never carried out post-mortems on the ones he got wrong. He just observed that if you are right more often than you are wrong, you are likely to stay in profit.

Not surprisingly, my parents were very concerned about my friendship with a communist bookie and far from ecstatic when I proudly told them that I wanted to go into the turf accountancy profession. I had rehearsed my speech carefully, but I did not anticipate the violence of my mother's reaction. The day I walked into 'that place' to start a permanent job, she said, was the day I would walk out of her house!

In desperation I started looking at advertisements in the *Worcester Evening News*. There was one for 'bright young men wanting to earn over £20 a week'. I wrote to the box number, and was asked to attend an interview with the managing director of the Household Goods Trading Co. Ltd in Worcester. Immaculately dressed in my only suit, shoes polished, A-level certificates carefully filed in my new briefcase, I arrived at the correct address – a room over a newsagent's shop in a Worcester back street. The managing director was a middle-aged lady with the most enormous bulging eyes, who told me that that the road to financial success was via door-to-door selling.

It was not exactly what I had in mind, but I decided to give it a go. For the next four weeks I knocked on hundreds of doors trying to sell metal tongs for getting clothes out of washing machines, 'best-quality' cutlery and rose-patterned soup bowls. I earned no commission in the first two weeks, £2 in the third week and £3 in the fourth; it cost me more than that in bus fares and shoe leather. I could not afford to continue!

Then I saw something much more promising: 'A career at Lloyds Bank will give you £1000 a year at the age of 30.' But it was not for me. As I walked through a large office towards the interview room, I looked at the sad faces of the clerks, young and old, working away at desks that would not have been out of place in a Dickens novel. I turned around and walked out of the building. (I often wondered if the very keen young man who escorted me halfway to the interview room before I bolted was Brian Pitman, who came from Cheltenham and worked his way up through the local branches to be chairman of Lloyds, before he was chairman of NEXT.)

I was more hopeful when I went to see a local firm of chartered accountants. The office atmosphere was very relaxed, almost cheerful compared to the bank, and I recognised two of my chess team who had left school before me. But that too was a dead end for me – because as an articled clerk I would have had to pay to work there, and I had no money.

In desperation I returned to the idea of going to university, thereby putting off the day when I would have to decide what I was going to do for a living. I applied to dozens of universities for a place in September 1961, but received only one invitation to interview: from Exeter, to study economics and politics. It took me six hours to get there on four different trains, and I arrived very late and in a bad mood. The grey walls of the university felt uninviting and everyone I spoke to was unfriendly. Again, I turned round and went home.

There had to be something better – but what? I was beginning to get lazy, lying around in bed in the mornings and becoming more and more depressed. Mum and Dad were getting worried and irritated by my lack of effort to find a job. I was in a rut that I did not know how to get out of. Then Dad said that he had arranged an appointment for me to see a youth employment officer called Mr Howes, in Worcester.

Howes was a tall, softly spoken man with a bald head of which a chunk was missing, the result of a German grenade. He took a special interest in me – I think he was used to trying to find jobs for young people with absolutely no qualifications, so to have someone with three A-levels was a form of light relief. He advised me to apply for a commercial apprenticeship with one of the large companies in Birmingham: one of them was Albright and Wilson, which did something with phosphorus; the other was Stewarts & Lloyds, in steel. The interviews seemed to go well, but no offers arrived.

I could not get enthusiastic about any of the career paths that Mr Howes suggested and although he was very understanding, he made it clear that he was not going to waste any more of his valuable time on me. Almost in desperation, he advised me to find a temporary job and when I had made up my mind what I wanted to do for a career, to go back and see him.

'Where can I apply for a temporary job?' I asked him.

'Try Kays,' he said. 'They're always looking for temps. They'll take anyone.'

It wasn't exactly a stunning recommendation for a future employer, but I wrote to Kays of Worcester and to my surprise I received a prompt reply inviting me to see a Miss Dunn on the following Friday. All I could find out about Kays was that it was a mail-order company sending out large, illustrated catalogues to agents who ordered goods on behalf of their friends and neighbours, who then paid for the goods at so many shillings a week. It was a new concept to me because my parents never bought anything on credit, but they told me that our neighbour Mrs Whitehouse was the agent for Goodson Road and I spent a few hours with her studying the catalogue and finding out what she did.

The interview was not quite what I expected. First, I was asked to write down my name and address to prove that I could write. Then Miss Dunn wrote down five numbers on a sheet of paper and asked me to total them. In fact I had added them up as she wrote them down, and gave her the answer before she handed me the piece of paper. It took her a good deal longer to confirm that I was correct. She eventually told me that I had passed, and I could start work at 8.30 the following Monday morning, at £4 17s 6d a week – better than my target of £4 – plus 5s a month bonus if I was never absent or late. I can proudly say that I never missed my 5s bonus.

On my first day – wearing a new yellow sweater specially knitted by my mother – I was the first of about 30 new recruits to arrive in the anteroom of the personnel office. Just before 8.30 a.m., a very smart young man walked in and stood at the back of the queue. The door opened and Miss Dunn appeared. I stood up and took a step towards her, but she ignored me and called out: 'Mr Fell?'

The smart young man marched past the line of people into Miss Dunn's office – and my mind went back to Towndrow's when 'her ladyship' tried to jump the queue. But unlike my mother, I did not complain. Brian Fell turned out to be an assistant buyer in the watch and clock department; we became friends, and many years later I recruited him to solve a problem for me at NEXT (as I mentioned in Part I).

One by one the names of the new starters were called out until I was the last one waiting. After an hour I was finally called into the office, asked to sign a form and escorted to a vacant wooden chair in a row of about 20 male and female clerks of all ages, shapes and sizes. The office seemed to be the size of a football pitch, with dozens of rows of clerks working away with their heads down. In front of each one was a cabinet with three shelves stuffed full of brown folders. Every three rows or so there was a manager surveying his little empire to ensure that everyone was working – rather in the manner of a slavemaster in a Roman galley, though without the whip.

I had no intention of staying more than three months, but I decided to give the job my full attention because I have never liked just coasting along. Throughout my life if I have got involved in something I have given it 100 per cent commitment. I had already seen how an agent operated, thanks to Mrs Whitehouse, and I was keen to find out how the other side of the business worked.

Each brown folder in front of me contained the records of a Kays agent. The agents would send in orders for goods, and the goods would then be sent out to the agents by post for delivery by hand to the customer – who if they liked the item would keep it and start paying for it on a weekly basis; if not, they would give it back to the agent to be returned to Kays. The agents would collect payments from all their customers and send the cash to Kays every week with a summary of their accounts. They received 10 per cent commission on all monies collected. My first thought was that the bad debts on this business must be enormous. But I learned that agents only dealt with people they knew in their own neighbourhoods, because if they did produce too many bad payers they could lose their agency.

Kays had been one of Britain's first mail-order companies, starting as a supplier of watches. It dated its origins from 1794 or even earlier, when a clock and watch maker called John Skarratt opened for business in a small shop in what is now St Swithins Street in Worcester. In the 1880s, Skarratt's descendant was joined by an assistant called William Kay, who eventually took over the business, gave it his own name, and ventured into selling watches by post. Each watch cost 20s and was supplied to groups of 20 people who had clubbed together to buy watches: each paid a shilling a week to an organiser, who sent the money to Kays. Each week one watch was sent to the organiser, who allocated it to one of the club members. If you were lucky you received your watch early on in the 20-week period; if you were the unlucky one, you had to wait until last.

After a while Kays decided to send all 20 watches after the first weekly payment came in, and trust that all the customers would honour their debts. This was the origin of the '20-week club', which developed into the agency mail-order business, which in turn grew in the post-war decades to provide almost every category of goods that a household could possibly need.

My existence in those first few months at Kays was dominated by the 125 agents whose records were neatly filed in the cabinet in front of me. One I shall never forget was a woman in Somerset who every Friday sent me about 20 statements, in immaculate handwriting, each containing the records of 15 customers, so 300 in all. Unfortunately her maths was not as good as her handwriting: it took all day to balance her accounts. If I could not do it on the Friday, I would smuggle her file out of the building and complete the task at home over the weekend. We were allowed to make a 5s adjustment in the accounts of agents with a large number of customers if we could not balance them completely – but I never used this concession because to me that would have been an admission of defeat.

As a result, I became the dumping ground for all the difficult agents whose records other clerks were unable to balance. We all had to fill in time sheets to show the number of agents we handled each day. It became obvious that my work rate was well ahead of most of the others'.

One evening as I was leaving the building, I was approached by a group of trainee buyers and merchandisers who were doing a stint in the accounts office. They had just had their three-monthly assessment and their time sheets had been compared unfavourably to mine, with a warning that they had better buck up their ideas if they wanted to go on to greater things. They suggested, rather firmly, that I might like to slow down a bit and stop showing them up.

I was not particularly bothered. I was not out to spoil their prospects or impress anyone. I was working hard because it satisfied me. After the 'friendly warning' I continued working at the same rate of knots, but simply omitted some jobs from my time sheet. That way, everyone was happy.

One Friday when I had balanced my agent from Somerset in record time, I started playing with my figures for the week. My 125 agents had sent in about £2000, which equated to £100,000 in a year. There were 24 clerks in my group, four groups in the office and four offices in the building – which meant a turnover of more than £38 million a year – and there were other Kays offices in Leeds, Glasgow and Wales.

To me, that made it a mighty big and impressive company. I had caught the mail-order bug: it eventually became an addiction and dictated the course of my business life.

Chapter 6

'Give that boy a 10 shilling increase!'

O ne Monday morning in January 1961, when I was a month short of my eighteenth birthday, my group manager at Kays called his clerks together and told us that the chairman of Great Universal Stores, our parent company, would be making his annual visit the following day. We were to tidy our desks and cabinets before we went home, he said, and we were to come in early the next day, because the chairman liked to arrive very early to catch people out.

I took this to heart and arrived at 7 a.m. I made certain not only that my own desk and cabinet were tidy but also the rest of the group's. If there was going to be a prize for tidiness, I wanted my group to win it.

At exactly 8 a.m. a short, slightly stooping, white-haired man in his mid-60s made his entrance, wearing a long black coat and a benevolent smile. This was Sir Isaac Wolfson, one of the great British entrepreneurs of the twentieth century and the head of a dynasty that has played an enormous part in my life from that day to this.

He smiled at us all as he came in, but the entourage of men in dark suits who followed him looked notably sombre. Mrs Maine who sat next to me, and who had worked at Kays all her life, whispered that the figure immediately behind the great man was his brother Charles, and behind Charles were other directors of GUS and the directors of Kays. I did not pay much attention to the supporting cast: my eyes were focused on the great man.

We had been told to keep our heads down and not stare at the visitors, so I started to balance one of my smaller agencies. Once I got stuck into the work, I was oblivious to what was happening around me. I did not notice the column of dignitaries slowly progressing down our line. Sir Isaac stopped right behind me, and I nearly jumped out of my skin when Tom Rallings, a Kays director, barked: 'Jones, show Sir Isaac what you are doing!'

It was startling enough that Mr Rallings knew my name, never mind that Sir Isaac wanted to know what I was up to. I launched nervously into an explanation of what an agency clerk did all day. Sir Isaac kept asking more questions: 'Show me your biggest agent... How much did she spend last year?'

Luckily, there was nothing I didn't know about my biggest agent. I even had a photograph of her with her two dogs, clipped to the front of her file. But this historic meeting of minds was brought abruptly to a close when the chairman of Kays, George Lodge, suggested that they move on to the merchandise offices. As he left, Sir Isaac put his hand on my shoulder and thanked me for what I had told him. Then he added: 'Give that boy a 10 shilling increase!'

I was on cloud nine, but I was brought back to the real world an hour or so later when Mr Rallings came past again and said quietly: 'Well done, Jones, but you can forget about the rise.'

I had to do just that, but I never forgot my first encounter with Isaac Wolfson. He was one of the most extraordinary men of his generation. The son of a Russian Jewish cabinet maker who had settled in Glasgow, young Isaac had first gone on the road as a salesman for his father's furniture workshop. He was selling clocks and mirrors at a stall in the Manchester exhibition hall in 1926 when he fell into conversation with the head of a 'club trading' mail-order business, Universal Stores, which recruited him as a buyer.

Renamed Great Universal Stores in 1930, the company was already a leader of the growing market for mail-order clothing sales on credit to working-class customers. GUS acquired Kays in 1938, and many of the older Kays staff remembered the day that two men in long black coats and black hats – presumably Isaac and Charles – had arrived to take charge.

Isaac became joint managing director in 1932 and chairman after the Second World War – during which, he once told me, he exploited the opportunity to sell fancy photo frames to the thousands of parents who wanted to display pictures of their sons serving in the forces overseas. After the war, by a series of bold takeovers he built GUS into one of Britain's most powerful retailing empires, selling clothing, furnishings, shoes and household goods. A quarter of the British population were his customers, and he had fingers in many other pies besides, especially the commercial property market. He did it all with a twinkling eye, a rumbustious Glaswegian charm and a relentless appetite for deals, but in his personal life he was modest and abstemious and extremely generous to those who asked him for help.

He encouraged the careers of a number of bright young men who worked for him, including Jeffrey Sterling, who eventually became chairman of P&O, and David Young (a cousin of Isaac's daughter-in-law, Ruth), who became one of Margaret Thatcher's ministers and later chairman of Cable & Wireless. David Young had a good description of Isaac in his memoirs: 'He had a magnetic personality and seemed to part charm, part hypnotise people into accepting his terms for almost anything he wanted.'

Though I was still very junior at Kays in the early 1960s, I would like to think that I caught Isaac's benevolent eye as a lad with future potential. In later years I spent happy times listening to his stories and absorbing his wisdom.

But back in January 1961, something else was about to happen to me. I was transferred to the finance department to fill in for a staff member who was on holiday. The work consisted entirely of adding up columns of figures – this was before we even had adding machines – and because it was only a temporary transfer I was expected to carry on doing my agency clerk's work as unpaid overtime. When in due course I reported back for normal duty, I was told I was to be transferred permanently to organisation and method

(O&M). This was a new department under a manager, Richard Pugh, who had recently joined Kays from Grattan Warehouses, another mail-order company based in Bradford.

I had no inkling that Richard and I would later become competitors for the top job in the company, or that Grattan, a name that then meant very little to me, would come to mean so much. The O&M department was established to find a way of mechanising the manual agency accounting system. The project was not popular with the rest of the office because it was seen as a threat to jobs. The staff need not have worried, because it all proved to be a complete waste of time and money. The system never worked and the accounting machines were quietly laid to rest in the basement where the auditors would not find them, because no one wanted to admit that they had to be written off.

O&M was very boring, so I was glad when the team was disbanded and I was asked to transfer permanently to the finance department. Within weeks of this move I had my second encounter with Isaac Wolfson. He was due to visit us the following day and once again we were instructed to be at our desks early. I took some ribbing from my colleagues, who said that because my desk was the nearest to the door he would undoubtedly ask me one of two questions: 'What is the square footage of this building?' or 'How much cash did you send to head office yesterday?'

On the way to work the next day, I repeated to myself over and over again '120,000 square feet' and '£234,000'. At 8 a.m. as usual, Sir Isaac arrived. His cheerful manner and cheerless entourage were just as before. He offered me his outstretched hand with the question: 'How much did you send to head office yesterday?'

I was so taken back at being asked to shake his hand that I mumbled, '120,000 square feet, sir'.

'Good,' he said, without batting an eyelid, 'Very good!'

I volunteered for any extra work that was thrown at me. Most people in the department had no professional qualifications, and I thought I might have a better chance of progressing if I went for one. I had become quite friendly with Richard Pugh and asked for his advice. He suggested that a good 'general' qualification was that of Chartered Secretary. I enrolled in a correspondence course and within 12 months had passed the intermediary exams.

I enjoyed my job enormously, and put in many hours of unpaid overtime. Before long I was preparing the monthly, half-yearly and year-end accounts, administering the directors' and senior executives' monthly payroll and taking part in various committees to plan the development of the business. Another chat with Richard Pugh convinced me that I should also go for an accountancy qualification and he recommended that I studied to be a certified accountant. I worked very hard at home and 12 months later I passed both the final exams of the Chartered Institute of Secretaries and the intermediary exams of the Association of Certified and Corporate Accountants.

Despite my work and my studies, I managed to fit in a very full social life. Kays had an active social club and a theatre group that put on an annual pantomime, in which I graduated from the chorus to my most celebrated role as the goose in Mother Goose. I also played football, cricket, tennis and skittles, and acquired a driving licence and my first car, a black Morris 1000.

And I spent a good part of my time chasing pretty girls, dancing and listening to music. This was the era of the Beatles, Elvis, Acker Bilk, Kenny Ball and of course Roy Orbison. When Roy was touring in England I would follow him round the country – no matter how many times I saw him on stage I still went back for more.

On Saturdays a group of us would go to dances at venues as glamorous as the Winter Gardens in Malvern and Droitwich, where all the boys would gather on one side of the dance floor eyeing up the talent on the other side, who were desperately trying not to look interested. The first bloke to make a move across the dance floor was always rebuffed, so I learned to wait until the evening warmed up a bit. And I devised a Plan B – if I asked a girl to dance and she refused, I told her I had been bet 10s that she would not dance with me and I would split it 50/50 with her if she would. It was expensive, but it did my reputation as a bird puller no harm at all.

I was growing up in a lot of different ways in those years. I developed an interest in the stock market, which came about through Joe Sanderson, an agency office manager who had also come to Kays from Grattan. A blunt Yorkshireman, he did not make the career progress that he might have done because his aggressive style did not fit the reserved Worcester culture. But he started an investment club that did so well that even other managers who resented his ambitions joined it, and he asked me to be its treasurer. One of the secrets of his success was his skill at 'stagging': subscribing for large numbers of shares in oversubscribed new issues, and receiving a scaled-down allocation that would shoot up in value for a quick profit once the shares started trading.

And when I was 24 I had my first thorough medical, which brought a startling revelation; though it gave no indication of the onset of Parkinson's. It included a hearing test: the doctor put some headphones on me and told me to press a button when I heard a bleep. After a while he cursed the machine for not working properly and went to get another one. We started again, but still I did not press the button. Finally, he took the headphones away and told me I was deaf.

'I am not,' I protested indignantly.

So he put a newspaper in front of his face and carried on talking – and I had no idea what he was saying. This was astonishing to me, but it turned out that my hearing was really very poor and I had subconsciously made up for it by lip-reading. When I got home I turned on the television with the sound off and realised that I could still 'hear' what people were saying. I did not tell many people about the problem and I never wore a hearing aid: I could get by, provided that I was looking directly at people speaking and they did not mumble.

There were even some advantages to my lip-reading skill. Many years later I was on a train to London when four businessmen sitting opposite me started discussing in very low voices a takeover bid that they were about to launch for a competitor. I was not in any conventional sense an 'insider' – they should have been a lot more careful in their conversation – so I did not feel guilty about having a small punt on the target company and collecting £565 profit when the bid was announced and the shares soared.

Growing up within the GUS organisation also meant learning the tricks of the trade that were used in Kays' accounts – and those of many other mail-order companies – and learning about issues that would recur time after time in my later career at Grattan and NEXT. For example, Kays normally achieved its sales budget for the year to 31 March sometime in January. So from the middle of January until the end of March, only a small proportion of actual sales were entered in the books. Unrecorded sales forms were secretly hoarded in a safe in the cellar, the existence of which was known only to a small number of people. I was its key holder. I could never understand why the auditors did not query the fact that the sales during March were always so low, but April's sales were always huge as the unrecorded sales from the last three months were retrieved from the secret safe and entered into the books of account.

One lunchtime in March 1965, the finance director found me in the canteen and told me to take the afternoon off, but to leave the safe keys with him. The following morning he told me the auditors had got wind of the sales forms in the safe and had demanded to inspect it. They had not been able to do that yesterday because I had taken the afternoon off – and I was of course the only key holder. But they could this morning, now that I was back. I escorted the auditors to the cellar, opened the heavy door of the safe – and revealed a completely empty interior. The auditors went back to their ticking, and shortly afterwards, the unrecorded sales forms went back to the safe in the cellar from wherever the finance director had hidden them overnight.

Then there was the business of managing the company's cash. Every day I had to send a cheque to GUS's head office, Universal House in Tottenham Court Road in London, representing the surplus cash for that day. If I was unable to send a cheque because there was no surplus cash, I would receive a reprimand from the finance department at head office: 'We are going to have to report to Mr Leonard that Kays sent no cash today.'

This was my first encounter, albeit at one remove, with Leonard Wolfson. He was Isaac's only child and had been a director of GUS since 1952, when he was 25. He became managing director in 1962, gradually taking over power in the group in the years that followed as his father took a less active role. It was never my impression that father and son were emotionally close, but there is no doubt that Isaac wanted to give Leonard every opportunity to become a great man of the business world. I have read that he even went to the Bank of England in 1961 to discuss the possibility of buying a bank, so that Leonard could become a figure in the City as well as in commerce.

Isaac was an autocrat, and that is what he taught Leonard to be. The threat transmitted by the finance department on Leonard's behalf was somehow perfectly characteristic of his management style. It was also a very useful lesson in the importance of cash-flow control.

In response, I contrived a plan to ensure that I was always able to send a cheque – and if I was short of funds to cover the daily cheque, I would stick a pin through the magnetic numbers on cheques issued to suppliers, thus rendering them unable to pass through automatic bank sorting machines and adding one day to the clearance time.

As each year-end approached, I was instructed that as far as possible no payments were to be made, except wages and agents' commission, between Christmas and 31 March so that the year-end balance sheet would show an incredibly healthy cash position. This, not surprisingly, resulted in a lot of very unhappy suppliers, and I had to deal with regular, desperate telephone calls, some threatening legal action, others pleading for payment because there was no money to pay wages. While I admired the discipline of looking after the cash, I was distressed by the effect this had on our suppliers, and confess that on many occasions I disobeyed orders and made payments to small suppliers that I believed would have gone bankrupt.

The Wolfsons themselves were great philanthropists through the charitable foundation that Isaac had endowed with a large block of GUS shares some years earlier, and that has given literally hundreds of millions to good causes. But GUS as a company was never famous for its commercial generosity; quite the reverse, in fact.

There were many examples of this during the 20 years I was there. I suppose I should not have been surprised that many years later it was a lack of generosity towards me that was the cause of my leaving the company.

My first disappointment had been the 10 shilling bonus offered by Isaac Wolfson but never actually awarded. In 1966, when I was earning £725 a year, I was hoping for a good increase in the annual April review because I had taken on more responsibility and was working long hours without any overtime pay – and a favourable review would have taken me past £780, which was the qualifying level for the company's non-contributory pension scheme. But when I opened my review letter my salary had been increased to £775: the £5 difference meant that the mean bastards had saved themselves a year's pension-fund contributions.

I have always maintained that money does not motivate me, but that unfair treatment positively demotivates me. I started to look for another job and had several interviews, but nothing really appealed. After the fourth interview I rationalised the situation: in the end, what difference would one year's delay in joining the pension scheme make when I was only 23 years old?

So I stayed, and I was soon glad I had because I started to work closely with David Wolfson. David was the son of Isaac's brother Charles, but I think in some ways Isaac thought of him like a second son of his own. He had joined Kays in 1962, having collected an undergraduate degree at Cambridge and an MBA at Stanford in California. He was still only in his late twenties and was tall and handsome; the office girls competed to deliver his post in the mornings. He was initially responsible for menswear, but was soon involved in every aspect of the business – and took me along with him. He told me that everything affecting the bottom line was my responsibility, giving me authority to ask questions throughout the business, including the merchandising and buying departments. I also began helping him to develop new agency accounting, stock-control and buying systems.

And I once saved his life (or perhaps he saved mine) when the lift doors opened in front of us on the top floor of Kays' head office, Elgar House, but the lift was not there.

Most weekends I would take piles of work home with me. One of my regular weekend chores was to check expense claims, and I soon developed a nose for false ones. I used to give a hint to those who erred that I had spotted something amiss, and that was usually enough to stop them. But I did catch one very greedy manager who was really taking the company for a ride. His job involved visiting suppliers three or four days a week and his expenses in total were not excessive. However, one weekend I noticed that his weekly claims were always backed up by the same type of receipts.

I looked through his expenses for the previous year and found that all his receipts were numbered sequentially – he had obtained receipt books for car parking, meals on trains and in certain restaurants and was using them week after week. I laid the 52 claim forms in long lines down the length of the board table, then rang him to say that my boss wanted to see him in the boardroom. As soon as he walked in he saw what was on the table and said without apology or remorse, 'OK, you've caught me. What are you going to do about it?'

I was extremely upset when he got off scot-free in return for reimbursing a nominal portion of what he had effectively stolen from the company. But justice was done some years later when he lost his job for another misdeed.

I was having fun; I was learning a lot from David Wolfson; I had finally passed all the exams to become a chartered secretary and certified accountant; I believe that I was building a good reputation within the GUS group. And suddenly a really big opportunity opened up for me. Rumours started to circulate that my boss George Peters, the finance director and company secretary, was leaving the organisation.

Peters seemed quite happy to give me more and more responsibility, which made my job all the more interesting and satisfying: I soon became his number two, overtaking a number of older, longer-serving, unqualified accountants. Peters himself had two sidelines, running an agency for Littlewoods pools and supplying eggs to a large number of the middle and senior management from the chickens he kept in his garden. While the old management of Kays was prepared to turn a blind eye to this situation, David Wolfson, who by this time had become joint managing director, was not. As the rumours grew that his days were numbered, Peters spent most of his time in his office behind a closed door, while I worried that if someone else were appointed finance director he would not allow me to retain all the responsibilities I had assumed over the last four years.

Because Peters became almost a recluse in his office, he asked me to do his daily chore of going to see the Kays chairman, George Lodge, whose office was in another building, to get his signature on cheques and other documents. I was always fascinated watching the chairman signing his name. He had the most precise, perfect signature of anyone I have ever known, with two dots under his name always in exactly the same place – to this day I have tried to maintain a legible, flowing signature of my own, and tend to look down on those who seem to be proud of their illegible scribble.

On my first visit on behalf of my boss I was standing in front of the chairman waiting for him to finish signing, and my eyes strayed over his desk. On the left-hand corner – I had long ago mastered the art of reading upside down – was a handwritten list of four candidates who were going to be interviewed for the soon-to-be-vacant finance director's position. I was not on it and I would not have paid washers for the four who were, all of whom I knew.

I went back and told the finance director what I had seen. He broke down, sobbing. He had been hoping that the pressure on him

Top left: Brother Fred holding
baby David at Cwm

Top middle: My first portrait
aged three

Top right: With one of the
gang outside St. Leonards
Church, Newlands in Malvern
(I'm the one on the left)

Middle: My first year at King's
School, Worcester

Bottom: Our wedding day,
24th August 1968

Four Wolfsons from three

Left: Lord (Leonard) Wolfson of Marylebone – "could be charming, kind and thoughtful, but most of us were frightened of him."

This portrait is by Andrew Festing, National Portrait Gallery, London

Right: Sir Isaac Wolfson – the charismatic founder of the Great Universal Stores.

Photo: Kays Heritage Group

generations - and me

Left: With two NEXT chairmen: Michael Stoddart (left) and Lord (David) Wolfson of Sunningdale – "the most outstanding businessman that I have met."

Below: Handing over the chief executive's role to Simon Wolfson in 2001 – "a brilliant young man."

Left: With George Davies in happier times

Opposite page:

Top: With the Prime Minister, Margaret Thatcher, and George Davies opening the new head office at Enderby, Leicester in 1987

Bottom: Learning to fold my arms like Prince Edward

Left: NEXT board of directors 1987/88: from left to right, Peter Lomas, John Roberts, me, Liz and George Davies, Tom O'Malley, John Whitmarsh

Above: At the Charity Ball
at the Battersea Arena with
friends Philip and Tina
Green (left and right)

Photo: Edward Lloyd

Right: Holding the Webb-
Ellis trophy - the Rugby
World Cup - with the captain
who won it, Martin Johnson

Photo: Edward Lloyd

Opposite page:

Top: Trying to look as cool
as the designer Bruce
Oldfield (right).
Left to right: Jacqui Wykes
(Barnardo's), Sue Myatt
(NEXT) and me at a
presentation for the
Barnardo's charity

Bottom: Meeting HRH the
Duke of Edinburgh at a
Charity function at St.
James's Palace

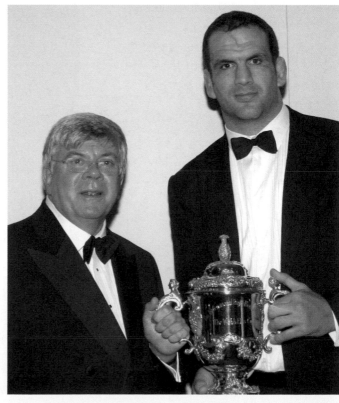

Above: Receiving an honorary degree in 1989 from Sir John Harvey-Jones, Chancellor of Bradford University

Above right: My first day as chief executive of Grattan in Bradford, 1981

Below: Raising money for Parkinson's with HRH the Duchess of Gloucester

Right: After receiving my CBE in 1999

The Parkinson

Winter edition 2001/2002

NEXT Ball:
David Jones' Event Raises £275,000

would blow over and everything would carry on as before, but the fact that people were already being interviewed indicated that there would be no reprieve.

He was told to leave the following day and I helped him to clear his office. He shook my hand and wished me luck – and I never saw him again. I spent the weekend considering what I should do, and by Monday I had made up my mind. On that morning's trip to the chairman's office I waited until he had signed all the cheques, then launched uninvited into a carefully rehearsed speech: 'Mr Lodge, I would like you to know that I can do the finance director's job.'

It was immediately obvious that he did not like the fact it was common knowledge that the finance director had gone for good – officially he had been sent on holiday while the situation was resolved. But the chairman's next remark really knocked me off guard: 'Who are you and what do you do?'

I had been preparing the company's accounts for about five years and he did not know who I was. My reply had a touch of anger in it. 'Among a lot of other things I pay your salary every month!'

I could not believe I had actually said something so stupid. I was dismissed with a wave of the hand. On the way back to my office I passed David Wolfson's open door and saw him smoking a Monte Cristo, staring out of the window deep in thought. I knocked and entered. As I walked towards his desk he turned with a look of irritation because I had interrupted his train of thought. I hesitated; maybe it was the wrong time. But the words were already flowing out: 'I'd like you to know that I can do the finance director's job.'

His reply was even more abrupt than the chairman's: 'Close the door on your way out.'

I returned to my office pretty depressed. I had certainly cocked that up. To take my mind off my failure, I started work on the monthly profit figures. They were looking good, helped by a number of cost-saving measures that David Wolfson and I had devised over the previous six months. I was putting the final percentages into the monthly statement the next morning when I was suddenly aware of someone standing in front of me. I looked up to see David smiling at me: 'You really think you can do the job?'

I nodded.

'OK! You've got six months to prove it. Good morning.'

He had turned to go when I said: 'There's one condition.'

He turned back to glare at me, probably thinking I was about to ask for a salary increase.

'Can you keep Leonard off my back?'

'That's impossible,' he laughed. 'You'll have to take your chances like the rest of us mortals.'

I went back to my profit statement and it was several minutes before it hit me. I had just been given the job (although not necessarily the title) of finance director of the company that I had joined nine years earlier as a temporary clerk. I wanted to tell Mr Howes, the youth employment officer who had tried so hard to help me. I rang his office only to find he had retired, but I tracked him down a few months later and was able to tell him over a cup of tea that I had at last decided what to do with my life.

When my appointment was confirmed, my new title – following a precedent in GUS itself – was 'joint secretary' responsible for the financial side of the company, while Eric Hilliard was to be the other joint secretary responsible for secretarial matters. The division of duties did not concern me – I never did enjoy the laborious paperwork associated with company secretarial duties and I was just thankful that no one else had come in above me. The only job I actually handed over to Eric was the senior payroll, and that was a boring monthly task.

In those days Kays had monthly board meetings, which started at 10 a.m. with a private discussion between George Lodge, David Wolfson and the other joint managing director, Vernon Watson. Then Eric and I would be summoned to go through financial and secretarial matters, and we would be joined by the other board members responsible for merchandise, the commercial side and the catalogue. I had been in the job for about three months when I received the usual call to join the board meeting, but this time the chairman's secretary – Cynthia Crawford, always known as 'Crawfie' – said I was to come up on my own.

Crawfie, incidentally, was a very significant person in her own right, and she and her husband Ray are still good friends of mine. We have seen each other's careers flourish: she became David Wolfson's secretary and went with him to Downing Street in 1979. There in due course she became Margaret Thatcher's personal assistant, accompanying her on official trips all over the world.

As I drove over to the head office, I racked my brain to try to anticipate whatever it was the top men wanted to talk to me about. Everything seemed quite normal when I joined them in the board-room. I went through the monthly figures, which were way ahead of budget, summarised the annual stock-taking results, also showing a dramatic improvement, and finally handed them a schedule of the senior executive salaries for the forthcoming April review. It was and still is one of my hobby horses that everyone should know their new salary level before the actual review date.

There was a pause that seemed to last for an age. David and Vernon were looking at the chairman, who was looking at his papers. Finally, George Lodge cleared his throat and, without look-ing up, said that the board thought I was doing a good job and had decided to promote me to the position of finance director at a salary of £2250 – a £500 increase! They all shook my hand, and David Wolfson added a typical dry comment: 'Now you'll really have to start working for your living.'

The promotion brought me my first company car, a gleaming white Triumph 2.5Pi – and when I thanked David Wolfson he said it was only self-preservation that had prompted him to give it to me. A few weeks earlier I had met him at the Witney Blanket Co., which had recently been taken over by GUS. It was a cold, wet day and he asked me for a lift home – in my ancient Ford Escort with no seat belts, heating or demister. In such murky conditions I could barely see at all through the steamed-up windscreen, and David spent the entire journey with his eyes closed, clutching his briefcase in front of him. When we finally arrived at his house, he was so relieved that he invited me in for a cup of tea and to meet his wife Susan and his baby son Simon – who would become such a valued colleague 20-something years later.

Under David's leadership in the 1970s, Kays became the most successful mail-order company in Britain – not the biggest, but by far the most profitable. But first, David had to take over from George Lodge as chairman, and George did not want to go. The only way he got the message that he had passed his sell-by date was when he returned from holiday and found his office dismantled! Many of our mail-order competitors had ageing chairmen who had done wonders in their day but stayed too long. George was an unworldly figure – he once gave his chauffeur a £5 note to fill his Bentley with petrol – and Kays was his whole life. Fortunately for the business, David was on hand to cut the cord, but if anyone ever writes a history of Kays I hope it is kind to George Lodge, because in his heyday he improved Kays' merchandise range beyond recognition and he knew instinctively what was right for the business.

I saw an example of this one day when I accompanied George Lodge to London for a meeting with Leonard to go through the year-end profit figures. To my amazement the figures were not discussed because Leonard had a different bee in his bonnet that day: for some reason he had the knife out for the suppliers of branded merchandise such as Black & Decker tools and Morphy Richards irons. He instructed us, and the people from our sister company BMOC, that all the branded merchandise was to be taken out of the catalogue and replaced by own-brand products.

On the train back to Worcester, between visits to the bar to replenish the chairman's gin and tonic, I asked him what he was going to do about this startling directive. 'Forget it,' he said, and we did – while BMOC did what it was told and took every branded item out of its range. George Lodge was wise enough to know that Leonard would eventually change his mind, which he did, forcing BMOC to backtrack and reinstate all the suppliers it had axed.

Rumour had it that George drank half a bottle of gin with his lunch and the other half with his dinner. Not long before he retired he was taken very ill, sank into a coma and was not expected to last the week. But he came round, and seeing his wife at his bedside barked: 'Peggy! Get me a gin and tonic!' Peggy asked the doctor, who said it could do him no harm at this stage. Three double g-and-ts later, George was on the road to recovery. He was back at his desk in three weeks.

But finally he let go of the reins and David Wolfson's era began. It was a time of rapid growth throughout the mail-order industry, which – because it was a labour-intensive business – also led to rapid growth in staff numbers. In the early 1970s that meant that we were increasingly at the mercy of the power of the trade unions, as wage rates started to rise sharply and our profit margins began to suffer.

The answer to this threat was the introduction of computer-based office systems and mechanised distribution centres. Fortunately for Kays, David Wolfson was ready to take decisions on these issues, despite some rather strange internal politics. David was always in Worcester on a Monday and would tell me what he wanted me to do that week. Vernon Watson, who had been joint managing director with David and was now managing director under him, was based in Leeds and would come to Worcester from Tuesday to Thursday. As David did not come back to Kays until Friday, the two senior executives would go for weeks on end without actually meeting. This inevitably resulted in the creation of two camps, which was distracting to some people, although not to me, because I was very firmly established in David's camp.

This was the time that I was able to gather round me a dedicated team of like-minded and talented people. We spent hours in the Lamb & Flag or the Crown at Wychbold discussing ways in which we could improve the business. Apart from my two close friends John Whitmarsh and Dick Swain, there were John Cutts, Dick Stokes, Dave Fortey, Ray Sheward, Brian Young and Mike Bottomley.

One of David Wolfson's finest hours as a decisive, hands-on manager was during the postal strike of 1971. The mail-order industry relied on the post at every stage: agents posted orders and payments to us, and most of the goods ordered were delivered by post, as were the items that were returned to us. We could not let the business grind to a halt, so we set up networks of local shops to which agents could take their orders, which were then delivered to Kays by courier. Parcels were delivered using our own transport and hundreds of small van operators. Cash collected by agents was remitted through the bank giro system.

Within a short space of time we had created an emergency system that was capable of receiving and despatching almost 80 per cent of the orders that we would normally have expected. More importantly, the strike resulted in the mail-order industry greatly reducing its dependence on the Post Office. It was not long before orders were placed by telephone, payments were made through the banking network and GUS set up its own parcel delivery service, called White Arrow.

There were other things besides day-to-day business in those years that taught me lessons about money and risk. One of them was the boom and bust of the housing market. In 1972 I had the opportunity to make my first speculative property investment. The landlord who owned Cwm and the house next door died, and his widow offered the two houses to my father for £1000. Though Dad now had a good job and a decent salary, he had no capital, and he did not want to borrow money even to buy the family home.

I was mindful of the fact that I had never repaid the £500 my parents had given me to buy my first car, so I decided to ask Barclays for a loan to buy the two properties. I proudly handed the deeds of Cwm to Dad, and kept No. 11 next door as an investment.

In the early days the return wasn't fantastic – the tenant paid me £1 per week rent. Many years later I was able to increase this to £10 per week. In 1987 the tenant, Mrs Collins, finally died at 93, having outlived three husbands, and I was advised by an estate agent friend in Malvern to auction the house, which was unmodernised and by that stage in pretty poor repair. We settled on a reserve price of £25,000, and I almost fell off my office chair when June told me a message had arrived to say that it had sold for £49,950, multiplying my money almost 100 times in 15 years.

Cwm did not achieve that sort of return, but it proved to be far more important to me for other reasons. The property market sometimes offers amazing profits, but it can also be full of perils.

In 1973 Ann and I decided that as the size of the family was increasing and very soon we would have to think about schools, we should move to Worcester. When we got married in 1968 we had bought a house at Collettes Green, Powick, outside Worcester, for £3950; five years on we found a buyer for it at £12,000 and agreed to buy a bigger house with a large garden, closer into town, for £18,000.

Then disaster! The property market collapsed – after I had signed for the new house, but before we had exchanged on the old one. However, I had an idea: Cwm was comfortable enough in its way, but it was still old and draughty and without central heating. Collettes Green, on the other hand, would be ideal for my parents. If they could sell Cwm, they could move to Collettes Green and buy a share in it, reducing my mortgage burden. My father liked the idea not only because it was better for Mum but also because he would have a garage for the pride of his life, his Ford Classic. So we sold Cwm for £6750 and my parents bought a half share in the house at Collettes Green, where they lived happily until my mother died in 1978. Dad stayed there until 1984 when he decided to come and live with us at Ilkley – and when we sold it his half share was worth £20,000, which helped him to keep some independence and 'pay his way'. Cwm was a humble home, but it served us remarkably well.

Back to business. In 1974 I was appointed joint assistant managing director of Kays, alongside Richard Pugh – putting us in
competition for the managing director's position when Vernon
Watson retired. It was also about this time that Leonard decided to
introduce monthly meetings of the mail-order directors in the GUS
group at head office. These meetings again highlighted the differences of style between Kays – where business was going very well
– and our sister company BMOC, where it was not.

The difference between the two companies dated back to the era
of George Lodge and his BMOC opposite number, Reuben Harris.
Both were lieutenants of Isaac's, but that was all they had in common. George's philosophy was 'don't change a winning formula –
and always keep it simple', whereas Reuben's seemed to be 'if it's
not complicated, don't do it'. When Reuben also reluctantly retired,
David Wolfson became chairman of both companies, spending
Tuesday to Thursday at BMOC in Manchester. He told me later that
he liked Kays because it had an informal atmosphere in which
everybody got stuck in to solve problems if they arose; at BMOC, by
contrast, everyone was very status conscious, and very concerned
with watching their own backs.

The main topic of discussion at the monthly meetings was the
construction of a new BMOC warehouse at Wigan. At each session
we would be treated to another new model of the layout of the
warehouse, a complicated report on how it would operate, and a
schedule showing the ever-increasing cost of the project. In four
months the projected cost rose from £9 million to £13.5 million. The
plan was to build a four-storey 'picking and packing' warehouse
with reserve stock stored in an adjacent high-bay warehouse,
where cranes automatically picked boxes or pallets of merchandise
and delivered them to the picking floor via conveyors.

It was an exciting new concept, but it was being developed by
people who had never worked in a mail-order warehouse and were
planning everything on the basis of theory rather than practice.
Leonard was becoming irritated by the delays in completing the
building and the soaring cost – as far as he was concerned, it was

his own money they were spending. The final straw came when the managing director of BMOC announced that the cost would increase to more than £17 million. Leonard went ballistic, and told him that £13.5 million was the absolute limit. This row would in due course alter the path of my career, but first there was another row to contend with – the VAT saga.

Value added tax – introduced by the Heath government in 1973 to bring the British tax system into line with what we then called the Common Market – was levied on the price of most goods supplied to our customers, with the important exception of children's clothing. We accounted for VAT on the cash collected from the agents, rather than on recorded sales – which was a concession to the mail-order industry, because it meant that we never paid VAT on cash we had been unable to collect.

The initial VAT rate was 8 per cent, but in 1975 there were strong indications that the rate would increase, maybe to as high as 20 per cent. Someone convinced Leonard that this meant mail-order companies would incur huge losses, because we would have to account for the higher rate of VAT on cash paid for goods that had been sold at the old 8 per cent rate.

In fact, the way we accounted for VAT ensured that there was no profit impact if the rate increased. It would be too tiresome to unravel the detail of this here, but suffice it to say that unfortunately Leonard had been misadvised on the issue – and it became a personal battle between him and his cousin David. An instruction came to both Kays and BMOC from Leonard's office to send a letter to all agents notifying them that 'in the event of an increase in the rate of VAT, the price of all goods held on approval will be increased by the amount of the tax increase'. It was clearly unnecessary, but BMOC went ahead and had millions of letters printed to send out to agents.

Leonard then rang me and warned me to do likewise or 'face the consequences'. He brushed aside my attempt to explain that there was no real problem if the VAT rate increased. He had obviously given up trying to persuade David, and had opted to give me a direct order instead.

If the instruction was to be obeyed, we would start distributing the letters the following Monday. I called an emergency meeting with my colleagues and we decided to hire a coach to take us to head office to tell Leonard how strongly we all felt about a palpably ridiculous instruction. I telephoned David in Manchester to tell him what we intended. He told me not to do anything yet, but to meet him at the Giffard Hotel in Worcester that evening. In the hotel we composed a letter explaining why the instruction was madness, and that the directors of Kays would not take responsibility for the consequences. It was posted that evening to the home address of each GUS main board director, and a copy was sent to Sir Isaac Wolfson, to be delivered on the Saturday morning. I went home on Friday wondering if I would still have a job on Monday.

On Sunday morning, David rang me at home to tell me to be at Universal House in Tottenham Court Road in London at 10 a.m. on Monday, and to tell the management at Manchester to do nothing with the letters until they heard from us. I enjoyed passing this on to the managing director of BMOC. The animosity was evident in his voice as he acknowledged the instruction with a sharp 'Right!' He quizzed me about the meeting and it was clear that he had mixed feelings: if this was an important event then he should be there, but if there were going to be fireworks, it might be better to keep a low profile and let an upstart like me take the flak.

I arrived early at Universal House. I had not slept because I had been going over my speech and I became more and more nervous as I waited in the reception area. One by one the main board directors arrived. They all looked very serious, and they all ignored me.

Then David arrived, looking cheerful and relaxed. I was concerned about my job and my mortgage, but he was actually enjoying the fight. We walked into the boardroom together and sat in two vacant chairs at the far end of the table. No one spoke.

Then Leonard walked in and took his place. He looked at his directors one by one as if to say 'You know what's required of you', then eyed me at the far end with David. 'Come and sit up here,

Jones,' he commanded, no doubt with the intention of isolating David even further.

He then summarised the issue. It was quite an impressive speech – he knew all the facts and expressed them clearly – it was just the conclusion that he got wrong. He did not appreciate that mail-order companies paid VAT on cash collected rather than 'sales'. He concluded by saying that he had ordered a letter to be sent to all agents and that BMOC had accepted the instruction, but that Kays had not and that the chairman of Kays was challenging the authority of the GUS board. He therefore wanted his instruction ratified by the board. He never once referred to David by name. It was clear to everyone present that this was more than a commercial issue: it was very personal.

Leonard did not call for a show of hands. He asked the directors to vote one by one to build up pressure on David, who was not invited to vote. David looked at me and shrugged his shoulders as if to say: 'It's a fait accompli, don't risk your career arguing about it.'

The pantomime continued until the last director was asked to vote. His name was Morrison and he had joined GUS when it bought the Paiges fashion chain. He turned to the chairman and said that he was not an expert on mail order and would like to hear what the mail-order directors had to say. Someone had forgotten to give him a copy of the script!

I suppose it was a measure of the esteem in which the elderly Mr Morrison was held that Leonard kept his cool. He did not ask David to comment, but turned instead to me. I looked at David and once again got the 'don't try to be a hero' signal. I cleared my throat and started my well-rehearsed speech – no one knew the subject better than me. Everyone was listening intently. As on that later occasion when the Grattan board had to be convinced of the merits of a deal with NEXT, it felt like *Twelve Angry Men*.

I got into my stride and instead of stopping the monologue once I had stated the VAT facts, I launched into a passionate plea to abandon the course of action that we were being instructed to follow, as to do otherwise would have very serious consequences for our businesses.

Then there was silence. No one looked at the chairman in case eye contact was followed by a direct question. It was Mr Morrison who came to the rescue: 'Leonard, we pay these people to run their businesses and Kays is hugely successful. We have to trust their judgement.'

At that point Leonard left the meeting. I thanked Mr Morrison for his help, but I don't think he quite understood why. I have never seen him since, but I am grateful to him for rescuing my career that morning. I followed David out of the boardroom and into his office. He shook my hand and told me to take my wife out to dinner that evening on the company to celebrate. As I left, he reminded me that we had won the battle but not the war. Our victory served only to increase the tension between him and Leonard and did not help the relationship between Kays and BMOC, where the management had been made to look like foolish yes-men.

Then Trevor Spittle arrived on the scene. David asked me to give 'a guy called Spittle' an induction to the mail-order business: he was a partner in Deloittes (GUS's auditors) who might be joining the group. I took an instant liking to Trevor. He was a man's man, a rugby fan who liked a pint and a smoke, and we quickly found ourselves in the local pub talking very frankly about what made GUS tick, how Leonard ran it like a private fiefdom, and why its salaries were significantly lower than in comparable companies. Trevor's appointment as finance director of GUS was confirmed the following month, and he made it clear that the mail-order division was going to be one of his prime interests.

Just before Christmas 1975 I received a call from Leonard, who simply said 'Would you move to Manchester?' with no explanation offered. I mumbled that I was prepared to do anything he wanted me to, and the call ended. Within five minutes I received another, this time from Trevor Spittle, and just as mystifying: 'That conversation you just had with Leonard. Forget it.'

I rang David to find out what on earth was going on. In an uninterested tone he said that he had no idea. But on the day before the Christmas holiday began, he asked me to call in at his office after we had finished our turkey lunch.

I walked in to find him grinning from ear to ear. He came straight to the point. BMOC was in a dreadful mess. The new warehouse was not working; there were no stock records or stock-location systems; 50 per cent of the goods ordered could not be found in the warehouse and were having to be cancelled and not despatched. In short, the warehouse project had brought BMOC to its knees. He wanted me to go and sort it out.

My first reaction was: 'But I don't know anything about warehousing.'

His reply was typical: 'You and I know that, but don't tell anybody else.'

I spent a lot of time over Christmas thinking about the move to Manchester. But when I returned after the holiday nobody mentioned it. David told me to be patient, but patience is not one of my virtues and I started to wonder if there had been a change of mind. Then on 28 January 1976 I received a message from Leonard: 'Meet me at Wigan at 10 a.m. tomorrow.'

I was about to be appointed chief executive of the largest mail-order company in Britain – and I was still four days short of my 33rd birthday. Looking back now, I ask the question that I did not ask myself or David then: why did they give me the job?

In Leonard's case I think it was desperation. He did not trust BMOC's senior management, and there was no one else in the group capable of doing the job. As far as David was concerned, I think he gave me the opportunity because he knew he could implement his ideas through me. Between the two of us, we could turn disaster into success.

We did, and the BMOC experience turned out to be a very good rehearsal for what we achieved 20 years later at NEXT.

Chapter 7

'I have 12 casting votes!'

Thanks to my excellent primary education, I knew that Wigan was one of the cotton towns of Lancashire. I planned my route estimating that the journey would take about four hours from Worcester and left in good time, at 5.30 a.m. All was going well until I noticed a sign: 'London 83 miles'. I had taken the southbound exit at Spaghetti Junction by mistake, and as a result arrived at BMOC's Martland distribution centre in Wigan 20 minutes late.

I parked in a vacant space in a row marked 'Directors only'. Before I could open the car door, a security guard who was a dead ringer for Mussolini told me to move.

'I am a director of Kays. I have an appointment with Mr Leonard Wolfson. And I'm late.'

'Well you can't park here. Directors only.'

In desperation I tried, 'Look here, my name is David Wolfson,' but Il Duce was not going to let me leave the car in that space, so I moved to the only other vacant one I could find, on the far perimeter of the car park. At least I could pretend it was the guard's fault I was late.

Once inside the huge warehouse, I found Leonard, flanked by his entourage from head office, shouting at the BMOC directors with the picking staff within earshot and enjoying every moment.

I walked towards the group hoping to slip in unnoticed, but Leonard spotted me.

'Ah, David.' He had never called me by my first name before. 'Gentlemen, meet your new managing director.'

There was a stunned silence – not surprisingly, since the incumbent managing director and his deputy were there.

'What's going on?' I heard a whisper. I shrugged my shoulders. I wasn't sure I knew any more than they did.

In due course we all moved on to lunch at BMOC's head office in Devonshire Street, Manchester. It was a bizarre occasion from start to finish. During the first course Leonard said that he had been wrong to leave the running of the mail-order division to his cousin, and that henceforth he was going to be much more hands-on. During the second course he formally introduced me as the new managing director who would take the business forward under his guidance and wisdom. When the pudding arrived, he went round the table advising each person in turn whether they were staying, going or being demoted. The director responsible for the new warehouse was fired there and then, as was the IT director. But strangely, the managing director was told that he would be staying.

I wanted to question that decision, but stopped myself. I remembered what David Wolfson had said to me before I left Kays: 'Anything can happen. Whatever is said, say nothing.'

I knew that I could not operate through the old managing director, but I would have to fight that battle another day.

What Leonard said over coffee did not please me either. I was to have two assistant managing directors. One, Michael Harris, was a good choice. We knew each other pretty well. He had earned his spurs as managing director of Marshall Ward, the direct mail-order catalogue subsidiary of BMOC, and I knew I could work with him.

The other was Jim Morris. He worked at the Nottingham headquarters of Midland Household Stores, GUS's furniture retailing arm. He was the protégé of Harold Bowman, who had recently been appointed deputy chairman of the GUS group. I had nothing against Jim, but his appointment would frustrate a key element of my own plans, of which more in a moment.

The final piece of the jigsaw was that Trevor Spittle was to become the deputy chairman of both Kays and BMOC – making life a little more difficult for David Wolfson.

These appointments helped to explain why there was such a delay after Christmas telling me what was going to happen. They had all been jockeying for their own positions first.

By way of light relief from all these machinations, there are some nice stories to be told about Harold Bowman. I believe that he joined GUS when his family business was bought by Isaac Wolfson, and he quickly became Leonard's right-hand man and press handler. He was basically a nice man who probably never imagined that he would reach such heights. Having got there, he was determined to make the most of it.

Once Ann and I were on holiday in the south of France at the same time as Harold, and he invited us to have dinner with him and his wife on the first night of their stay at a five-star hotel. They met us in the foyer and we followed them into a magnificent dining room. Harold called the head waiter, explained who he was, that he was staying at the hotel for the next three weeks, and that he wanted the very best table overlooking the harbour reserved for him every evening.

A momentary hesitation from the waiter was dispelled by a very large tip. During the exquisite meal that followed, Harold let me into a secret. People usually tip if they have had good service at the end of a holiday, but he always tipped heavily at the start. That way the service was immaculate – in expectation of a similar tip at the end, which would not be forthcoming.

At the end of dinner the head waiter came to ask if everything had been satisfactory, which it certainly had. He then wished the Bowmans a very happy stay at the hotel, as he was taking his own annual holiday beginning the following day. The dark cloud that descended over the Bowmans' side of the table hid the cheeky wink the head waiter gave us. I thought for a moment that Harold was going to ask for his tip back.

Another legendary Bowman story had its setting in a different grand hotel, the Savoy in London. When Harold became a director of GUS, he decided that a person of his position should always lunch at the smartest place in town, the River Room. One day he entered the restaurant and sat straight down at the best table overlooking the Thames, only to be told that it was reserved for a regular customer, as was virtually every other table in the restaurant –

but if he was lunching alone they could fit him in at a small table by the door. Harold had patience: slowly but surely over the succeeding years he moved closer to the treasured window table as other River Room regulars retired, died or fell from grace.

After hundreds of lunches of smoked salmon, steak and kidney pie, and vanilla ice cream – I had this meal with him there on many occasions – he was just one step away from the best table in the best restaurant in London. At last its regular occupant, who had frustrated Harold's ambitions for so long, suffered a fatal heart attack in mid-lunch. In the confusion that followed, no one noticed the heir apparent slip into the premier seat. I don't know if this story is entirely true, but I heard it at that very table from Harold himself.

Harold was considered by Leonard to be a very skilled negotiator. He may well have been, but I was upset to receive an instruction, not long after my appointment at BMOC, that all contracts over £250,000 had to be referred to him. This meant that after I had negotiated the best deal I could and shaken hands on it, I would have to take the supplier to see Harold, who would screw a little bit more out of him. I considered that this practice undermined my own integrity, because if I shook hands on a deal I did not expect someone else to reopen negotiations.

So I worked out a solution to keep everyone happy. When I had finalised a negotiation and shaken hands on a deal, I would tell the supplier to add back a certain figure to the agreed price so that, when he had the inevitable encounter with Harold, he could reduce his price again to finish up at our agreed figure. The supplier was happy because he knew where he stood. I was happy because my credibility remained intact. Harold was happy, because he had been able to squeeze that little bit extra that only he could extract. Leonard was happy, because 'that little bit extra' would help to pay for Harold's chauffeur-driven Rolls and his lunches in the River Room.

Back to BMOC's lunch of the long knives. After it was over, Leonard was off to visit other GUS companies in the Manchester area. As he left he said to me in a loud voice, so that everyone heard, 'Right, get on with it. Meet me for dinner tonight and I'll go over your plan.'

What plan?

I telephoned David Wolfson and told him what had happened. Even he was surprised that Leonard had gone as far as he had. He told me not to worry about the managing director because he would sort him out next week. He was not concerned about Spittle being deputy chairman, but like me, he was not very happy with the appointment of Jim Morris.

David and I had talked about the problems at Manchester long before my appointment. One of our plans was to replace the computer systems in BMOC with Kays' systems, which had been developed by the best IT team in the mail-order industry, led by John Whitmarsh – and which actually worked, unlike BMOC's. The fact that Morris had been made responsible for IT would make it more difficult to bring John over and convert to the Kays systems, because Jim would want to develop his own.

But that problem would have to wait. First I had to get though dinner with Leonard. I sat down in the boardroom and thought about 'my plan'. I rationalised that there was only one short-term objective: to get that warehouse running properly. If we failed to do that and continued to cancel 50 per cent of the orders because we could not find the merchandise, there would be no business left to plan.

I met Leonard and Trevor Spittle at the Midland Hotel that evening. The first half of dinner was dominated by a repeat of Leonard's rant against his cousin David. Despite David's advice to keep my head down, I argued that he was the real architect of Kays' success and that I needed his help and advice to get the new warehouse working efficiently. In response Leonard stared coldly, and I wondered if he was about to change his mind about me.

'How old are you, Jones?'

I panicked. If he knew that I was not yet 33 years old, he might use it as an excuse to rescind my appointment.

'Thirty-eight.' It just came out. The moment passed, but forever afterwards I had to remember that if Leonard was involved I had to add five years to my age. As for my plan, I told him that the most pressing task was to get the warehouse working.

'*No*! What is your plan to make BMOC a good business again?'

I really did not know what to say, but came up with some verbiage about looking after the customers, the suppliers and the employees. It sounded quite good to me, but not to Leonard.

'What about the shareholders?'

'If those three groups are happy, we'll have a successful company and that will make the shareholders happy.'

That seemed to satisfy him.

'Is there anything else?' he asked, more to Trevor Spittle than to me, as he got up to go.

I responded, 'What about my salary?'

It has often amazed me that those who have plenty of money don't realise that other people need it to live on. Trevor Spittle said he would deal with it, and it then took me six months to negotiate an increase from £10,500 per annum to £12,000 - to run a business with over £500 million turnover and 20,000 employees. There were no fat cats in GUS in those days.

My first task was to sort out the new warehouse, at the time the largest mail-order distribution centre in Europe – and to cope with the very different culture of BMOC. Kays was an informal company, with an open-door policy and no barriers to constructive discussion about improving the business. Everyone was on first-name terms and if there was a problem, we all mucked in to sort it out. People really cared about the business: it was a way of life as well as a job. We would spend hours in the pub in the evenings and in one another's homes at weekends, debating ways to improve what we were doing. And we had a guiding light in David Wolfson, who told us to keep it simple, to concentrate on the important issues and not get sidetracked by trivia, and to climb the mountain by taking one step every day. This was to be my gospel for many years ahead.

But the British Mail Order Corporation was different. It was a collection of independent departments that communicated with each other only at a very senior level. There was a 'keep your head down and look after yourself' attitude. If someone else was having a hard time, so much the better; it kept the pressure off you. No one used first names, and nobody went to the pub to make the really important decisions.

Two examples help to illustrate this culture. BMOC's company secretary was a delightful man called Aubrey Baitup who had joined the group when GUS bought the Witney Blanket Co. He was not a director of BMOC so he could not lunch with the board, but his status was higher than the senior managers, so he could not lunch with them either. It was decided that he should have his own dining room, where he ate in isolated comfort, fussed over by his own chef and waitress. The only time he had anyone to talk to was if there was a visiting company secretary – but if that person was also a director of his company he was invited to the directors' dining room, leaving Aubrey on his own. When my inquisitive nature prompted me to open the door of his private dining room, he explained the situation.

'Tomorrow you'll eat with the directors,' I said. It was my first executive decision at BMOC. When Aubrey walked rather nervously into the directors' dining room the next day, several people started to say, 'But he's not a dir…' The look on my face stopped them from completing the sentence.

There was more of this sort of thing to come. At my first meeting with the warehouse management, I was introduced by the warehouse director as 'Mr Jones from Kays', not as 'David Jones, our new managing director'. I let that one pass as he introduced his team. I knew all their names and job titles from the report that the personnel department had prepared for me. I greeted each one with a handshake and called them by their first name, despite the fact that they had been introduced by surnames only.

The warehouse director beckoned me to join him outside the room, where he advised me, 'We don't use first names in BMOC.'

I replied firmly that I would address people as I wished to, and that I expected to be called David.

We rejoined the team, who could not help notice the black cloud hanging over their director's head.

I continued the meeting using my usual technique of asking what they thought the problems were, and how they would solve them. At first they were very reluctant to talk. Their director had a 'don't you dare open your mouth' look on his face, but after a while they relaxed and my probing led to a healthy discussion.

The star performer was a short, elderly man called Joe Wild, who had spent his entire working life in the company's warehouses and was due to retire the following month. He identified the problems and offered opinions on how to solve them. His revelations about the shortcomings of the IT systems were too much for the director, who told him to shut up. It was my turn to beckon the director out of the room. But this time we did not stop walking until we got to the front door. I now had a vacancy for a warehouse director.

Happily, I persuaded Sam Nelson, who had planned Kays' warehouses in Worcester and Leeds, to come and join my team. He was helped by a rejuvenated Joe Wild, who delayed his retirement for a year at my request. For many years afterwards I used to receive a kind note from him on a Christmas card. I never did get a Christmas card from the ex-warehouse director.

I did not have to be an expert on warehousing to identify the problems at the Martland distribution centre. The concept was that the mechanised high bay (about 40 metres high) would house all the reserve stock on tall racks, with automatic cranes taking boxes and pallets of merchandise off the racks and delivering them to the appropriate floor for 'picking' to fulfil customer orders. The fact that Leonard had frozen capital expenditure on the project meant that the racking and cranes had never been installed. The high-bay warehouse was used to store the reserve stock, but only on the floor of the building. As there was no computerised information about the location and quantity of stock, finding any particular item was a nightmare.

We employed hundreds of people who would be given an item number, a quantity, a packed lunch and a supermarket trolley each day, then sent into the high bay with an instruction not to come out until they had filled their trolley with the correct product and found a way out of the maze. When I first walked round the teetering mountains of stock and kept bumping into these lost souls, I wondered what on earth I had got involved with.

So my next major decision was to sign the contract for the high-bay equipment. I decided there was no time to persuade Leonard to agree: we were simply never going to solve the problem unless we got the high bay working properly.

The other major problems were on the picking floor, where the aisles that handled bestselling merchandise items resembled King's Cross station in the rush hour, while other aisles that handled poor sellers had people hanging around with nothing to do. Each item was allocated the same-sized 'bin' on the picking floor, so that if we sold 1000 a day of one item, its bin would have to be replenished twice a minute – an impossible task even if we could find the reserve stocks of that item in the high bay.

The result of this chaos was that over half of all customers' orders had to be cancelled because we could not find the stock in the high bay or could not get it to the picking location quickly enough. I brought over a team from Kays and set about the task of rectifying the problems, making certain that whatever we did had David Wolfson's approval.

One weekend was spent counting the stock and establishing proper stock locations. We relocated the items across the picking floors to even out the workload. We solved the replenishment problem for bestselling items by creating locations for them that could hold at least one day's anticipated demand. Within four months we had solved the cancellation problem, and within twelve months we had the high bay fully kitted out and working smoothly. We climbed the mountain one step at a time. It was quite an achievement.

In June 1976 – five months into the task at Martland – I was warned that Leonard was about to embark on his annual tour of inspection in the north of England. These tours had a comic aspect to them. They were conducted from a large, elderly Daimler limousine, driven by an even more elderly chauffeur. On one occasion when I was accompanying him back to Manchester, the limousine broke down on a busy motorway. Leonard simply got out of the car and stood in the middle lane with his hands raised, forcing an approaching Mini to stop inches from his knees. He then stooped down, opened the door and got into the passenger seat, instructing the startled driver to carry on – and leaving the chauffeur and me to fend for ourselves.

I was told Leonard's preferred route round BMOC's sites, so I did a dummy run to familiarise myself with it and check that there were no problems. Everything seemed in good order, except our returns warehouse at Chadderton near Manchester. This was where we processed items returned by customers who had ordered them 'on appro' but did not want to keep them. The vast majority of items were returned in perfect condition and put back into stock to be despatched again – which was particularly important at the end of the season when we were short of stock on winning lines. But solving the problems that had caused so many order cancellations at Martland had created a new problem at Chadderton: we had a sudden increase in returns as a result of the higher level of despatches from Martland. We had about two weeks' worth of unprocessed returns, piled high in post-office sacks on the first floor.

When Leonard arrived I actually enjoyed his company for the first time. We spent the day in the back seat of his Daimler visiting all our offices and warehouses across Lancashire. We talked about my family and his, and we even compared our school days at King's Worcester. Every time we passed an old cotton mill he would treat me to a potted history of it and the company that had owned it.

When we arrived at Martland there was a reception committee of GUS hangers-on who now wanted to be associated with the distribution centre because it was working so much better. I wondered where they had all been five months previously. Almost as if he had read my thoughts, Leonard murmured as the car door was opened by six different hands, 'I hate these reception committees of big shots.'

I replied without thinking, 'I don't see any big shots!'

He stopped, and I thought that I had gone too far. But he was smiling: 'You're right. The only big shots here are in this car.'

Even his poor old chauffeur chuckled. The visit was going well, and Leonard was in a very relaxed mood.

That was no reason not to be on our guard, however. I had been told that Leonard always inspected the gents, because he had a theory that if the toilets were in good working order then the rest of the building would be OK. At one of the old textile mills that served as a warehouse and was due to be closed when Martland was running at full capacity, he asked me to direct him to the nearest washroom. I remembered that there was one near the lift on the floor we were on. I was slightly surprised when we got there to find that it was signed 'Ladies', but not to worry: that meant that the toilet on the floor below had to be a Gents. But strangely, that too was a Ladies. At this stage, Leonard lost the urge and decided to move on – which was fortunate, because the sign on every Gents had been changed to 'Ladies' five minutes before he arrived, and would be changed back as soon as he left the building!

We had not reached the returns warehouse yet. When we did, he jumped out of the car and almost ran towards the doors leading to the first floor. Had he been tipped off? I closed my eyes and waited for the explosion. But when I opened them, all I could see was a highly polished floor and not a post-office sack in sight.

I looked at the warehouse manager, but he would not catch my eye. I rang him afterwards and without prompting he told me that the post-office sacks had been loaded into containers and had spent the day being driven up and down the M6, to be brought back that evening. I could not really hold this against him: the visit had been an enormous success, BMOC had been seen to be back on course, and I was the hero of the hour.

The Martland distribution centre had had a short but eventful career to date. It had caused four directors of BMOC to lose their jobs, almost brought BMOC to its knees, and greatly assisted in the upward path of my own career. It was about to play another major role, as the scene of my first industrial dispute.

While we were sorting out Martland's problems, the trade unions kept a low profile. We had meetings with their officials and local representatives and I thought I had struck up a good relationship with both. I was naïve enough to believe that if I treated people well, they would repay me by working hard and not making trouble.

I had been managing director for almost a year when the annual wage negotiations came around. I did not expect an easy ride, because inflation was very high and unions were very militant in that winter of 1976–77, when there were strikes everywhere and the British economy was probably at its lowest ebb in modern times. In our particular case, everyone knew that BMOC was doing much better than before, so the shop stewards' expectations were high.

The negotiations began well. Heading up the union side was Jack Day, the Manchester regional officer of USDAW (the Union of Shop, Distributive and Allied Workers), a thin chain-smoker who coughed endlessly. His reputation was that he was moderate, honourable and trustworthy. He would drive a hard bargain, but when he gave his word he stuck to it.

Roy Reece, BMOC's personnel manager, reported that after three routine meetings to go through the usual excessive claims and counter-claims, they had got down to real discussion and were not a million miles apart. I had high hopes of a quick settlement, which would have been another feather in my cap, because a number of GUS companies, including Kays, were having difficulty reaching satisfactory wage agreements that winter.

Then suddenly the Martland shop steward, Jimmy Rowe, decided that Martland should have its own negotiations. As it happened, the Wigan area was handled by the Liverpool office of USDAW, and I suspected a bit of a power struggle between Manchester and Liverpool. But Jack Day told me that he had seen this ploy before and would continue to negotiate centrally. According to him, Martland's shop stewards would come back into line when they realised they were being ignored.

But it did not work out that way. Jimmy Rowe often had difficulty expressing himself, using long words in the wrong context. Nevertheless, he could deliver a good speech rallying the workers against the oppressors, and he persuaded the senior shop steward of another warehouse at Eccles to back his cause. By lunchtime all the other warehouse representatives had walked away from the table and joined them.

Jack Day called off the negotiations, saying that he would not continue until the breakaway representatives came back into line. I had just got this news when a cheerful Leonard Wolfson came on the telephone: 'Have you got an agreement yet?'

I hesitated. 'Not yet, the union officials are having a slight problem with the Martland shop stewards.'

There seemed no point in telling him that all the other warehouses had joined the Martland militants. He replied that we should never have built the place, but we could not change that. He had every confidence that I would sort it out, and I was not to give way to the militants under any circumstances.

When the request arrived for separate negotiations with Jimmy Rowe and his rebels, I refused to have anything to do with it. It was the union's problem and it was up to the union to sort it out. Jack Day repeated his assurance that they would soon come back into line. But when I arrived at the office at 7 a.m. the next day, the security man said in a matter-of-fact voice, 'Martland is on strike.'

I rushed to my office and rang the security office at Martland. 'There is a line of pickets, six deep, across the entrance stopping everyone coming into the building,' I was told. 'Even transport with stock deliveries is being turned away.'

Apparently, Jimmy Rowe had called a meeting the previous evening and told everyone that the company was refusing to talk to democratically elected shop stewards, so he was calling an indefinite strike – without a vote first. By lunchtime he had picket lines organised at every BMOC warehouse.

I was livid with Trevor Head, the personnel director, and Roy Reece, because I thought they had totally misread the situation. Why hadn't we known about the meeting the previous evening and taken steps to head off the problem? Trevor was distraught, because he had genuinely believed that Jack Day would be able to control the militants. Roy was more phlegmatic: I think he quite looked forward to the battle.

I told Leonard what had happened. Not surprisingly, he was very agitated and instructed me to get the warehouses back to work before the weekend. I had not the foggiest idea what to do. I could talk to the USDAW officials, but not to the unofficial strikers. But the officials would not talk to the unofficial strikers either, nor would they recommence the wage negotiations while the unofficial action was going on. Meanwhile, orders were pouring in at the normal rate, and we could not despatch a single item.

I failed to fulfil Leonard's instruction to 'get them back before the weekend'. On Monday morning, he told me that he was sending up the big guns – Harold Bowman, Trevor Spittle and GUS's special adviser on industrial relations, Geoffrey Finsberg MP – to sort out the problem 'that you are incapable of sorting'.

They were due to arrive on Tuesday morning, so I called everyone together for 10 a.m. Besides my own team, there were the USDAW officers from Manchester and Liverpool, Jack Day and Jack Gardner. They both had to be persuaded to come to the meeting and did so, I think, purely out of curiosity as to what these City heavyweights were like.

Jack Day was on his fourth cigarette when the London mob walked into the boardroom.

Harold Bowman started. 'I am the deputy chairman of Great Universal Stores Limited...' He paused for them to grasp the significance of his status. 'We are all very reasonable people. So can you please sort out this minor problem and we can all get back to normal.'

Jack Day lit another cigarette, coughed several times, then said politely but firmly that he did not give in to unofficial action and that we should sit tight and wait for the militants to run out of beer money.

Harold looked across at Geoffrey Finsberg, who took his cue and stood up as if in Parliament. 'I am Geoffrey Finsberg. I am a member of the shadow cabinet and was a minister in the last Conservative government...' Again, a pause for impact. 'GUS is a good employer, we employ hundreds of thousands of people...'

When he had finally finished his political speech, I could have sworn he was waiting for cheers from his own back benches. But Jack Day simply lit what must have been his eighth cigarette and indicated with a shrug that he had already answered the question 15 minutes earlier. Why waste good smoking time repeating himself?

There was an uneasy silence, interrupted by the telephone ringing. I had instructed that no calls were to be put through unless it was Leonard.

'That will be Mr Leonard,' I said.

I picked up the telephone. Leonard wanted to speak to Harold Bowman, who was about to head for the washroom.

'Yes, we're still talking,' Bowman told the boss, jigging about urgently. 'Have a word with Geoffrey.' But Geoffrey had already gone to the washroom. 'Then David will explain. He's doing a good job, he'll have them back in no time.'

He handed the phone to me and darted for the crowded washroom, where Trevor Spittle was also ahead of him. Before I could explain that the situation was not quite as Harold had described, Leonard said, 'Well done, David. I'm in France until Monday. I'll call you then. Don't pay them too much.'

The bemused USDAW officials left the room – grateful, no doubt, to have had their prejudices confirmed about the ineptitude of top management at work.

When the washroom brigade reappeared, Harold set off to leave with a cheery, 'Well, that's that!'

Geoffrey graciously indicated that he was glad to have helped, and Trevor gave me a look that seemed to say, 'Well, someone has to be the sacrificial lamb.'

I was left wondering whether this was the real world or whether I might suddenly wake up from a nightmare.

It was Roy Reece who brought me round. 'Well, that was an education. What do we do now?'

Although it was barely lunchtime, I said, 'I've had enough for one day. I'll see you tomorrow.'

I went back to the Piccadilly Hotel where I was staying – I had not yet moved the family up to Manchester – and lay on the bed going over and over the problem. Jimmy Rowe and his gang were about to ruin everything for me. I was not going to sit there and do nothing, but who could I talk to? I could not reach David Wolfson. The USDAW officials had made their position very clear. And I could not talk to the strikers because…

Because of what? Who said I couldn't talk to them? They may be on unofficial strike, but they were still employees of BMOC.

I jumped up, telephoned my driver, Kevin, and asked him to pick me up at six that evening. I rang the security office at Martland and told them that I would be arriving there at 7 p.m. That would certainly be relayed to Jimmy Rowe, ensuring he would be there when I arrived.

When I got to Martland I wondered whether it had been such a good idea. The call to the security office had brought a full turn-out of pickets, but no sign of Jimmy Rowe.

As the pickets gathered round the car I got out and said in as normal a tone as I could manage: 'Hi fellas, is Jimmy around?'

At that point Jimmy appeared from the door of an old Portakabin that served as his battle headquarters. I suggested that we had a chat over a cup of tea.

We sat round a table for three hours drinking gallons of tea, before we both signed a scribbled note that was the basis of a wage agreement to end the strike. I went back to the hotel in a happy mood. Now we could get on with the job. We just had to tell Jack Day to convene a meeting of all the union representatives and it would all be over.

Or so I thought. The following morning I arrived at my office early and telephoned David Wolfson with the news. He was never at his best first thing in the morning.

'A bit unorthodox,' was his comment. 'You've taken a big risk. Let's hope you get away with it.'

What risk? All I had done was to get off my backside and do something, instead of wandering around like a headless chicken. Trevor Head and Roy Reece came in as I was finishing the call. I thought that at least they would be pleased I had broken the dead-lock. I went through the events of the previous evening.

As the story unfolded Trevor got paler and paler. Then he got up and asked to be excused to 'consider his position'.

'What's the problem?' I asked Roy.

'You've broken all the rules,' he said gravely. 'Trevor will lose his credibility with the regional officers, and Jack Day could well decide to make the strike official.'

Instead of solving the problem, I had apparently made it ten times worse by uniting the union officials and unofficial strikers against me.

'Give me five minutes with Trevor,' said Roy, leaving me to con-template this self-inflicted disaster.

They returned an hour later. Trevor, almost back to his normal colour, calmly explained that the details of my outing last night had already reached Jack Day's ears, and that he was hopping mad and demanding an immediate meeting with us. There was now a strong possibility that USDAW would make the strike official, and the best we could do was explain the situation to Jack Day and 'hope for the best'.

At midday, Jack Day walked into my office. I knew straight away that it was not going to be an easy meeting because he was without a cigarette in his hand. My fears increased when he refused the offer of one of mine – this strike was the only time I ever smoked cigarettes.

I had already decided on my tactics, which were best described as grovelling. 'I have made a big error of judgement,' I began, going on to describe the pressure I was under, what with Leonard expecting the strike to be over by Monday and my job being on the line if it wasn't.

Jack Day said nothing for a long time, then lit up his first cigarette of the meeting. 'Don't you ever do anything like this again.' A long pause. 'I'll call a meeting for 10 o'clock Monday.' Another pause, and a tone of extreme seriousness. 'And destroy that piece of paper you signed.'

I asked for his lighter, and the agreement I had signed with Jimmy Rowe went up in smoke there and then.

So on Monday morning we went in to bat with Roy Reece leading our team, Trevor in reserve if for tactical reasons we had to refer anything to 'higher authority', and me nowhere to be seen to avoid the likelihood of Jimmy Rowe claiming that I had agreed to things we no longer wanted to agree to.

At about 11 a.m. Leonard rang for an update. 'No, they're not back at work yet,' I told him, 'but we're in negotiation with the regional officer and the shop stewards and I'm confident that we'll work out a solution.'

He asked for updates every hour. I rang David, who asked me to ring him every hour too, just before I rang Leonard.

The meeting dragged on through the day, with Roy Reece skilfully organising regular adjournments 'to consider our position'. These breaks meant that everybody had to hang around getting bored and hungry, the more so as opening time approached. I made two phone calls on the hour as instructed, and during the 2 p.m. call with Leonard, he told me that he was going home for his afternoon nap and would I please not finalise the negotiations until he was awake again. David, by contrast, said he was so excited that (contrary to his Jewish faith) he had eaten a ham sandwich.

At 7 p.m. we signed a deal. Everyone's weekly wage would increase by £1 plus 4 per cent. It was a fair offer, and was accepted by a large majority when a vote was taken the following day. Within a week we were back to normal.

No one ever knew that the agreement I had negotiated with Jimmy Rowe was £1 plus 5 per cent; I was certainly not going to tell anyone. I became a hero again – my colleagues nicknamed me 'Golden Halo'. But I knew I was lucky to get away with this one, and I owed a great deal to Trevor, Roy and Jack Day.

I wrote a short note when the dust had settled thanking Jack for his understanding. He did not reply.

After the strike, life at BMOC returned to what passed for normality. It was not easy running a company with a culture so different to the one I had been brought up in, but it was a challenge that I relished. I would like to think that some of the Kays philosophy eventually rubbed off on BMOC.

One of the good things to come out of the strike was that its resolution strengthened my position within the GUS hierarchy, and I was able to replace Jim Morris with John Whitmarsh from Kays, which he had joined when David Wolfson set up the computer department there. He and I became very close friends and I regarded him as an IT genius. He worked incredibly hard to convert BMOC to the tried-and-tested Kays computer systems.

There were many other flawed aspects of BMOC's modus operandi. For example, the marketing director's main purpose in life was to recruit new agents at the lowest 'cost per starter' that he could achieve. Unfortunately, the cost was not calculated by including the bad debts that often occurred with new agents in their first year.

On paper it looked as though the marketing director was hitting his recruitment targets, until you saw the unacceptable level of bad debts that the new agents were creating. It turned out that he was advertising for agents in low-grade local newspapers read by people who were less likely to keep up their weekly payments. So I brought up from Worcester another close colleague, Dick Swain, to take over responsibility for marketing and credit control. 'Uncle' Dick was a one-off – a fixer rather like the character portrayed by James Garner in *The Great Escape*.

My life in this period came to be dominated by the mail-order meetings on the third Thursday of every month at GUS head office in Tottenham Court Road. You never knew what was going to happen at them. The starting time of 9.30 a.m. meant that we had to travel down to London the night before – which I did not mind because we usually had dinner with John Sterling, Leonard's brother-in-law, who kept us amused with all the latest GUS gossip.

At the meeting itself, Leonard sat at the head, with me on his left and my BMOC directors down my side of the long table. David Wolfson sat opposite me, with the Kays board down his side. At the far end on the Kays side was Trevor Spittle, who took the minutes. David and I used to have a bet on whether Trevor would be asleep before 3 p.m., thanks to the large amounts of gin he consumed over lunch. I invariably won, and Leonard never found out why David always tossed a 50p coin across the table at about 2.35 p.m.

On one occasion I raised the subject of capital expenditure authorisation. The procedure was that all items over £5000 had to be formally approved by the GUS finance meeting that was held each Tuesday. It would often take weeks to get approval, and so I suggested that the authorisation limit should be increased to £100,000.

Leonard was not in favour and implied that he would not trust us to make decisions of that magnitude. I pointed out rather aggressively that every week we were responsible for buying tens of millions of pounds worth of merchandise.

I wished I had kept my mouth shut, because it prompted Leonard to reply, 'No one should buy any merchandise without referring to me, and if I am not available the buyers should talk to David (Jones), and if he is not available too, they should talk to Vernon (Watson, the managing director of Kays) and if he is not available they should talk to Richard (Pugh, the assistant managing director of Kays) and if he is not available and the worst comes to the worst, they should make the decision themselves.'

We all had to be excused to go to the washroom to relieve ourselves of the pent-up hilarity. The laughter exploded in the closets. When we got back to Manchester we commissioned plaques for our offices: 'If the worst comes to the worst, make the decision yourself!'

But the meetings were not always amusing; they could sometimes be quite upsetting. One month the BMOC contingent was on a high because profits were good, the new catalogue had started very well, costs were falling and everything seemed to be coming together nicely. I went to the meeting in fine fettle. Maybe I appeared too cocky for Leonard's liking: he really gave me a hard time. I withstood the abuse until he called me an idiot, at which point my usual calm nature deserted me. I closed my file with a bang and left the room, shaking with rage.

After a few minutes Trevor Spittle came and asked me to rejoin the meeting.

'Trevor, I don't deserve this treatment,' I said, and left to catch a train back to Manchester.

When I arrived at my office the next day, my secretary told me that Leonard had telephoned the previous afternoon to congratulate me on the excellent profit figures. That was his idea of an apology.

Perhaps with hindsight I allowed Leonard to have too much effect on me, but it is hard to overstate the influence he had on the lives of the people who worked for GUS. I saw him turn normal, robust adults into quivering wrecks. To the outside world GUS was a very successful company with an enviable record of annual increases in profits. But inside the company the majority of senior managers were scared of the chairman. Looking back, I have to wonder why so many of them put up with it. I also believe that Leonard had a little respect for me because I was a bit of a rebel who stood up to him when it mattered.

Around this time there was another example of the penny-pinching that was another aspect of the way GUS was run. The qualifying salary level for the group pension scheme had risen to £3500 per annum, and it happened that an increase I had agreed for a large number of the middle management would take them over that figure and therefore entitle them to the benefit of a non-contributory pension scheme. In fact, I used entry into the pension scheme as a way of thanking many people who had worked hard for me in the turnaround of the business.

Then, without discussion, I received a circular from head office saying that the qualifying salary was now £6500 per annum! I went mad, and demanded an immediate meeting with the trustees of the scheme. I could not persuade them to lower the salary level, but I was able to delay the implementation of the change to allow people who passed the £3500 barrier that year to join the scheme.

On another occasion Leonard rang me one Monday morning and, in the course of a quite friendly conversation, said that he was worried about the outlook for the economy and that I should reduce the staffing level by 10 per cent. I did not take him seriously. I pointed out that fortunately we were bucking the trend and sales were very buoyant – to which he replied magisterially that 'as the controlling shareholder of GUS' he expected me to carry out his instruction.

I explained that it was not possible to do what he had instructed and that if he wanted to do it he should come to Manchester and do it himself, because I certainly would not. I was told to 'come down and see me immediately'.

When I arrived at his office at 3 p.m. he had departed for the day, leaving a message for me that he had changed his view about the economic climate.

The decision-making process in GUS was a nightmare. A typical example was the saga of IBM versus Amdahl. Kays had always been a user of IBM computers, and when we introduced Kays systems into BMOC we naturally replaced its ICL equipment with IBM mainframes.

We needed to upgrade our equipment in 1979 because of the increase in business volumes, and were about to present a case for a bigger IBM machine when John Whitmarsh was invited to visit the headquarters of Amdahl, a new competitor of IBM set up by a former IBM scientist, Gene Amdahl. John returned very embarrassed because he had changed his mind and now recommended that we purchase an Amdahl machine. We negotiated hard with the European head of Amdahl and agreed a price of £2.3 million, a saving of about £1 million on the IBM equivalent.

I decided to put the proposal to Leonard on his June visit to Manchester. We were joined at lunch by his wife, Ruth, whom I immediately took to because, while he was ranting at us during the first course, she suddenly said, 'Leonard! Shut up and let these people eat their lunch!'

I whispered to her, 'I could work for you!'

Undeterred, Leonard brought up the subject of IBM versus Amdahl and put it to the vote, asking each director round the table which supplier they wanted. By the time he got to me it was Amdahl 10, IBM 0. But I was not given the opportunity to vote. Leonard just said, 'I have 12 casting votes. You'll have IBM.'

We did get the Amdahl machines in the end, but only after a lot of canvassing of the inner circle of people who were able to exert influence on the ultimate decision maker.

During this period the relationship between Leonard and David Wolfson deteriorated quite significantly, so much so that when David rang me one Monday in 1979 to say that he was on his way to Manchester and would meet me for dinner, I somehow knew that he was about to leave the group. I was right: he told me that he had had enough, and was leaving to work for Margaret Thatcher, as secretary to the shadow cabinet.

Although not unexpected, this was still shattering news. For over 15 years he had been my boss and mentor, and his support and guidance had got me to the position I then occupied. It did not improve my frame of mind when he said that I would be out of the business within a year, because 'Leonard will drive you mad'.

In fact I lasted a little longer than that. Early in 1980, Leonard agreed – after a lot of lobbying – to promote me to associate director of GUS. I was still only 37 years old, although my 'official' age within GUS was 42. Trevor Spittle had replaced David as chairman of BMOC and Kays, but we were all rather disillusioned with him. All his good ideas about improving our terms and conditions had come to nothing after he joined the yes-men who surrounded Leonard. I knew that I could not rely on Trevor in a crisis.

Over the Christmas period and well into January 1980 there was a lorry drivers' strike. This was particularly damaging to the mail-order industry because it coincided with one of the busiest stock-intake periods of the year, the launch of the spring/summer catalogue. It did not last long, but resulted in hundreds of containers of new stock being held up at the docks. When the strike was over there was a huge backlog that would take months to clear unless we did something positive.

Leonard had recently issued an instruction that no new buildings were to be acquired for any length of lease without his personal agreement. I decided that the only way I could solve the delivery backlog problem was to take a large warehouse unit at Trafford Park, unload the containers, send the urgent merchandise to the picking warehouse and leave the non-urgent merchandise in the temporary warehouse until we could come back and deal with it. I talked to Spittle about this and he agreed that we should take the building for six months, but not tell Leonard. If he ever found out, Spittle would of course support me.

So we took the temporary warehouse and cleared the backlog of deliveries in record time, stealing a march on all our competitors – even, in this context, our own sister company Kays – because our stock availability became so much better than theirs.

On a visit in March, Leonard was walking round the merchandise floor when he bumped into one of my merchandise managers and asked him how things were going. The manager replied that his department was operating very well, mainly because we had cleared the backlog of deliveries so quickly through the temporary ware-house that I had taken at Trafford Park.

'What new warehouse? Did you know about this, Trevor?'

'No, I didn't.'

So much for Trevor's support. For the first time since I joined Kays 20 years earlier, I was beginning not to enjoy my job.

The wage negotiations in March 1980 were held against a background of very high inflation and high interest rates, and the fact that everyone knew the company was doing very well. Not surprisingly, the union wanted a bigger slice of the cake. After several meetings, we settled on a general wage increase of 17 per cent. This sounds very high by today's standards but it was not then, and I was pleased with the outcome.

Traditionally in GUS, the percentages awarded to higher earners were reduced because it was assumed that the higher paid did not require the same percentage on their salary to keep pace with the increase in the cost of living. I had some sympathy with this argument, but over the years the level of executive pay in BMOC had fallen well below industry averages. I proposed that all grades received the same 17 per cent increase.

A barrier to this proposition was that Leonard himself was paid a very low salary – he had an enormous dividend income to supplement it – and nobody could be paid more than him, so senior executive salaries were all squashed into a narrow band between £22,000 and £27,500. My salary for running a company of by now almost £1 billion of turnover was £25,000. I argued the point with Trevor Spittle and after a while he reluctantly agreed that I could award 17 per cent to everyone up to assistant managing director level, but 'you'll have to negotiate your own salary with Leonard, and don't mention that everyone else has got 17 per cent'. As ever, Trevor was watching his back.

I was prepared to take my chances with Leonard. Having trebled the profits of BMOC in three years, I was confident that he would recognise my success with a good increase.

My confidence was further boosted by a memorable retail ana-lysts' visit to Martland distribution centre. GUS was and had always been a very secretive company, supplying the barest details of its business even to its own shareholders. No one knew how much profit was made by each company in the group. All the outside world knew was that aggregate profits increased every year and that the accounting policies were very conservative. So there was great excitement in the City when the retail analysts for the various stock-broking firms were invited to visit BMOC and Martland.

I laid on two coaches to transport them from Manchester station to Wigan, and on each coach there was a question-and-answer ses-sion, with me on one coach and Trevor Spittle on the other. The questions on my coach were very penetrating and I had to ask Sidney Robin, who was joint deputy chairman of GUS with Harold Bowman, how far I should go.

'Tell them what they want to know,' he said casually, having taken advantage of the bar on the train from London.

The impact of that journey was such that most of the analysts crammed into my coach on the return. By this time Sidney was doz-ing, and the conversation was very free-flowing. The analysts went back to London a lot wiser than when they left, and a number would prove very helpful to me in future years.

Meanwhile, I tried to arrange a meeting with Leonard to discuss my salary but he kept putting it off, so that although the review date was 1 April, I still had no increase by the middle of June and was very upset about it. I rang his secretary and said that I was going to camp outside his office until he saw me. He agreed to see me and after half an hour of haggling he said that 10 per cent was as far as he would go. An extra £2500 per annum was the biggest rise that I had ever been offered, so reluctantly I agreed.

As I got up to leave he added, 'and make it effective from 1 October.'

I could not believe it – having screwed me down to 10 per cent, he then halved my increase for the year to 5 per cent. I was so stunned that I just kept on walking, and I was still seething when I reached my office late that afternoon. As I walked in my secretary told me that a Miles Broadbent wanted to speak to me urgently. I did not recognise the name, but assumed that he was one of the retail analysts who had been calling me regularly since the Martland trip.

When Miles came on the line he introduced himself not as an analyst, but as a headhunter. It was the first call I had ever received from a member of that profession, and even the word 'headhunter' was unfamiliar to me. I said 'I hope you find one', but he ignored that and went on, 'How would you like to be the finance director of Grattan plc?'

'Why would I want to do that?' I asked. 'I'm already managing director of the largest mail-order company in the country. Offer me the chief executive's job and I might think about it.'

Miles said he would come back to me. Within minutes he did so. 'How would you like to be chief executive of Grattan plc?'

'Let's talk!' was my instant reply.

Chapter 8

'The mail-order business is like sex...'

I arranged to see Grattan's chairman, Michael Pickard, that evening at a hotel near Coventry. It did not take us long to agree the terms on which I was prepared to move: a salary of £50,000 – double what GUS was paying me – plus 100,000 share options and a Daimler.

We talked about the difficulties at Grattan. It was one of the best-regarded companies in the mail-order trade, having been very successful in the 1960s and early 1970s. But since then it had lost its way, mainly by falling behind on the computer systems side. Its warehouses were old-fashioned and labour intensive. Most recently, it had poured money into an agent-recruitment campaign that had brought high bad debts, ruining profitability and driving the share price down.

I explained my view that recruitment of new agents went in cycles, very often for no apparent reason. It was vital that you recognised when a downturn was coming and accepted the fact that the recruitment of new agents was going to be difficult. I had my own method of testing the climate, because the worst thing you could do if there was a downturn was to increase the recruitment spend, since the resultant bad debt would be horrendous. I suggested that we recruit two people immediately – an IT director and a marketing manager – and, surprise, surprise, I had two ideal candidates, John Whitmarsh and Dick Swain. Michael Pickard agreed that I should approach John, and suggested that Dick Swain should 'apply' for a job on the marketing side that was currently being advertised.

The following weekend I went to Worcester to talk to John. He was playing cricket, so I arranged to see him at the match. Dick was also there as a spectator. When John was run out, I took a quiet walk round the ground with him and filled him in on what was happening. I asked if he would come with me. In a way it was a stupid question, because John, like me, had lost motivation when David Wolfson left, and he said 'yes' straight away.

When we came back to the pavilion, Dick simply asked, 'Well, when are we going to Grattan?' How he heard our conversation, I shall never know.

John and I signed letters of intent the following week and were told that formal contracts would be drawn up for us as soon as possible. I was due to resign on the following Monday and John on the Tuesday. I telephoned Trevor Spittle on Monday morning and said that I was going: I had enjoyed my years with GUS, but felt that it was time to move on.

'Is it Grattan?' he asked.

I could see no reason to lie.

'Leonard will be very upset. He'll make it difficult for you.'

'Why should he?' I asked naïvely. 'I've been a loyal company man for 20 years. Why shouldn't he respect my decision?'

'I won't say anything until the finance meeting at 10 tomorrow. Think carefully about it and let me know before then if you change your mind.'

The line went dead before I could reply, 'Why should I change my mind?' I did not bother to telephone Trevor again before his meeting. I just sat in my office awaiting developments.

Harold Bowman was first to call – they put the big guns in early. But his heart did not seem to be in it. Maybe he was still cross with me for easing Jim Morris out of BMOC. He just said that Leonard was upset and had asked him to ask me to change my mind. I replied politely that I would not: I had decided that it was time for me to move on, and that I wanted to become the boss of a public company.

Louis Speelman was the next to call. Like Dick Swain, he was often known as 'Uncle' Louis. He was a GUS merchandise controller, one of the small team that Leonard surrounded himself with to keep an eye on merchandise departments around the group. This gang, with one or two exceptions, was pretty unpopular within the subsidiaries because they reported every little detail they picked up back to Leonard. Louis obviously thought money would change my mind and it was just a question of how much.

'David, how are you?'

'A little confused, Louis. I've decided to move on, and now I'm being put under pressure to stay.'

'Have you ever heard of Trevor Francis?' Of course I had: he had become Britain's first million-pound footballer when Birmingham City sold him to Nottingham Forest in 1978. But I could not see the relevance of the question.

'He was paid £100,000 to transfer. Well, I'm offering you £100,000 to tear up your contract with Grattan, and we'll indemnify you against any legal action from them.' That was quite an offer by GUS standards – four years' salary!

'Louis, I've signed a contract and I'm not reneging. My reputation and integrity are worth far more than £100,000.'

'How much more?'

'Do me a big favour, Louis. Go back and tell Leonard I don't want any bad feeling. I've had a wonderful career at GUS, I owe them a lot, but they owe me a lot too. Let's be gentlemen and accept the situation and get on with our lives.'

The telephone went dead. Who would be next to have a go?

There was a knock on my door and BMOC's personnel director Trevor Head appeared. I had intended to tell my colleagues as soon as I knew that Leonard knew, but the stream of phone calls had side-tracked me. Trevor was as white as a sheet. He had just had a call from Sidney Robin asking for a copy of my employment contract.

I told him everything that had happened, including my frustration over the salary review. The tragedy of the situation was that if Leonard had not been so mean as to defer my pay rise until October, I would have never discussed Grattan's offer. I was leaving the group because of £1250!

'Of course, send Sidney a copy of my contract.'

'That's the problem. I don't have a copy.'

That was absolutely true. In all my 20 years' service in Kays and BMOC I had never been offered a contract and never asked for one. Trevor was obviously a very worried man, because he knew that if he failed to produce an employment contract for me at this crucial juncture, all the anger that had been generated by my resignation would undoubtedly be vented on him and it would be the end of his career in GUS.

I did not see why he should suffer because of me. 'Get me a contract,' I told him. 'Six months' notice on both sides. Backdate it to when I was appointed managing director of BMOC and I'll sign it.'

Ironically, I was signing the contract when my secretary told me that Leonard was on the line. I gave the contract to a relieved Trevor, took a deep breath and told her to put him through. For some reason I switched on the pocket tape recorder that I had been using when Trevor brought the contract in.

Leonard's voice came on the loudspeaker – and I could hear that he too was on a loudspeaker phone, so I assumed that all his directors and advisers were in his office listening. They were probably recording the conversation as well.

'David, what's all this about? You know I'm grooming you to be my successor. You're not going to give that up, are you? I made a mistake with your salary. I realise you have young children and responsibilities, so we'll match whatever Grattan are offering you. Is this a deal?' He obviously expected me to say 'yes'.

'It's not a question of money, Sir Leonard, it's an opportunity for me to be the chief executive of a major public company. I'm flattered that you considered me as a possible successor, but with respect you'll still be running this group in 25 years' time when I'll be thinking of retiring.'

His conciliatory tone changed to rage – and threats of legal action. I decided to play for time and agreed to go to London the following day to talk to him. I telephoned Michael Pickard to tell him what was happening and to seek some assurance that Leonard could not harm Grattan. Michael was away until the Friday.

When I arrived at Leonard's office he greeted me like a long-lost son. It was as though the previous day's conversation had never taken place. He took it for granted that I had changed my mind simply because I had turned up for the meeting. He said that he had an important meeting to go to and left his office without another word.

I set off to talk to Trevor Spittle. On my way I bumped into Harold Bowman.

'Is everything OK?' he asked cheerfully.

'Yes, thank you,' I replied.

When I found Trevor, I told him I was worried that Leonard might go as far as to try to persuade the banks to withdraw support from Grattan. He said that Leonard certainly had 'friends in high places' in the City.

On the Friday morning I telephoned Michael Pickard and gave him a full update of events since last we met. I told him about my concern, and said I wanted assurances that the banks would continue to support Grattan.

Michael became very angry, because he thought I was changing my mind. I assured him that I wasn't, but said I thought I owed it to myself and my family to take every possible precaution before jumping ship. He calmed down and said that he would arrange for me and John Whitmarsh to see him and his financial advisers at a flat in London owned by Morgan Grenfell that evening, which happened to be Friday the 13th.

When John and I arrived at the flat, Michael Pickard was already there with Roger Seelig and Chris Knight from Morgan Grenfell. Over a pleasant dinner Roger, at his most eloquent, said that it was not possible for GUS somehow to undermine Grattan's financial stability, other than by beating us in the marketplace. He ruled out the possibility of a bid for Grattan by GUS because he thought it would be blocked by the Monopolies Commission – and indeed, not long afterwards, the Commission blocked GUS from acquiring Empire Stores.

John and I were happier with these assurances, but kept asking questions until two minutes after midnight – neither of us was particularly superstitious, but we still did not want to sign the contract on such an unlucky date.

Once we had finally signed, they took the contracts and left. We were staying at the flat for the night. We telephoned several of our colleagues whom we had already asked to join us, then sat back with an expensive bottle of brandy. An elderly night porter knocked on the door to see if we wanted anything, so we offered him a brandy. He picked up a tumbler and held it out. I started to pour, but he omitted to say 'when' until the glass was full to the brim. He was about to take a swig when Roger Seelig came back in, having forgotten his car keys. The porter quickly put the tumbler in his trouser pocket and walked out, with brandy splashing down his leg onto the plush carpet. Strange how insignificant images stay in the mind in the midst of all these tensions and excitements!

We both handed in our resignation letters on Monday morning, and at lunchtime we were told to go home on 'gardening leave' pending the agreement of our release date – or so we thought. That evening, John and I went to Grattan to meet our new colleagues. Some of them were a little subdued, particularly Michael Place, the managing director. I had met him a few times: he was a very pleasant man, perhaps too nice for the cut and thrust of corporate life.

John and I were both getting very excited about our new careers, so much so that when we got home from Bradford, we stayed up most of the night planning our campaign to revive the fortunes of Grattan. The strange thing was that once the decision to leave GUS was made, the joys and frustrations of BMOC, and of dealing with Leonard, quickly receded into history. Only the future mattered.

However, the euphoria was dispelled when the post arrived the next day. Here was a letter from GUS's solicitors, Paisner & Co, advising me that I had agreed a verbal three-year contract with Leonard and that my contract with Grattan was therefore invalid; if I did not rescind my notice, I would be sued.

I rang Michael Pickard immediately to ask for advice and he recommended me to use Addleshaws, a law firm based in Manchester. I rang them straight away and arranged to see one of their partners, Ken Perkins, that afternoon.

In effect, GUS wanted to keep me away from Grattan for as long as possible. I was quite willing to stay away for six months and start my new career on 1 January 1981, but Leonard wanted more. Apart from the verbal contract claim, he and his lawyers argued that I had so much confidential information in my head that moving to a competitor would inevitably harm GUS. But I refused all attempts to delay my starting date with Grattan, because if it was delayed beyond 1 January 1981 my new contract would be null and void.

Despite all the assurances from learned counsel that there was no way I could be prevented from taking up the new job, the period of enforced gardening leave was the worst time of my life. I had looked forward to playing some golf, getting a little fitter, seeing more of my wife and children, and planning the future with plenty of time to think. But the legal action that GUS brought ruined all those intentions and put me under appalling pressure, which made me very depressed. I was accused of taking documents and computer files, and it became possible that a court would order an extension of the gardening leave to nine months, in which case my Grattan job would evaporate – and I could hardly envisage GUS having me back.

During this very harrowing time there was one act of kindness that I will never forget. One morning I received a call from David Alliance, the Iranian-born chairman and principal shareholder of N. Brown, a small, well-run and very profitable direct mail-order company, based in Manchester.

Back in 1978, David Wolfson and I had agreed to buy N. Brown for 50p per share, valuing the company at £6 million. We had shaken hands on the deal and I had confidently organised a meeting for David Alliance and myself to see Leonard. Part of the agreement was that if we had to part company with any of N. Brown's senior management, we would do so on generous terms. What was supposed to be a polite meeting over cups of tea rapidly became an 'I'm better than you' battle as Leonard haggled over every conceivable point. When he started making difficulties about the generosity of the proposed pay-offs, Alliance – who is a proud man, and not easy to do business with – snarled that he would never sell his business to GUS, and walked out.

But I stayed on good terms with him, and while I was in the thick of my own battle with GUS he invited me to lunch with him at his office in Manchester. I gave him all the gory details, and he sat back in his chair and said that if GUS succeeded in delaying my release longer than Michael Pickard was prepared to wait, then he would employ me on the same terms as Grattan had offered. This took a huge load off my mind and enabled me to take a more aggressive stance in the discussions with GUS.

By October, nothing had been resolved. Ken Perkins of Addleshaws was concerned that GUS would wait until January before applying to the courts to keep me away from Grattan, delaying the legal action so that I could not honour my start date. We decided to test the water and agreed that John Whitmarsh should telephone Trevor Spittle and tell him that he was going to start work at Grattan the following Monday. This instantly produced an injunction from GUS, forcing John to appear in court.

The gambit paid off for us. Although the proceedings were about whether John could start at Grattan immediately, it was really a foretaste of the case that GUS might bring against me. The judge was Harry Woolf – now the Lord Chief Justice – and I am certain that he realised this significance, because in his summing up he confirmed, in GUS's favour, that six months' 'gardening leave' was appropriate because John's contract with GUS clearly stated that he would have to give six months' notice. But he went on to say that any longer period would be inappropriate, irrespective of the contract term. This was a clear indication that even if GUS were able to convince a judge that I had agreed a three-year verbal contract, I could not be kept idle for more than six months.

There was one comical incident in that courtroom. The judge was going through one of my affidavits that referred to a telephone conversation with Leonard in my office. I had switched the sound to the loudspeaker so that John Whitmarsh, who was with me, could hear both sides of the conversation. In my affidavit I referred to the telephone loudspeaker as a 'squeeze box', as we always did.

'What is a squeeze box?' asked the judge.

Our QC did not know, so he turned to his assistant sitting behind him. He did not know either, and turned to Ken Perkins sitting behind him. Ken did not know, and turned to me sitting behind him.

'A telephone loudspeaker,' I said to Ken.

'A telephone loudspeaker,' Ken said to the assistant.

'A telephone loudspeaker,' the assistant said to the QC.

'A telephone loudspeaker, m'lord!' the QC said to the judge, who had already heard the answer three times.

The following Monday Trevor Spittle called us to a meeting. He said that GUS would agree that John and I could both start at Grattan on 1 January 1981, but he wanted our written undertaking that we would not approach or entice any other GUS employees to join Grattan. Ken Perkins advised us that this undertaking was not worth the paper it was written on, because nobody could stop an individual applying for a job. I told Trevor we would sign the under-taking but that we wanted our legal fees reimbursed, our salaries paid up to the end of December 1980 and our company cars until the end of January. To my amazement he agreed, and my 20-year career with GUS came to an end.

There were many good things about those years. They gave me a solid business training that enabled me to face the challenges ahead. Most importantly, I built a team who would be with me through all the excitements of the 1980s at Grattan and NEXT. And I will never forget the inspirational leadership of David Wolfson.

Finally, I am grateful for the opportunities I had to talk to Sir Isaac Wolfson, who as he got older started to repeat his favourite stories, but it never mattered – they were still wonderful to hear. Early one morning in the mid-1960s he came into my office and asked me to take him on a tour of Worcester, where he had lived many years earlier. In the car he asked me how long I had worked in mail order, and told me it was a fine choice of career. 'The mail order business is like sex,' he chuckled. 'When it's good it's very good, and when it's bad it's still good!'

Some years later we organised a special lunch for his golden wedding anniversary. In a marvellous speech he said, 'People ask me what's the secret of a happy marriage, and I tell them that on our wedding night, Edie and I agreed I would make all the big decisions and she would make all the small ones. You know something? In 50 years of married life, there've been no big decisions to make!'

Regrettably, most of the less good things that I remember about GUS relate to Isaac's son Leonard, on whom the reader might be thinking I have been too hard. I do not want there to be any feeling of sour grapes in this account. Leonard could be charming, kind and thoughtful, and was often very interesting company. But he could also be very abrasive and dictatorial. He once told me that he was basically shy and that shouting at people was his way of overcoming that shyness. When my wife met him at a party at Claridges to celebrate Isaac's birthday, she said that she could not understand why I was so afraid of him. But the truth remains that I was.

Nevertheless, I learned three vital things from Leonard. First, the importance of cash flow: profit and loss accounts can hide a multitude of sins, but you can never fiddle your bank balance. Secondly, always make a decision: if it's the wrong one, you'll soon know and you can change it, but the worst thing is not to make any decision at all.

And thirdly, I'm afraid, it was by observing him that I believe I learned how not to treat people if you want to get the best out of them.

started at Grattan on 5 January 1981, along with John Whitmarsh and Dick Swain, who to no one's surprise had been successful in his job application. We decided that Dick would look at the agency side of the business, John would concentrate on the IT department, and I would investigate merchandise and warehousing; then we would meet at a pub called the Feathers each evening to report back to one another and discuss what needed doing most urgently.

At the first of these sessions, John was depressed that Grattan was so far behind Kays. He did not relish having to go over old ground and complete another conversion to the Kays systems. I tried to convince him of the opportunity we had in our hands. Grattan had a good reputation in the home shopping industry (we stopped calling it 'mail order', incidentally, after the introduction of telephone ordering), but it had not moved with the times. Once we had updated the systems, it would be in a very strong position again.

But if we wanted to implement the Kays systems quickly, we would have to recruit the people who developed them with us at Kays and BMOC, because GUS would certainly not license the systems to us. We made a list of the people we wanted and systematically planned our campaign to get them.

Over a period of months we got almost everyone we wanted, and it really was a unique team. I have already described John Whitmarsh as being close to a genius. 'Whit' lived for his work, and it was fortunate that his wife Olive, like mine, recognised that she was often the second priority in her husband's life. In the early days at Worcester, Olive rang me at home one Saturday to say that John had not been home for two nights and she was getting worried. I tracked him down in the computer room at Kays, where he had been working on a new program for almost 72 hours non-stop.

He graduated from a brilliant programmer to a formidable analyst, who could solve any problem you threw at him. He was also our conscience – he stopped us getting complacent. We all owed him a great deal, and his outstanding work, first at Kays and then in sorting out BMOC, Grattan and NEXT, entitled him to an early rest. He retired at 50 to get his golf handicap down and see more of his wife and his two fine sons.

Dick Swain had first joined me as an internal auditor in 1972, but really made his mark when Kays became involved in credit-scoring systems. In earlier days the vetting of applications to become agents was done individually, by experienced managers who had a feel for which ones might go bad. When agents had become established they provided an element of credit control for their own customer lists; but we also encouraged every agent to buy goods for themselves and their immediate family from the catalogue, so continuous monitoring and control of the level of bad debt was a very important management issue for us.

Credit-scoring systems were designed to automate this process and give us better control by assessing the odds of a new applicant becoming a bad debtor. When David Wolfson asked me to send someone to San Francisco to assess whether a system developed there by a company called Fair Isaacs Inc. was suitable for Kays, I selected Dick to go. He became our expert on credit as well as on agency systems.

When I realised that bad debts were a problem in BMOC – because the marketing department merrily went on recruiting new agents who were not creditworthy – I decided to combine the marketing and credit-control functions under Dick. It was vital to translate that experience to Grattan, and Dick had his own special way of communicating it. When we were having difficulty getting Grattan's agency office staff to accept the new computer systems, he stood up one day and declared: 'Look! We're in the shit here! David and I are in it up to our arses and we need you to jump in and help us to get out of it...' After that, we had their full cooperation. Dick also retired early, at 55, and achieved his ambition to buy a boat, which he keeps at Palma, Majorca, where he now spends most of his time.

During the first three months of 1981 there was a steady flow of resignations from Kays and BMOC to join us at Grattan. Each Monday was a 'hit day', and after a while Trevor Spittle started to telephone me on Fridays to find out who was resigning on the following Monday. Mike Bottomley was the first to arrive to take over computer operations, and he in turn recruited Dave King and Dave Abbot from Kays' Leeds operation. Such was the confusion in Kays that no one seemed to realise that Dave King had actually left – he and his new Grattan team went back to the Leeds office several times to study the Kays systems.

Eventually we took the heart out of Kays' computer department by appointing eight more of its people, led by Dick Stokes as John Whitmarsh's right-hand man. We also recruited Brian Young to head up merchandise control, and Colin Tranter and John Williams to run the buying side. We were extremely unpopular at GUS, and even our own chairman Michael Pickard began asking questions about how many people we were poaching.

Meanwhile, the installation of new computer systems – using Amdahl mainframes – went well. We had experienced managers who had done it all before, and they found good juniors in the department who were ready to learn. We also had the advantage of being able to write new software that was far more efficient than the Kays systems written a decade earlier.

The agency offices were our next priority. Savings had to be made, which regrettably meant redundancies, but I explained to the trade union representatives that we had to make these changes or the whole future of the company would be in danger, and everyone might lose their jobs.

The buying department was more difficult. It was effectively a mafia, and I found it very difficult to penetrate. After monitoring it for three months, I decided to make the entire band of senior managers redundant. I put John Williams – whom I had recruited from Marshall Ward – in charge of the whole of buying and merchandise, with Colin Tranter in charge of overseas sourcing. John Brenton was recruited from Kays to head the non-clothing department.

There is an interesting little anecdote about John Williams' departure from GUS. His salary was £12,500, and he and I agreed a starting salary at Grattan of £17,000. GUS put John under extreme pressure to stay, even offering him a salary of £17,500. But he had given me his word and he joined us after his compulsory gardening leave. He came to see me at the end of his first month to say that I had made a mistake with his salary. We had agreed £17,000, but I had paid him at the rate of £17,500 as a reward for loyalty. This became known as the '£500 factor': the best motivation is to reward people when they are not expecting it.

Colin Tranter and I had become very friendly during my last two years at BMOC and I learned a lot from him, particularly about buying from the Far East. When he joined me at Grattan, it quickly became obvious to us that we were paying more for garments than GUS had done. While GUS's quantities were bigger, the main reason for the differential was that Grattan was buying through importers, which had to make a margin for themselves.

I went on my first Far East buying trip with Colin with the intention of gathering information about what was involved. But when I discovered that the main routine was for the British importers we dealt with to turn up at the Hong Kong hotel where we were staying with all their samples for selection, I immediately sent the Grattan team home. We did not need to travel to Hong Kong for the pleasure of meeting importers who could just us well bring their samples to us in Bradford.

It seemed obvious that we could do much better by cutting out the middlemen and going straight to the manufacturers. I put Colin in charge of Far East purchases and he set up a Grattan Far East office – which was the model for the NEXT Asia office that I set up 10 years later.

It was on this first trip that I had my first taste of Chinese corporate hospitality. I had just got off the plane, worn out after 16 hours in economy class – Grattan could not afford Club and in those days there were three stops on the journey – when Colin told me that he had organised dinner that evening with Sidney Ho, the owner of Jan Sin Mee, one of the biggest garment manufacturers in the Far East.

He told me that we would be sitting at a large round table, that Sidney and I would sit opposite each other, and that the rest of the party would sit on either side of their respective bosses. The more senior they were, the closer to the boss they sat.

He warned me that it was sport for the Chinese to try to get a visiting boss drunk, and that their best brandy drinker would be seated on Sidney Ho's immediate right. Throughout the meal, this ringer would repeatedly fill his glass with Hennessy XO, clink my glass and down it in one. I would then be expected to do the same.

But the secret that Sidney Ho's crew did not know was that behind me were 48 bottles of Chinese beer. The Chinese can drink endless quantities of brandy, but unlike any self-respecting Englishman, they have no capacity for beer. Colin whispered to me that after I had struggled to down my glass of brandy, I should hand the champion boozer, whose name was Jack Lee, a bottle of beer. I should then proceed to swig a bottle of beer myself. He was honour bound to do the same.

As the evening progressed, poor Mr Lee got more and more drunk. I became cocky and started to drink two bottles of beer each time, and he had to follow suit. When he finally slipped under the table unconscious, our host decided that it was time to go home. We watched the disgraced Lee being shovelled unceremoniously into the back of one of a pair of gleaming white Rolls-Royces, and waved an unsteady goodbye to our generous hosts. As the cars disappeared round the corner I collapsed, and had no knowledge of anything else until the following afternoon; fortunately it was a Sunday.

We had great fun on those Far East trips. We worked hard and played hard, and followed a strict set of rules. Everyone had to wear the company 'uniform': grey trousers, white shirt with a tie, and a blazer if a jacket was required. Buyers from the other home shopping companies were always out there at the same time as us, and I used to be appalled at their scruffy jeans and T-shirts. I wanted Grattan buyers to stand out for their smartness and professionalism. Everyone had to be at breakfast at eight, leave for their first appointment by quarter to nine, and report back on progress at the hotel at four.

There were many amusing stories. One that passes the censor involved a night out with one of the suppliers whom we liked. I had two rules about being entertained by suppliers in the Far East: I was very selective who I went out with and where, and we always split the bill. This supplier was a good guy and we had a lot of fun, but he was well the worse for wear when we pushed him into his room at 3.30 a.m. By nine that morning he had not appeared, so I went and knocked on his door. After a while he opened it, still dressed in the clothes he had been wearing the night before, and apologised for not coming down to breakfast because 'I've been working on my faxes'. I might have believed him if the chocolate that the chambermaid always leaves on the pillow at night had not been stuck to his left cheek.

By 1982 we were making real progress at Grattan. The share price, which had been 54p when we joined in January 1981, had risen above £1, and the retail analysts in the City were writing good things about us. But I was increasingly concerned about the structure of the agency home shopping business. As more and more agents were recruited, the number of customers per agent reduced to the point at which the majority of our agents were in fact customers who had a catalogue for their own use and took the 10 per cent agency commission as a discount for their benefit.

At that stage, Grattan had just one trading brand – its agency catalogue. To give us more flexibility, we set up two direct catalogues, Look Again and You & Yours, which charged the customer for postage and packing and for credit and did not pay the 10 per cent agency commission. I was also keen to get into the 'direct-response' market (in which customers buy from advertisements, rather than from catalogues) and was in the process of discussing how to do this when I had a call from Malcolm Field, the chief executive of WH Smith. It owned Kaleidoscope, a well-established direct-response company, and wanted to sell it. We met in the Queen's Hotel, Leeds the following day and shook hands on a deal for £250,000.

By the strangest of coincidences, the following week I had a call from John Wallis. I had known John well in my days at Kays: he had been recruited by David Wolfson to put some life into the childrenswear ranges there. John inevitably suffered the same loss of motivation as the rest of us did when David left GUS, and he had gone to work for Terence Conran. That did not work out for him, and he left Conran to take up a senior position with Kingfisher. He told me that Kingfisher had now had a change of direction and he was out of a job: did I know of any suitable vacancies? I offered him the job of managing director of Kaleidoscope. He accepted, and did a very good job building up a direct-response division for Grattan. Two years later we bought another good name in the sector, Scotcade, and by 1986 the division had a turnover of over £80 million.

We were engaged in a number of development projects in this period that subsequently became standard practice in the home shopping industry. The most exciting was the setting up of the 'Super Agents Network', later known as the courier service.

John Whitmarsh, Dick Swain and I were in the Feathers one evening discussing how we could improve Grattan's profitability to Kays' level. One of the areas in which Grattan was well behind Kays was the cost of sending goods to customers and getting returns back. We still used the Post Office parcel service, whereas Kays and BMOC used the White Arrow van delivery service that GUS set up after the postal strike in 1971. Grattan could not duplicate the van delivery operation because our volumes were too small to make it viable. We had to think of something else, and we hit on the idea that our big agents could deliver not only their own customers' parcel but also the parcels for other, smaller agents in their area.

John then proposed that we used our wives to test the new scheme. So Ann, Olive Whitmarsh and Judy Swain became the first home shopping couriers. We delivered goods to them at home, where they repacked them and delivered them to customers in their area. This was the start of the delivery method used by all major home shopping companies in the 1990s, which NEXT still uses to provide a 24-hour delivery service.

We continued to look for other ways to improve on what we had done at GUS, and that led to the setting up of Westscot Data. During the 1970s someone in GUS had the exceptionally bright idea of bringing together all the bad-debt information from the two mail-order companies, Kays and BMOC, and combining it with the electoral roll, which we could input by buying all the printed electoral registers. It was a big project, but it created an enormously useful credit-referencing bureau. It was initially available only to GUS subsidiaries, but as the quality of the information improved over a period of time it began to attract outside clients as well. The business still exists as a subsidiary of GUS, trading as Experian.

We were aware of the potential of this business and decided to set up our own version of it. One of the team was introduced to Gordon Pollock, a canny Scot who had successfully set up a credit-referencing bureau and debt-collecting agency for Scotland, based in Glasgow. We bought the credit bureau, Westscot Data – leaving the debt-collecting side of it behind – and built it up into a new UK-wide bureau. It was slow to get off the ground, but began to make reasonable profits by the late 1980s.

By another coincidence, at round about the same time we helped to set up another business, Scorex. As I said, Kays had been one the first UK companies to use computerised credit scoring, and Dick Swain was my man looking after it. He and I became very friendly with a brilliant technician in this field called Jean-Michel Trousse, who worked for Fair Isaacs, the US company whose system Kays had imported. Early in 1983, Jean-Michel told Dick that in his spare time he had developed a new style of reporting the results of the credit-scoring process. To put it simply, whereas the Fair Isaacs system could only be interpreted by someone with a master's degree in applied mathematics, Jean-Michel's new system could be managed by a mere accountant like me, or a marketing director like Dick.

For some unaccountable reason, Jean-Michel's superiors would not adopt his system – probably because they had not yet recouped all the set-up costs of their own systems, and did not want to offer an alternative that would require far less expensive back-up from them. So Jean-Michel left Fair Isaacs and spent a year out of the industry (having signed a non-competition clause when he resigned) quietly refining his system.

He brought his system to me at Grattan because he wanted to set up his own credit-scoring company, but had no capital with which to do so. It is always a problem when a good friend comes into your office asking for financial support, because if you invest the company's money and it goes wrong it is very embarrassing – as it might have been some years later when I was approached by Fran Cotton and Steve Smith to bail out their Cotton Traders Company. In both instances I delegated the decision to my finance director; in Jean-Michel Trousse's case, that meant Peter Lomas.

Peter assessed Jean-Michel's business plan and came to the same conclusion I had reached: that it was worth a punt. Grattan invested £250,000 for a 40 per cent stake and Scorex, as the business was called, flourished as Westscot did, after a slow start. Both companies became part of NEXT in the merger in due course, and reluctantly both had to be sold when we needed the cash. Our stake in Scorex raised £7 million and Westscot raised £23 million.

Tragically, Jean-Michel and his second wife Françoise were killed in a plane crash in the Caribbean while on honeymoon. We had agreed that if anything ever happened to him I would take over as chairman, and the business continues to go from strength to strength.

With agency, buying and merchandising all sorted out, the bad debts under control, the direct home shopping catalogues launched and Kaleidoscope under our belt, we could now turn our attention to the warehouses. We knew that we would encounter resistance to change in that area, so we had concentrated on getting the rest of the company into good shape first. The previous management had effectively abdicated responsibility for running the warehouses to the union.

We were now ready to introduce new warehouse systems that would greatly improve efficiency and cut costs. We went through the correct consulting procedures with the union, but got nowhere. This was still the early days of Margaret Thatcher's government, before she began to win the battle against the excesses of trade union power. But I was prepared to face a confrontation if I had to. I felt that we had no alternative but to impose the changes we wanted, and see what happened.

Not unexpectedly, our warehouse staff promptly went out on unofficial strike. But the new spirit we had engendered at Grattan suddenly came to the fore. All the agency office staff and head office staff volunteered to work in the warehouses in the evenings and weekends to clear the picking and packing. All the directors – including me – put in as many hours as they could, and I shall long cherish the memory of John Whitmarsh running up and down the picking racks of the Gifts Galore catalogue, overtaking every other trolley in the aisle.

There is no substitute for doing the job yourself, and the experience we gained in the warehouse during the strike resulted in many beneficial changes that helped improve profitability. But our success in keeping the warehouse picking and packing up to date led to a much bigger problem: Post Office lorries would not cross the picket line to take the parcels away.

We were not to be denied! One night my most trusted crew met at the house we rented at Bramhope near Leeds, then drove in convoy to Morrison's supermarket car park, which was close to Grattan. We walked into the despatch area of the warehouse, loaded all the parcels into vans, and drove the vans to the Post Office sorting office – to the immense surprise and irritation of the night shift there. The only hiccup was the arrival of the police when we were halfway through the loading: someone had spotted our suspicious gang in Morrison's car park and thought that we were raiding Grattan.

Despite the late night we all turned up at our offices as usual in the morning. The pickets must have wondered why I had a smile on my face. When I walked in I was confronted by a distraught Mike Davies, the head of security: 'Someone has stolen all the parcels!' In the excitement nobody had thought to tell him what was going on.

This escapade seemed to demoralise the majority of the warehouse strikers, who now realised that I was prepared to take them on – and that I had the vast majority of Grattan employees behind me. They returned to work on the following Monday and caused no more trouble as we implemented the necessary changes.

But we still had not solved our fundamental warehousing problem. We were giving a better service, offering better value and quality in our product range; we were reaching more customers through the Look Again and You & Yours catalogues and the direct-response businesses. All of that meant that our warehouses were beginning to creak at the seams.

We looked at the alternatives. We could increase the number of warehouses, but it would be expensive and inefficient to increase the number of locations from which we operated. We could build a large new warehouse on a greenfield site, somewhere with very good road communications. That was a better idea – but where would we get the skilled staff from, and what about the redundancy costs and our social responsibility in Bradford, where we employed thousands of people?

So the third and best option was to build a large new warehouse actually in Bradford, as near as possible to the existing warehouse. But where?

I was looking out of my office window pondering this problem when I spotted the solution. Along Thornton Road was a large, derelict site with some old buildings and a tall chimney stack, and a few hundred gypsies living on it. When we eventually got the site we found that there was a stream running through it – not as charming as it sounds in the centre of industrial Bradford – and it had been a dumping ground for anything and everything, including hundreds of old television sets.

The site was owned by a number of landlords. We had to persuade Bradford City Council to issue compulsory purchase orders so that the site could be assembled and ultimately sold to us. Gordon Moore, the chief executive of the council, and Gerry Sutcliffe, the leader, were both extremely helpful. Not only were we able to buy the site, but we also secured grants from the council and from European funds to pay for putting in foundations and diverting the stream. The Listerhills warehouse took two years to complete, and at the time was the largest and most up-to-date home shopping warehouse in Europe.

During my time at Grattan I met some extraordinary people. Not long after I joined, I had a telephone call from Robert Maxwell. Before he discovered his true destiny as a newspaper proprietor, he was on his mission to take over the world's printing industry and wanted Grattan's business. I was very reluctant to give him any, because one of his companies had let me down at BMOC. But we had several meetings and eventually I relented and gave him a trial order to bind 20 per cent of the next issue of the Grattan catalogue. I should have followed my instincts, because he let me down and I had to ask a favour from another printer to get the job done in time. I did at least have the satisfaction of threatening Maxwell with legal action and receiving £50,000 compensation.

For some reason Maxwell kept in touch, despite the fact that I never did business again with him or any of his companies. Ann and I went to several parties at his home, Headington Hall in Oxford, and I got to know him reasonably well. He was always supremely confident that he could solve any problem, so I remain deeply sceptical about the theory that he committed suicide on his yacht.

A less famous entrepreneur who crossed my path was Cornelius Donovan, known to his friends as Con. I was first introduced to him by Colin Tranter in our BMOC days. Con had a manufacturing business at Hadleigh near Southend in Essex that supplied us with skirts and I met him when he made one of his infrequent visits to Manchester, but I did not know him well.

Not long after I joined Grattan he telephoned my secretary asking for an appointment to see me. At the meeting he explained that he had decided to give up the skirt business because he could not beat the competition from overseas. Instead, he was keen to start a retail business selling clothing at discount prices. He already had one shop at Hadleigh that sold the overruns from the skirt factory, and was looking for more product to sell in that shop and other sites he had identified in the area.

I had inherited at Grattan a mountain of old stock that remained on the books at full cost value because the effect on the accounts would have been disastrous if it was marked down to its real value. As I could not be held responsible for the errors of my predecessors, I had taken a full provision against the old stock, but I still had the problem of getting rid of it.

Although we had set up our own small chain of Manorgrove discount stores, we continued to have far too much old stock taking up valuable space in the warehouses. We agreed to launch Choice stores, a 50/50 joint venture between Con Donovan and Grattan, to be run by the Donovan family and to sell Grattan surplus stock. In the early days Con also organised auctions all over the country to get rid of huge quantities of stock, accumulated over many years, that would not easily sell even in discount shops.

It was very much a family business, with four Donovan sons all working in it. When NEXT sold Grattan to Otto Versand in 1991, I told Con that he could decide whether he wanted to stay with Grattan or become part of NEXT. Without hesitation he opted to transfer to NEXT, and he still has a good operation selling NEXT surplus stock and Directory returns. It has made a healthy return for a small initial investment by Grattan back in 1981, and the interesting fact is that I did not have a signed agreement with Con until the late 1990s. Our partnership was based on a handshake and he never let me down. He is one of those delightful characters who have the ability to make money whatever the circumstances.

One illustration of this was the saga of the slimming capsules. One Sunday morning in 1984, Con telephoned me at home to tell me he had a great idea. Through a friend called Jack Hamilton he had met a Dr Watson, who had 'discovered' a miraculous formula enabling you to slim while you sleep!

Con was always ringing me with ideas, most of which were quite sound, but I swiftly formed the view that this was not one of them. He kept on ringing me, however, and finally got my full attention when he told me he was discussing the concept with GUS on the following Friday.

'I'll see you on Thursday,' I said, and duly had a meeting with Con, Jack Hamilton and the worthy Dr Watson, who apparently specialised in dietary planning for athletes. Among his testimonials was one from the great Kenyan runner Kip Keino. He explained that a combination of two amino acids, arginine and ornithene, taken three hours after dinner before going to bed, could make you slim while you sleep. Con, rather surprisingly, had embarked on a clinical trial using overweight volunteers and every one of them had lost weight.

We immediately formed a company called Natural Vitality in which Grattan, Con, Jack and the doctor each had 25 per cent. There followed six months of hectic activity during which we cornered the world's supply of the two amino acids, sold over a million packs of slimming capsules at £9.99 a go, and made three happy people overnight millionaires.

One of the ways we marketed 'Slim While You Sleep' was in the *Sun* newspaper. That involved several meetings with its infamous editor, Kelvin MacKenzie – well, not exactly meetings. Although Con and I were in his office, Kelvin carried on editing the paper and dashing around the editorial floor shouting and swearing at anyone and everyone. I had never met anyone quite like him and was convinced that he would soon burn himself out. Happily I was wrong, and he is still going strong. He is one of those big, unforgettable characters that you meet very occasionally. The world needs more of them.

One story I was told about him may not be entirely true, but I hope it is, and it's worth retelling anyway. Kelvin never stopped working, and if he wanted to speak to someone he took no account of the time of day or night. At an unearthly hour, he telephoned one of his young, female executives to discuss an idea that had just come into his mind. She was used to these calls from him and picked up the receiver – but answered in a series of breathless gasps that suggested she was on the verge of a spectacular orgasm. Kelvin was so taken aback that when she said, between gasps, that she would ring back when she had finished, he meekly put the phone down. Twelve hours later, she called him back: 'Hi, Kelv, I've finished!'

As for our slimming capsules, we had nothing but favourable comments from users, but Con and I decided to sell the business when Esther Rantzen's *That's Life* programme started to investigate complaints from people who had suffered side effects from other, untested slimming formulas. Con remains a very good family friend. He has been a generous supporter of my charity work, and is a genuine entrepreneur whom I like and admire.

Meanwhile, during these Grattan years I was learning to live with Parkinson's – which at that stage in its progression was relatively easy to manage and conceal, once I got used to the routine of taking so many pills. As I said in the Introduction, the diagnosis in July 1982 came just at the time when the changes we had made to the business were starting to bear fruit, and it was also a time when our family life was very happy, cushioned by the rising value of my Grattan shares and despite Ann's initial reluctance to move to the Bradford area.

Bradford itself did not have a good reputation as a place to live in those days, and the Yorkshire Ripper was still at large around Leeds, which was no fault of either city, but added to Ann's resistance. We decided not to move to Yorkshire until August 1982, because to have transferred earlier would have interfered with the children's education. When the time came, Alison passed to go to Leeds Girl's High School, while Richard and Stuart both won places at Leeds Grammar.

We chose our location in Yorkshire by drawing a series of circles with Bradford and Leeds as the centres. Where the two circles met was the area we decided to look at: around Otley, Guisley and Ilkley. We found the answer at Ben Rhydding, a hillside on the edge of Ilkley, in the form of a delightful late-Victorian house called Whinbrae, which we improved by adding, among other important things, a full-sized snooker room.

We settled happily there and I enjoyed every aspect of my job. But Britain was a rapidly changing consumer society in the mid-1980s and I had a nagging worry about the future of home shopping.

It was still part of our team culture to meet at the Feathers after work, and inevitably we started to debate over our pints how we were going to keep up the momentum and the profitability of the business. Home shopping had had a very good run, but inevitably things would have to change.

The agency mail-order business had started to expand in the 1950s when the part-time agent took over from the full-time door-knocking salesman and collector. Catalogues became bigger and glossier, well-known brands increased the credibility of the offer, and clothing was photographed in a much more attractive way. But 25 years on, the entire format of the traditional catalogue was beginning to look very tired.

Perhaps more importantly, the traditional advantages of the industry – commission, credit and convenience – were being eroded. The commission was far less important because so many agents sold only to their immediate family and regarded commission as a discount on the items they bought rather than as part of their income. And the industry had lost its advantage as a provider of credit to lower-income customers who had no hope of a bank overdraft; now credit cards were being promoted very aggressively and anyone could have one, or even several.

The convenience of home shopping was still a factor, but that too was being eroded as the product began to look expensive by comparison with more competitive high-street prices. If, on the other hand, we tried to reduce selling prices but maintain our gross margins, the inevitable result was a drop in quality.

Brands were becoming increasingly important to consumers, but there was no real brand identity in the home shopping industry. All the catalogues looked very similar, and no one ever boasted that they were wearing Grattan. Any preference for one catalogue over another was based simply on habit or whim. There was very little difference in the way the agents worked, and the level of stock availability and delivery performance was standard across the industry. Market research, for what it was worth, indicated that GUS's catalogues were considered to be the most price competitive, Freeman's was the most fashionable, Grattan had a reputation for the best quality, Empire Stores was credited with having the fastest delivery, and Littlewoods was known for nothing much except being totally unmemorable. But the truth is that the differences between us all were very small.

In this rather depressing survey of the state of the industry, Grattan was at least as well placed as any of the major players. We had a good spread of business across our traditional agency catalogue, two direct catalogues and the direct-response business in Kaleidoscope and Scotcade. But still we had no brand, no name that was worth anything in its own right beyond the value of the outstanding cash owed by our agents and customers.

I concluded that there were two possible ways forward. The first was to increase the size of the business by acquisition and maintain profit growth by overhead cost reduction, taking advantage of the fact that Grattan's systems, being the latest to be implemented, were the most efficient in the industry. The obvious target for this was Empire Stores, which was slightly smaller than Grattan and was also based in Bradford.

One good connection between Grattan and Empire was that they were founded by the same family, the Fattorinis. Antonio Fattorini, an Italian immigrant from the shores of Lake Como, had first opened a jewellery shop in Leeds in 1831, and a branch in Bradford 15 years later. In the late nineteenth century, Fattorini Watch Clubs (like Kays in its earliest days) offered working men the opportunity to contribute small sums from their wages to buy watches, and later general household goods from a catalogue. That business became Empire Stores, but in 1912 a member of the family broke away and set up a competing mail-order company, which became Grattan.

Sadly, my attempt to reforge this sentimental link with Empire Stores was a complete failure. In hindsight that may have been a good thing, because it would have increased the problems we faced later, but at the time I was very irritated. I could not persuade Empire's chief executive Ralph Scott and his team that it was a good option for them. I suppose it was not surprising: they were very wary of us, particularly when I made it clear that Grattan would be the dominant partner in a merger and that our management team would run the combined group. The discussions swiftly came to nothing.

The second possibility was to link up with a well-known high-street brand and launch a new-generation catalogue using its name and product. It was this train of thought that took me first, and unsuccessfully, to talk to Marks & Spencer, and then, through Roger Seelig, to that meeting with George Davies on 15 June 1986. And that takes us back to where we started.

Part III

1996–2005

Living with Parkinson's

Chapter 9

'Retail really is detail'

By 1996, I really started to feel that we had turned NEXT into a successful company again. But something else was happening by then that also began to influence my thinking about the future. My Parkinson's condition was getting noticeably worse and increasingly difficult to hide. That focused my mind on what kind of business I wanted to leave behind when I eventually handed over to a successor.

At 31 January 1996 we had £173 million of net cash in the bank, and in March we announced that we had made a pre-tax profit for the year to 31 January of £142 million. I had been chief executive for over seven years – a period that had started very badly both for me and for NEXT but, after a lot of hard work and a certain amount of good luck, had ended well.

But NEXT had also been a highly successful company 10 years earlier – and within two years, from 1986 to 1988, it had taken itself to the brink of disaster. My job would not be complete until I had laid foundations that ensured it would never happen again.

I had long ago decided, irrespective of the Parkinson's problem, that I would not continue as chief executive for more than ten years. In my early days in the mail-order industry I saw many examples of bosses who did a fantastic job for their companies but then spoiled it all by clinging to power way past their 'sell-by' dates. Often they ended up being remembered chiefly for the fact that they had to be forced into retirement kicking and screaming after a series of profit warnings. There have also been some notable examples of the same syndrome in high-street retailing companies in the recent past.

Well, it was not going to happen to me. I like the American presidential system of a two-term limit – no one should run anything for more than eight to ten years, because by then you can become bored, complacent, outdated, over-comfortable, arrogant, lazy and out of touch with the real world. I do not believe that I had become any of these things, but I did not want to take the risk. In any case, after ten years in the top job, it was time to give a younger person the opportunity.

I set myself three important tasks. The first was to establish the principles of a long-term strategic plan that could be reviewed regularly and tweaked occasionally, but would always be there in the future to help us avoid the temptation to over-react to short-term difficulties. The second was to identify my successor. The third was to ensure that his business objectives were sound, and that he was thoroughly trained to do the job.

Throughout the recovery period, the guiding light for most of our strategic decisions was the fact that we were managing the business for the medium to long term, and not for short-term glory. We were helped considerably by the fact that in 1990 most commentators had written NEXT off as a basket case, and therefore mere survival was a bonus. The fact that our profits increased so dramatically each year meant that we were never under pressure to match retail analysts' forecasts. We did not have to find creative ways of increasing profits: NEXT's accounts were consistently prepared on the most conservative basis, something I had perfected in my years at GUS.

I will admit to having a certain degree of sympathy for my predecessor, George Davies, who was constantly under pressure to outperform the market's expectations – though I believe he did bring some of the pressure on himself by promising too much.

So what were the main principles that would ensure NEXT's ongoing success?

It was always my ambition that NEXT should be a company that people wanted to work for. I do not kid myself that we get everything right in this respect, but we have tried to retain the informality of a small company where employees feel that they are individually important. Various bonus schemes and wide coverage of share option grants ensure that everyone can share in its success.

There was no room for structured bureaucracy, because we always wanted to be able to react swiftly to opportunities and challenges. An example of this was the regular Monday morning property and capital expenditure meetings, where we made decisions quickly and often gained a useful lead over competitors who had more formal decision-making procedures.

The closure of NEXT Originals and the successful decision to have the same product range in Retail and the Directory proved beyond doubt that NEXT is one brand. It was clear to me that we should always resist the pressure to segment our offering to customers as we got bigger. Our product is aimed at the mass-market customer aged between 17 and 70 who wants well-styled, good-quality clothes at affordable prices.

In order to find out more about our customers, we installed video cameras in several stores. Not surprisingly perhaps, we found that most customers shopped in the same way: they saw something in a style they liked, then felt the quality and texture of the fabric, then looked at the price.

'Style, quality, price' became the simple way of describing our product ambitions.

Style is important because NEXT has always stood for fashion – not catwalk high fashion, but clothes that people feel good in.

Quality is vital. One of my very first slogans was that 'NEXT will never compromise on quality'. Everyone in the company is aware that it takes years to build a good reputation, but that it only takes a few poor-quality purchases to destroy it.

Price is always important. We continually strive to give our customers better value, so if we are able to lower our cost price from the manufacturer, we will either reduce the selling price or provide a better-quality item at the same price, or a combination of both. As we continue to make improvements in the sourcing of merchandise, reflected in better quality at lower cost prices, it would be simple just to make more profit. But that would conflict with our stated policy to manage the business for medium- to long-term benefit. I have said before: it is better to reduce the selling price when you can afford to, rather than be forced into it when you cannot.

It was and still is a great advantage that everyone in NEXT knows why 'style, quality, price' is important – it is our gospel. This was preached at all the meetings I had with the staff when I was finding out what the problems were, at product training with the store managers every six months, and at the informal meeting I used to have with all the managers who joined NEXT.

When asked what their priorities were in their previous companies, many of our new recruits would reply that they were instructed to increase gross profit (the difference between the selling price to the customer and the price paid to the manufacturer), reduce the amount of selling price reductions ('mark-downs') needed to sell the overstocks, and reduce the amount of unsold stock at the end of the season.

You can imagine their surprise when I told them that our objectives, by contrast, were to reduce selling prices rather than increase gross margin, and to maximise full-price sales, rather than worry about levels of mark-downs or unsold stock.

The fundamental difference between NEXT and many of our competitors is that the competitors would describe a good product line as one of which they bought 20,000 and sold 20,000, whereas we would describe a good line as one of which we bought 40,000 and sold 35,000. We had the best of both worlds – we maximised sales at full price and were able to sell the overstock very quickly at half price in the popular end-of-season sales.

In fact, we used to receive regular complaints from Marks & Spencer about the queues that started in the early hours of the first morning of our sale, because when their staff turned up for work they could not get through the thick line of shoppers waiting to get into the adjacent NEXT store that had opened at 6 a.m.!

In the early years of the recovery period, we had to reduce the amount of our selling space significantly as part of the plan to improve profitability. But by 1996, we were confident enough about our ranges – and about the future – to start a new expansion pro-gramme. Mindful of the problems that resulted from the uncon-trolled increase in the number of NEXT stores in 1987, after the acquisition of CES, we introduced some basic investment rules.

We decided that the cost of the new space had to be repaid by an increase in cash profit within a 24-month period, and that the new space had to achieve a net branch contribution of at least 15 per cent of sales before charging central overheads. We also took into account an estimate of the sales that would be diverted from exist-ing stores nearby.

We insisted that recommendations for new selling space came from the area managers, who presented their recommendations at half-yearly 'branch review' meetings. The logic was that the expan-sion was planned from the bottom up by the people who were responsible for its success. They knew, in turn, that if they failed to achieve their targets, they would lose out when it came to bonus time.

At first, the additional space came from within the existing stores, by building mezzanine floors or by converting storage space into selling space. When we had exhausted these opportunities, we identified locations where we were under-spaced and looked to relocate to a larger store. At the same time, we opened new stores where we did not have a presence. This was particularly important, because it resulted in NEXT being one the first clothing retailers to recognise the potential of out-of-town shopping parks that had hitherto been occupied only by 'hard goods' retailers like Dixons, Comet, MFI and B&Q.

It was not long before the improvement in sales signalled that our distribution facilities would not be able to cope in two or three years' time. I had to ensure that NEXT's distribution facilities were good enough to take us into the twenty-first century. As I described in Chapter 4, I went through the alternatives with my very experi-enced team and we spent many hours walking around derelict sites in South Yorkshire. Some £120 million later, we opened two very large, highly automated distribution centres without any major problems.

Another 'warehouse' success that pleased me was the returns department at Bradford. By far the least popular department in any retail organisation is the one that handles customers' returns. I had always been convinced that given the right equipment and systems support, there was a small fortune to be saved in this area, but it was impossible to prove it. This was the only major capital project in all my years at NEXT that was based on gut feeling rather than financial appraisal. Thanks to the hard work of George Bennett and his team, tens of millions of pounds have been saved by increasing the amount of returned merchandise that is refurbished and put back into stock.

So all the foundations for long-term success were in place. It was time for me to start thinking about my successor.

In 1994 I had reported to the non-executive directors that I believed I had identified the person who would take over from me as chief executive. I was talking about the person I referred to rather mysteriously earlier as 'my young personal assistant'. He was in fact Simon Wolfson, who started to work with me in October 1991.

A few months before that, David Wolfson had asked me if his elder son could work temporarily in one of the London stores before he started a career elsewhere. I said that if there was a vacancy, and if he passed the interview, then that was fine by me – as I would have said to anybody who asked for a favour in this way. We recalled the fact that this was the little baby I had seen on that damp day two decades earlier, when the poor state of my old car had terrified the chairman so much on the drive home from the Witney Blanket Company that he had given me a company car instead!

Simon started work as a 'junior sales consultant' in NEXT's Kensington store, but I purposely did not make contact with him because there was no need to do so and I did not want to embarrass him. But when he left a few months later, he wrote a detailed report about his experiences as a sales consultant and sent it to me. It was quite an eye-opener, full of sharp observations about the way we ran the store – right down to minutiae like where we put the labels on our skirts. I asked him to come up to Leicester one Thursday evening to go through it with me.

Simon was a rather shy, intense young man with his father's agile mind, and a list of scholastic successes that included a law degree from Cambridge. We got on well, and I asked him what he was going to do for a career. When he told me that he was joining a management consultancy firm, I suggested that he might prefer to work for me.

'I certainly would,' he said, 'but I don't think that my father would approve.'

'I'm offering you a job, not your father. It's nothing to do with him.'

That was how Simon joined NEXT as my personal assistant. He should take a significant amount of the credit for the improvements that we introduced in the early 1990s. He had that rare talent, just like his father, of being able to analyse a problem and find a solution very quickly. The first solution might not be the final answer, but he would go on worrying at the problem until he had an answer that worked. On one occasion, we sat in his office for a whole day until we had devised the store bonus scheme that is still in operation today. Another time Simon, David and I locked ourselves away together and – with David taking the lead – devised a new merchandise allocation and replenishment system for the stores.

Oddly enough, one of the advantages we had – and I realise what a strange admission this is – was that none of the three of us really knew what we were talking about, because none of us had ever worked in a high-street retail business before, so we could start with a blank sheet of paper. I believe that this was a great advantage because we did not have any preconceived ideas.

It did not take long for me to decide that Simon would be my successor. He had all the necessary qualifications. He belonged to one of the most impressive retail dynasties of the twentieth century, so the business was in his genes. He was well educated and ambitious, but very willing to learn. He was a good listener and had an amazing capacity to absorb information, but above all he had that most important gift, common sense.

I could now concentrate on my third self-appointed task, of ensuring that he had training in all aspects of the business so that when his time came he was fully prepared. It was almost like fate, because this was exactly the same opportunity I had been given in Kays 30 years earlier, by his father. Simon's first major promotion was to retail sales manager, then to retail sales director in 1995. When Bob Harrison, the director responsible for IT, retired, I asked Simon to look after that side too. This was an obvious move, because it came at a time when we were in the midst of upgrading our retail systems: as sales director he was able to specify exactly what he wanted, and by controlling the IT resource he was able to ensure that the change happened on time. His ability to get the best out of people was clearly evident when he took on the IT responsibility. He got the very best out of Ray Sheward, who had been one of the team who had joined Grattan from GUS in 1981, but had left Grattan to work at Empire Stores before rejoining NEXT in 1992.

As Simon took on more responsibility, he retained all his existing areas of management. This was an essential part of his training, because he had to learn the detail of each new area, and then set up a good management structure to control the department when he moved on to the next challenge.

From retail sales he graduated to the NEXT Directory and became one of the few people in retailing to understand the detail of both high-street retailing and home shopping – his father and I were probably the only others! This knowledge was extremely important when we set out to bring our two methods of shopping closer together, to make it easier for our customers to shop with us.

He thoroughly deserved his promotion to the main board of NEXT in February 1997, although it provoked the inevitable cries of nepotism. This was totally unfair, because in reality Simon had to prove his ability much more than might otherwise have been demanded of him, simply because he was his father's son.

I ensured that every other senior appointment I made during this period was discussed with Simon first. This was a lesson I had learnt from the Grattan days. When I took over NEXT, I appointed Mike Bottomley as my successor to run Grattan, because he was the best person for the job at the time. The problem was that the team he inherited was my team, of which he had been one. The others were accustomed to my ways, and they found it difficult to get used to one of their own giving the orders. By involving Simon in senior NEXT appointments from an early stage, I made sure – bearing in mind that he was younger than many of the managers who would eventually have to report to him – that he would not run into that problem.

Although we had solved one important succession issue, there was another one on the horizon at an even more senior level. The news that David Wolfson was going to leave NEXT came as a bombshell. Throughout the struggle to rebuild NEXT that I describe in Part I, we had been a fantastic partnership. But in 1996, he was asked to succeed Leonard (who was approaching 70) as chairman of GUS – which was, after all, the Wolfson family business. It was an invitation he could not refuse. I sensed that he did not want to leave NEXT, but I also knew that he felt a duty to return to the family fold.

David had been in his element during NEXT's difficult years. He used to come up to Leicester for one day a week, usually a Wednesday, and we would work together in the morning, have lunch, relax for an hour after lunch with a Monte Cristo No. 1 cigar (usually mine), then he would catch the 4 p.m. train back to London. I admired and liked him immensely, but not everyone could cope with his ruthlessly analytical approach and his cutting wit. After he had gone, I often had to spend the rest of the afternoon trying to convince one or other of my team that the chairman really did rate them, despite what he had just said, and that they shouldn't resign!

As I have said before, David was the most impressive business-man I have ever met. He had an extraordinary ability to identify the crucial problem and solve it in the simplest way possible. NEXT would not have become the great company it is today without his contribution – and perhaps without the particular combination of his talents and mine. An analyst once asked him the secret behind NEXT's phenomenal success. '10 per cent inspiration and 90 per cent perspiration,' he replied. 'I provide one and David provides the other. But we haven't yet decided which is which.'

David was not a natural chairman – it requires a lot of diplomacy and patience, which are not his strengths – and I suspect that he did not really like the role. His chairmanship of NEXT worked because he and I were a team. He could easily become irritated if people did not understand what he was saying. Perhaps his only real fault was the fact that he made up his mind about people very quickly and once he had done so, it was very difficult to change his opinion.

I was very sad when David agreed to return to GUS. He stayed there only a relatively short time, until he handed over to Victor Blank in July 2000. But he succeeded in modernising GUS and changing its direction. Under his chairmanship GUS bought Argos, one of the best retailers in the UK. It also bought TRW, a US credit referencing and database marketing company that, combined with GUS's information technology business and renamed Experian, became a major inter-national brand. David also persuaded one of America's top retailers, Rose-Marie Bravo, to join Burberry's, a strong brand within the GUS group that had not moved with the times. Her success led to the busi-ness being floated on the stock market in July 2002.

In some ways I would have liked to have gone to GUS with David. If it had been possible for GUS to buy NEXT I think he would have tried, so that he could have continued the working relationship with me and Simon.

But that was not to be, and David's impending departure meant that we suddenly needed a new chairman. I discussed the situation with the board. It was agreed that I should become chairman as well as chief executive – and that we should also appoint a heavyweight deputy chairman, someone with serious clout in the City. On my shortlist the top name was Sir Brian Pitman, the highly respected chairman of Lloyds TSB, and the man responsible for its emergence in the early 1990s as the market leader in the high-street banking market when NatWest, Barclays and Midland all fell into various kinds of trouble. I asked Marcus Agius of Lazards for his view, and he confirmed that Brian was an admirable choice, but doubted whether he would be interested or would have the time.

I met Brian and he agreed to think about it and visit us at Enderby. He was very impressed with what he saw and he agreed to become deputy chairman. But before we could announce the appointment, a serious problem reared its head. To put it simply, we had got our Spring/Summer 1998 womenswear range all wrong. It was a well-established practice to send out a Directory Preview catalogue to a cross-section of Directory customers before the season started, in order to identify the bestselling lines, but all we had picked up from the Directory Preview sent out in October 1997 were negative vibes.

The consensus response was that the range was too much weighted towards high fashion, and did not include enough basic and 'contemporary' merchandise. In my simplistic way, I describe as 'high fashion' the clothes that you feel comfortable wearing for up to six months before they go out of fashion; 'contemporary' means clothes that you feel you can wear for up to eighteen months; and 'basic' refers to items that you can wear forever. This time round, we had plainly got the balance between these categories wrong. The early weeks of trading in the stores in January 1998 confirmed that our retail customers thought the same.

And there was another problem, which only I knew about. Over the Christmas break I had become increasingly convinced that I had made a mistake agreeing to become chairman as well as chief executive. When we took that decision, I had not been concerned about the 'corporate governance' aspect of it – the fact that it was no longer considered good practice for one person to hold both top jobs. I had canvassed the opinions of a number of our institutional shareholders and they were quite relaxed about it, so long as we appointed a strong deputy chairman. But I was worried that it could expose me to severe criticism if something did go seriously wrong.

The failure of the womenswear range was not a crisis of that magnitude, because we were well equipped to put it right. But what if something major happened that a chairman and chief executive who was 100 per cent fit might have spotted and avoided?

In all the years since I had been diagnosed with Parkinson's, this was the only time it interposed itself in an important business decision – reflecting the fact that (as I shall describe in Chapter 12) the symptoms were gradually becoming harder to control. I did not feel ready to go public about the disease, but I knew that I could not go on hiding it indefinitely.

I discussed my worries with the family over Christmas. The motion that I should not become chairman was carried unanimously by Ann and the children, so I arranged to see Brian Pitman early in January. First, I advised him that we had a problem with womenswear. I told him I wanted him to know about it before we announced his appointment, in case it prompted him to change his mind. But he had no doubt that he still wanted to join NEXT: 'All good companies have the occasional hiccup,' he said reassuringly. 'You'll get through it.'

I then told him that I had reconsidered my own position, and that it would be stupid for me to take on the combined role when we had one of Britain's best chairmen already available on our board – him! This was entirely true, but it was not the real reason for my decision. I have since apologised to Brian for being so economical with the truth. He was certainly the best candidate for the job, but I could not tell him about my Parkinson's Disease, because it was still a closely guarded secret.

His answer was that he would do whatever the board of NEXT wanted him to do. His appointment as a director was announced on 1 February 1998, and he took over the chair from David Wolfson after the AGM in May. David was always going to be a hard act to follow, but the fact that such a hugely respected figure as the chairman of Lloyds TSB was prepared to be NEXT's chairman greatly enhanced our reputation. I met many people who had lunch or dinner with Brian during his NEXT tenure and they reported back to me that all he could talk about was what a marvellous company we were.

I am pleased that I did not become chairman in 1998 for all sorts of reasons, including the fact that it left me more room to ensure that when the time came for Simon to take over from me, everyone in the company would accept the change. Equally important, the outside world would accept him in the chief executive's role too, and this meant not only our shareholders but also the financial press and retail analysts.

By this time most of the analysts in the sector were genuine NEXT enthusiasts and supporters of our shares. I maintained close contact with the more experienced of them – Paul Deacon, Roy Maconachie, John Richards, Ray Bowden, Richard Ratner, Rod Forest and Brian Rayner – some of whom I had known since the celebrated coach trip to Martland in 1980. They had all kept an open mind about our chances of recovery during the grim early 1990s. Julie Ramshaw of Morgan Stanley became a solid supporter and introduced a number of American institutional investors to us. Nick Bubb, who was also at Morgan Stanley for some years and who famously said we had 'thrown the baby out with the bathwater' when we sacked George and Liz Davies, took a while to come round. But when he did, he too became a strong supporter.

One analyst who was consistently hostile to NEXT in the 1990s was Tony Shiret of Credit Suisse First Boston, who repeatedly accused us of overtrading. In late 1998 he issued recommendations to sell NEXT at £4.68 and buy Arcadia at £2.80 up to £4, advice that would have been disastrous to follow. I keep these two CSFB circulars framed side by side on my study wall, but I have never (until

now) reminded Tony of them, because nowadays he is much more positive about what we are trying to achieve.

Despite our differences of opinion, I always respected Tony and other analysts of his generation because they did their homework properly, and formulated their own views about the state of our business and strength of our profits forecasts. To digress for a moment – managing and responding to City opinion is, after all, a crucial element of any senior executive's job – I think that too many younger analysts do not go to the same depth of analysis, simply relying on what companies tell them about next year's profits.

From time to time there are investigations into companies whose chief executive or finance director or investor relations director has allegedly given preferred analysts an inside steer about future profit. It is difficult to be black and white about this: in principle no individual should be given information that is not available to all shareholders. On the other hand, if one or two analysts are wildly out of line in their forecasts compared to what the company sincerely believes the results will show, then the company has to try to find a way of pointing that out – simply to avoid wildly wrong forecasts being bandied about.

Usually analysts tend to note the forecasts published by the company's own stockbrokers, on the assumption that the in-house brokers have some additional 'inside' information. In the 1990s the smarter analysts also knew which of their own rivals in other City firms were closer to the company, and therefore of which other analysts to take most notice. Throughout my time at Grattan and NEXT, I believe that we handled the analysts fairly, without ever breaking the City code, and in the end they have been pretty fair to us.

It is interesting that the way in which we communicated with our shareholders was different in the 1990s compared with the 1980s. In the Grattan days, the usual format was to have organised lunches with retail analysts who invited a group of, say, ten fund managers to hear about the company and ask questions.

At NEXT in the 1990s this changed. We started having one-to-one meetings with shareholders, without outside analysts present.

This was obviously more time consuming but resulted in a closer relationship between the company and its shareholders – which proved very helpful when we wanted to discuss important matters such as senior management changes, directors' benefits or corporate governance.

The Spring 1998 womenswear crisis tested our good relations with the City. I can recall a meeting with one of our shareholders, Legal and General, when in response to my well-rehearsed speech about the problem and how we were going to put it right, one fund manager simply said, 'We don't expect mistakes from you, David!'

This became a standard comment – other retailers get it wrong, but not David Jones and NEXT. But embarrassing as it was, the episode turned out to be a blessing in disguise. I put Simon in charge of sorting it out and we replaced the senior management in that area. We also introduced controls to ensure that it could not happen again, and promised the City that the problem would be sorted by October – which it was.

The later part of the 1990s was far more relaxing for me than the first part! Simon was taking on more and more of the day-to-day responsibilities and, unlike some of my counterparts in other companies, I encouraged this gradual transition. He began to take the lead in presentations on a one-to-one basis with major shareholders and in the six-monthly analysts' meeting when we announced our half-year or full-year results. There were still comments about his age, not helped by his teenage looks: I remember one financial journalist asking me if he had started shaving yet! But on the whole I think that my presence by his side gave comfort to the financial community that the combination of an old, safe pair of hands with a young, energetic and talented mind was a very good formula for success.

Meanwhile, one of the many things that I learned from Brian Pitman was the importance of enhancing earnings per share. He pointed out that in the United States, when annual results are declared, attention focuses on earnings per share and the movement in EPS compared with the previous year. EPS was important to us, and the increase we had achieved since 1991 was phenomenal, but the improvement was a by-product of our success, not the main objective, and therefore we hardly ever referred to it. However, Brian taught us to think of EPS as the main measure of success, and we have tried very hard ever since to encourage retail analysts to look first at the growth in EPS before worrying about more mundane matters.

Too many retail analysts and financial journalists have a flawed bias towards like-for-like sales comparisons, or the level of selling space increases or capital expenditure, or the inflation or deflation in selling prices. Of course these are important, but they are only a few of the elements that influence the ultimate indicator of success or failure as far as our shareholders are concerned, which is the long-term enhancement of earnings per share.

This emphasis on EPS resulted in NEXT starting (and still continuing) a programme of buying our own shares back for cancellation: by simple arithmetic, the fewer shares we have in issue, the higher the earnings per share will be. Since we started this programme, we have bought back almost 30 per cent of our shares at prices of under £8 per share. This represents a strong statement about the confidence we have in NEXT – and the best investment for our money.

The City seems to have mixed views on share buy-backs. Pundits who do not like companies buying back their own shares tend to imply that the management must have run out of ideas – by which they really mean ideas that create trading opportunities for short-term investors and fee opportunities for investment bankers. But this is a dangerous view, because lesser mortals might be influenced by the criticism and spend their surplus cash unwisely just to prove to the City that they had not run out of ideas.

$\int$imon was now ready for the big step up. Taking responsibility for the product was the final part of his Master's degree in how to be a successful chief executive. The only task he had not undertaken was to manage the warehouses, but he could pick that up as he went along – just as I had to do when his father sent me to Manchester in 1976.

But there was still just one little obstacle: his age. He was only 31, and unlike me at almost the same age, he could not pretend that he was older because, apart from his youthful looks, he was already on the NEXT main board and his age was published in the annual report. Analysts and fund managers developed an aversion in the 1990s to any sniff of dynastic management in public companies. For example, they had not liked the idea that Arnold Weinstock might be succeeded at GEC by his son Simon, who in fact died tragically young. There had already been comments about nepotism when we made Simon Wolfson sales director, and the City would have to be very carefully prepared for the idea that he was about to go straight to the top.

The solution we came up with was perfect. Simon was appointed managing director of the NEXT brand, which allowed him to establish himself as the rightful successor within the company, before being exposed to the City. By the time we announced at the AGM in May 2001 that he would succeed me as chief executive that August – and that I would move to deputy chairman, and succeed Brian Pitman as chairman a few months later – there was no adverse comment at all, only applause.

His age, 33 by the time he took over, still made headlines in the financial media. The *Observer*, for example, called him 'extraordinarily young'. But the tone was generally admiring rather than cynical – and rightly so.

I am immensely proud that Simon has succeeded me. He is an outstanding young man, and the timing was right for both of us. The advance of Parkinson's was, in some ways, making me retreat from the corporate spotlight. In any case, to be brutally honest, I was starting to get bored as chief executive because I believe that I function best in a crisis, and the crisis was now long past.

The four most enjoyable periods of my career were the early 1970s at Kays, when we had to contend with the postal strike and the three-day week; the late 1970s, when I tackled the problems of BMOC, particularly at Martland; the early 1980s, when the challenge was to turn Grattan around; and finally, the early 1990s and, most exciting of all, the recovery of NEXT. The first three of those crises were a rehearsal for the fourth. If, on the strength of that track record, I am credited with a part in saving NEXT and rebuilding it, then I have no doubt that Simon will receive the credit for going on to make NEXT a really great name in modern retailing.

Not long after he joined us, he told my secretary June that his ambition was to 'have the steel of my father and the style of David Jones'. I regarded that as a great compliment, and I was happy to have completed my last big task as chief executive.

I held that title from December 1988 until July 2001, which is a good deal longer than my ideal timeframe of eight to ten years. In mitigation, I plead that in those first two 'wasted' years of 1989 and 1990 I was not managing NEXT in a conventional sense, but trying to keep it alive. And in the last two years Simon was running the core of the business, the NEXT brand, with me leaving him enough space to do things in his own way.

When we announced our annual results for the year to 31 January 2005, I paid tribute to my young successor for the remarkable progress that NEXT made in the first five years of his stewardship. I was also very proud to say in my chairman's statement: 'It is the sign of a well run business that when times get tough the management takes it in its stride, and does not run around like headless chickens.' Times were very tough at NEXT at its lowest point, and no doubt changing market conditions will one day make it tough for us again, but I am certain that we have the right people and the right philosophy in place to enable us to take it in our stride.

If I have one regret about my 13-year tenure as chief executive, it is that I did not have the money or the courage to lead a management buy-out of NEXT in the dark days of 1990. As I have said, I am sometimes a gambler, but never for high stakes. In this case the stakes – for me personally, for my family, for NEXT's workforce – were already high enough. Thank goodness, through a combination of luck, grit and common sense, the risks that we did take at NEXT paid off for all of us.

What about NEXT today and its competitors? Throughout my time as chief executive, I never made any public comment on other retailers. It was our policy to be very careful about what we said to the outside world on any subject. We never criticised the opposition, nor did we respond to comments that from time to time some of them made about us.

We even had a fear of winning individual or corporate awards, because some well-known business leaders and companies have fallen from grace soon after doing so. In the mid-1990s I finally ran out of excuses for not accepting the Retailer of the Year award, but fortunately the curse that came to haunt some earlier winners left me well alone.

One way or another, the competition probably thought we were thoroughly standoffish. NEXT has often been referred to as the 'Leicester mafia' because we tended not to associate with our opposite numbers. Being tucked away in Leicester contributed to this, and so did our pride in the NEXT brand and the fact that battling to survive always draws people closer together. We were a team who kept ourselves to ourselves, and that gave some people the impression that we were arrogant. Well, maybe we were; but we just did not see the need either to curry favour with our competitors or to badmouth them.

As far as the financial press was concerned, the only serious mistake that I can recall making was when I jokingly said to Kate Rankine of the *Daily Telegraph* that my wife could not find anything in our Spring/Summer 1998 range that she liked. This was the season when we really had got the product range wrong, and it badly affected the results for 1998/9 – our trading profits for the year fell from £176 million to £163.5 million, despite a strong recovery in the second half. My comment to the *Telegraph* was published in a light-hearted way as if Ann had spotted the problem before we had noticed it ourselves within the company – which was obviously not true, but was bad for market sentiment.

No real harm was done in the long run, apart from Ann having to put up with some good-natured ribbing at the golf club. But after that, I made certain that every conversation with journalists started with 'This is off the record', until the point at which I was prepared to say something very carefully phrased on the record.

I cannot go off the record now, but I can see no harm in commenting on the state of the retail industry today – including NEXT itself.

I have said before that one of the main reasons for the success of NEXT since 1991 was that, having identified exactly what we wanted NEXT to represent, we did not change the strategy, we merely tweaked it when necessary.

The NEXT doctrine was and is a consistent one:

We aim to achieve consistent long-term growth in earnings per share.
We do not compromise on quality.
We aim to give our customers a wide choice of well-styled, good-quality products.
We aim to give our customers the best possible value, by passing on the improvements that we achieve in the buying price in the form of better value or quality, or a combination of both.

We are often asked how we would react if one of our competitors targeted our prices and undercut them. Of course we monitor the competition, but our selling prices are based on the cost price we pay and the profit margin we require. We do not have loss leaders – low-priced items with reduced margins – because this is a recipe for disaster. You finish up selling more items at reduced margins and this inevitably leads to price increases on lower-volume, higher-priced items in order to make up the shortfall in gross margin. If one of our competitors did target our prices and seriously undercut us, I would want to know whether they were buying better – and if so why. But if the lower prices were the result of cut margins and this was affecting our sales, we would reduce our sales forecast. We would not attempt to undercut the competition if the result was lower gross margin.

We will continue to increase our selling space, but only on the basis of the strict financial criteria that we first introduced in the early 1990s.

These financial safeguards have stood the test of time, and they are our insurance policy to prevent a repeat of the uncontrolled space expansion of the mid-1980s. Many followers of NEXT criticise our space expansion programme when there is a dip in consumer spending. They do not seem to understand that we very rarely take a new store on less than a 15-year lease, so that to jeopardise many years of profitable trading because of a short blip is clearly not good logic. These doubters also seem to be obsessed with like-for-like sales. The success of the larger stores, particularly those in out-of-town parks, will have two noticeable effects: sales per square foot will go down, but profit will increase. Simon has a good one-liner that sums up our approach: 'We prefer profit before publicity!'

Our consistent approach over many years has been greatly assisted by stable management. There is a clear, long-term company philosophy that everyone understands. I have often said that the success of my stewardship of NEXT will largely depend on whether it is still just as successful, or even more so, in three years' time.

We also have the advantage of having two successful formats – a portfolio of good retail stores and the most successful home shopping catalogue in Britain – which gives customers the greatest possible degree of flexibility to buy from us in the way that suits them best. No other retailer in the UK has this advantage.

It was the ambition of creating a successful home shopping offer linked to a retail brand that led to the merger between NEXT and

Grattan. The NEXT Directory is, as I have said, the only successful 'big-book' home shopping offer to have been launched in the last 25 years, and probably even longer than that. Both Sears, which owned Freemans Home Shopping and a number of retail brands, and Littlewoods, which operated large stores as well as a home shopping business, had the opportunity to follow NEXT's example, but neither of them did so. It's now too late for Sears. Littlewoods could have done it if it had the courage to consolidate the product offer as we did, but instead it maintained a separate chain of catalogue-based Index stores that accumulated £100 million of losses over 20 years. The closure of the Index chain was announced in April 2005, and some of the outlets were sold to GUS, to be rebranded as Argos stores.

Over the last 40 years, three landmark changes have shaped our shopping habits. The first of these was the introduction of credit cards – starting with Barclaycard in 1966 and Access in 1972 – and the huge increase in consumer credit that fuelled the shopping boom in the 1980s and hastened the decline of the traditional credit-based catalogue business. The second was an enormous increase in car ownership, in turn leading to the development of out-of-town shopping centres, replacing the role of the traditional High Street in shoppers' habits and affections. That, in turn, has resulted in the move by big food supermarket chains to extend their offer into clothing – Asda's GEORGE range, designed by George Davies, being the shining example – as well as electrical and other household products.

The third great leap forward was the birth of the internet. Ownership of home computers has grown at a phenomenal rate, so that even my generation, who grew up without them, are becoming addicted. Our children, now in their twenties and thirties, use the internet constantly – and for their children it will be the absolutely essential everyday means of communication, source of information and tool of business and trade. Twenty-first-century retailers will have to refine and develop their internet shopping offer if they want to stay in the game.

Today books, flowers, electrical goods and CDs are the main products bought through the internet, as well as air tickets, hire cars and hotel rooms. Tesco.com has created a new mechanism for home-delivered grocery shopping, which is a boon for busy households. Trading secondhand goods on eBay has become a pastime for millions of people, and a profession for tens of thousands of them.

But internet-based clothing sales have been slower to take off – perhaps because people shopping for clothes like to take their time and think twice about their choice, feeling the fabric if they can and comparing one outfit carefully with another, so they do not necessarily want the 'one-click' speed with which they can buy a book on the Amazon website; and partly because in the early stages of website design, catalogue photographs and textile colours did not reproduce so well on screen. But colour reproduction is improving all the time, and technology is being developed that will enable shoppers to put their own images on screen and see how they look in a particular outfit.

In an amazingly short period of time we will experience a major change in the way we shop. Large supermarkets – and to a lesser extent petrol stations – are causing the demise of local newsagents and tobacconists, bakers, greengrocers, milkmen and butchers. This trend will accelerate, as more and more people find it more convenient to visit out-of-town shopping centres for a one-stop shopping experience. Those who don't shop out of town will shop more and more through their home computers and their web-linked mobile phones. Internet shopping will become the norm – but only those companies that have efficient delivery systems will survive. Traditional High Streets will no longer be the centre of retailing but will, in my opinion, become residential areas surrounded by all kinds of leisure activities – casinos, health centres, clubs, restaurants and bars. This may sound far-fetched, but what else could happen?

The success of the Directory has given NEXT a head start in the emerging area of internet shopping. The service started to take off during 2000, and doubled its sales in 2001/2 to around 11 per cent of all our home shopping sales; in the year to January 2005 that percentage rose to 30, and could well have reached 40 by the following Christmas. It will not be long before the catalogue is replaced by a highly sophisticated website that will feature every item we sell.

The end result of all these changes in society and technology will be an extremely competitive environment for retailers, even more so than today, in which only the fittest will survive and prosper. I believe that NEXT is one of the fittest. It has a strong out-of-town presence, it has efficient warehousing and distribution systems, it is at the forefront of internet selling, and it has a very strong brand.

But who will be our competitors? I do not have a crystal ball, but I will offer a few predictions.

The big supermarket chains will continue to increase their share of the clothing market, most probably at the expense of the old home shopping brands and the cheaper retail stores groups. But I expect some takeover activity in this sector, with other foreign retailers following the example of Wal-Mart, which came from the US to buy Asda in 2001.

There will be significant consolidation of non-clothing retailers. A small number will survive and flourish, Argos being the most obvious. Shoppers will select the items they want on the internet, order and pay for them, and either have them delivered to their homes or collect them from out-of-town stores. The clothing retail trade will be dominated by a handful of big groups, and many famous brands will disappear.

I will stick my chin out and say that well-known brands such as Boots, WH Smith and Woolworths may find themselves struggling to cope with the competition from the supermarket giants, as traditional high-street shopping loses its appeal.

And what about the people who run the retail industry? Over the years I have known all of them, and some – such as Rick Greenbury of Marks & Spencer – I have already talked about. During the 1990s I came across Geoff Mulcahy, my fellow King's Worcester alumni, who once asked me if I would be interested in joining him at Kingfisher; but there was no way I would have been tempted to leave NEXT at that stage, when I had such a huge job to do. I also regularly bumped into John Hoerner of Arcadia and Keith Edelmann of Storehouse, both of whom I think took a rather dismissive view of NEXT's chances of recovering to be a serious competitor – perhaps to their later regret.

But the one whom I really respected, then and now, and whom no account of the future of retailing could ignore, is the man who has changed the face of the British High Street and is likely to be the biggest player in whatever happens there over the next decade. He is, of course, Philip Green.

I have known Philip for over 20 years and we nearly teamed up in the late 1980s to buy a business. What fun that would have been, but it was the wrong time for NEXT. We have become good friends and I really admire what he has achieved.

There is so much rubbish written and said about Philip that does not do justice to the real person. Yes, he expects his people to work very hard – but he is a great motivator and people like working for him. If you put yourself out for him, then he will support you. He is very keen on giving young people the kind of opportunities that he did not have himself, and has introduced one of the best recruitment schemes in the UK for aspiring retailers of the next generation.

He is also a strong family man and enjoys his weekends with his family away from the pressures of business. He is extremely generous and has supported me in my charity work in many different ways. He is loyal to his friends, but does not like to be let down, or for people to take advantage of his generosity. He is a character, a modern-day Isaac Wolfson or Charles Clore, and the retail scene is richer because he is around.

The thing about Philip, to put it bluntly, is that he has balls. He is extremely confident of his own ability. He is willing to take big risks and he is very determined to succeed. But he is not boastful. He recognises that his success is largely due to the fact that he happened to hit his peak at a time when a significant part of the clothing trade was very badly managed, offering him huge opportunities. Like me, he bemoans the lack of talent emerging on the retail scene, and is irritated with retail leaders who sit in ivory towers, rather than involving themselves in the nitty-gritty of the business. Retail really is detail, as so many people (including George Davies) have so often said, and the difference between success and failure is very marginal. Philip is not just the billionaire wheeler-dealer the media likes to paint him as, he really knows the detail too.

He started his run of success when he bought Olympus Sports from Sears for Tom Hunter, and they both made a big profit when Tom sold out to JJB Sports. Philip then bought Sears cheaply and made an even bigger profit by selling off its various brands and properties – and what a sad ending that was for a business empire that was almost unrivalled 40 years ago. (Liam Strong, who succeeded Michael Pickard as chief executive of Sears just before its final decline, once told me that 'he was going to give me a run for my money'. He didn't, I'm afraid.)

Many people would have stopped there and enjoyed the fruits of their labours. Philip likes the good life and spends a lot of his time in Monte Carlo – but he also loves the cut and thrust of business. And he is a genuine trader, not an asset stripper. Everyone who knew him also knew it was only a matter of time before he struck again. But the next time it would be to pick up a business he could develop, not another one he could profitably dissolve.

So he turned his attention to Bhs which – like its team mate, Mothercare – has been struggling for years. I am not surprised that Bhs was never a successful business in recent times, because I could never quite understand where it fitted in the clothing market. In the same way, I could never get to grips with the product offer in C&A and Littlewoods. If the chief executive of one of their most successful competitors could not understand them, no wonder they were losing ground.

Mothercare, on the other hand, should have been very successful. It had everything going for it: a good pedigree, a fantastic name, a loyal customer base, good locations and a growing market. What else do you need? In my time at NEXT I only ever hankered after buying two other trading formats, Mothercare and Jaeger. Both had huge potential that was never quite realised.

Mothercare remains an independent company today, but in 2000 Bhs itself became the next scalp for Philip Green, and his swift success in turning it around suggests that he paid a bargain price for the business – a mere £200 million. In 2002 he bought Arcadia – the Top Shop, Dorothy Perkins and Evans fashion chains – for £850 million. With the benefit of hindsight, that was another fantastic bargain. Within a year Philip had doubled the operating profits of the group to £228 million and within three years he had probably quadrupled the company's value – though he has no intention of selling it again.

There are interesting comparisons between Arcadia and NEXT. Both companies had their roots in menswear: NEXT in J. Hepworth & Sons and Arcadia in Burtons. Both companies inherited strong freehold property portfolios, much of which were sold off. Both emerged in the 1980s with exciting new stores and clothing ranges that helped to revive British consumers' interest in fashion shopping. Both were managed in their 1980s heyday by larger-than-life characters – respectively George Davies and Ralph Halpern – who deserve full credit for changing the fashion world.

But the development of the two groups in the 1990s was very different. NEXT had a stable senior management team, while Arcadia went through several rounds of change. NEXT consolidated its product offer into one brand, whereas Arcadia retained a multitude of different fascias. A director of Arcadia once told me that they could not afford to close one loss-making brand because the asset write-off would be so horrendous; he seemed to forget that the assets were worthless anyway. At NEXT I took the decision to close over 100 loss-making stores, taking a huge asset write-off as I did so. But as so often, the long-term gain justified the short-term pain.

That brings me to Marks & Spencer. In the second half of 2004, Philip Green missed buying M&S by a whisker. In my view, he failed for three reasons. The new 'interim' chairman of M&S, Paul Myners – who had recently replaced Luc Vandevelde – was highly respected in the City, having spent most of his career as an institutional fund manager. He brought in a respected retailer, Stuart Rose (who had run Arcadia in better times), as chief executive. Thirdly, Philip has become the victim of his own success: everyone knows he bought Sears, Bhs and Arcadia at prices that subsequently enabled him to make spectacular profits, so it was not unreasonable for shareholders to suspect that his final offer for M&S might turn out, with hindsight, to be a winning deal for him too.

M&S shareholders now believe that they have an each-way bet. If Stuart Rose is successful they will gain. But if he fails, they expect Philip to come back.

My prediction? All I can say about Stuart's chances of success is that he faces an even harder task than the one I faced at NEXT in December 1988. I wish him the best of luck, but sadly I don't expect M&S to sparkle again over the next decade. The boardroom discontent has continued and another chairman, the former civil servant Lord Burns, has been named to take over from Paul Myners.

And Philip? I think he will concentrate on his existing businesses and triumph over M&S in a far less expensive way than actually buying it.

Finally, what about NEXT overseas? We have had our compulsory excursion and failure in the US, and small, relatively inexpensive expeditions to France and Russia have not been successful either. Although there are well-run, profitable NEXT franchise operations in the Middle East and Japan, we do not believe it would be sensible to take on the distraction of further overseas ventures when we still have so much to do in the UK and Ireland.

But one day…

Chapter 10

'Be reasonable, do it my way!'

I thought long and hard about whether I should become chairman of NEXT. More recently – with a different hat on, as a non-executive director of the supermarket group Wm Morrison – I have had to think long and hard again about a whole range of issues to do with how the board of a major public company should be made up, and what the respective powers of the chairman and his directors should be.

I have always tried to do the right thing in life, even if not everyone would agree that I have always succeeded. The issues of whether it is right to accept a job in the first place or to hang on to it, or how much power should be concentrated in the hands of a chairman or chief executive, or when it is right for non-executive directors to intervene and insist on change can be complex and highly charged. Despite all the efforts of the corporate governance industry, the textbook answers are not always the right ones: often the best way to analyse these issues is by means of real-life examples.

In the case of the chairmanship of NEXT, I had the example of a great retailer in Ian MacLaurin of Tesco, who selected his successor, Terry Leahy, trained him, handed over to him and left the business to pursue other interests, notably chairing the England and Wales Cricket Board, the Sports Council and Vodafone. On the other hand, there was also the example of another great retailer, Stanley Kalms, who built up an amazing business, selected his successor, John Clare, trained him, handed over to him and stayed on as an active, high-profile chairman. Both Tesco and Dixons did very well indeed on the strength of their own versions of succession planning.

Then there was a third example to consider: Rick Greenbury of Marks & Spencer. Rick had difficult relations with the media (when they criticised him, he sent them ill-tempered notes that came to be known as 'rick-o-chets') and eventually with many of his own colleagues. But he was a good ally to me and never said a bad word about NEXT. In fact, when he was asked on one occasion about the imminent demise of NEXT, he rebuked the analyst who posed the question, told him that NEXT was a good business that would recover, and that I was a good guy. So I am reluctant to be critical of him. Nevertheless, it always seemed to me that for too long Rick was reluctant to identify his own successor.

He had done an outstanding job for M&S for many years, but he held on to power as both chairman and chief executive until pressure from institutional investors finally obliged him to split the role and name Peter Salsbury as chief executive. However, by then the media and some of his own colleagues had turned against Rick and the power struggle that followed was very destabilising for the company. Arguably, it has never recovered. That was a path that I was always determined to avoid.

I needed to debate the issue of the chairmanship with myself (and with the family) not because I had any urge to leave NEXT – far from it. I would miss the excitement, and above all the people. My concern was whether I could get used to not being the boss, or whether I would try to cling to power and end up getting in Simon's way.

There was obviously another issue: my health. I had been incredible lucky to have been able to keep going at full pace for almost 20 years since I was first diagnosed with Parkinson's. But by 2001 it was even more obvious than it had been in 1996 that I could not expect to go on forever. I discussed the pros and cons with the family, and they all agreed that provided I felt up to it, I should accept the invitation to become chairman.

At no time in the decision-making process, I'm afraid, did I take any account of yet another new edict from the corporate governance gurus, frowning on the appointment of a retiring chief executive as chairman of the same company.

In my case the non-executive directors of NEXT agreed that I should be chairman, and the executive directors fully supported the decision. One advantage I had in my new role was that I had a detailed knowledge of every aspect of the business. This ensured that the executive directors could not get away with loose explanations or omissions in their reports to the board. I believe that their reports are better prepared because they are aware that, in most cases, I am likely to know as much about the subject matter as they do.

The working relationship between Simon and I has been a very good one – as I always expected it to be. In the same way that his father and I understood each other very well and I could always sense when David was unhappy about something, Simon knows me well enough to tell when I am concerned. The most important thing is that we are both dedicated to the company and its continuing success, and we have very similar views on how it should be run; hardly surprising, perhaps, as we both benefited from the training we had from his father.

I am kept fully informed about what is happening on a day-to-day basis. Simon always asks my opinion on his strategic plans and on anything he is doubtful about. At the end of the day, the performance of NEXT is the best indicator of whether or not we are both doing our respective jobs well.

I enjoy being the chairman immensely. Whether or not I am a good chairman is for others to judge. I consider myself fortunate that over the last 40 years I have seen a variety of other chairmen at work, and they all contributed to my ideas of how the job should be done.

I have already described my admiration for my two immediate predecessors, David Wolfson and Brian Pitman – and I think I have said enough about the attributes of two other chairmen who feature in this story, Leonard Wolfson and George Davies. But let me try to sum up the qualities of the others I encountered.

Going back to the beginning of my career, George Lodge of Kays was one of the last chairmen of the old school: autocratic and aloof, he called everyone by their surname and did not believe that a business decision was likely to be improved by discussion. He even had a plaque in his office saying 'Be reasonable, do it my way!' But he never panicked, he never lost control. Most importantly, he was always concerned about the long-term success of Kays, not his own or the company's short-term glory. He once said to me: 'The most important thing is the brand. Always protect it.' In the 1960s, brand management was by no means the highly developed science it is today, but George understood it intuitively.

Unfortunately, I think he stayed on too long – and the danger with that was that most people would remember him for the fact that the GUS powers-that-be had to demolish his office to get rid of him, rather than the fact that in the post-war decades he established Kays as one of the best mail-order companies in Britain.

Sir Isaac Wolfson was in the twilight of his career as chairman of GUS when I knew him, but he also made an enormous impression on me. He had a tremendous ability to motivate people. After a chat with Isaac you would follow him over a cliff. He could also be difficult and he would often chastise people for inefficiency or incompetence, but he never left you bloodstained on the floor. He would always pick you up and dust you down, so you were ready for the next challenge. I like to think that a little of his motivational ability rubbed off on me!

Trevor Spittle was my chairman at BMOC after David Wolfson left to go into politics. I liked Trevor. He was one of the boys, he liked rugby and gin and tonics, he was a heavy smoker and he was very overweight. He once said to me that he knew he had a very unhealthy lifestyle and that he probably would not wake up one morning, but he chose to live his life that way. Sadly, his prediction came true.

In the late 1970s a gang of GUS people used to go to rugby internationals at Twickenham and we always had pre- and post-match parties at Knellor Hall near the ground. When my team joined Grattan we continued to go to the England games and used to gatecrash the GUS party. At first Trevor tried all sorts of ways to keep us out, but eventually he gave up and made us all very welcome.

When he joined the GUS board he listened to our moans about pay and conditions and about Leonard's management style, and said that he wanted to put things right. But although he promised so much, he did not always deliver on his promises. In that sense he was a great disappointment, and his example made me vow never to promise anything I could not deliver.

Michael Pickard was the chairman of Grattan when I joined in 1981. He was first class, a perfect role model for anyone aspiring to be a plc chairman. His style was to pick the best person he could find to be his chief executive, debate the strategy, then leave him to get on with it. He also taught me how to handle the City: to treat analysts and journalists with respect and never lie to them. Most of all, he made me realise the importance of maintaining your own integrity.

Michael had to give up the chairmanship of Grattan when he became chief executive of Sears. His successor was John Hann, who had been managing director of Boots Retail and had been a non-executive director of Grattan for a couple of years. John – like David Wolfson, but for very different reasons – was not a natural chair-man. He was probably too gentle, but he was excellent with people and made certain that the interests of all Grattan's employees were protected when it was acquired by NEXT.

Michael Stoddart was the chairman of NEXT when I joined the company in 1986. With his background in merchant banking and the investment trust world, he knew everyone in the City who mat-tered, and I suspect that he did an enormous amount of work behind the scenes during the very difficult period after George Davies departed, reassuring investment institutions and bankers that NEXT would get it right. I always said that Michael was the man for a crisis, and he certainly proved that in December 1988. I also believe that if he got up one morning and there was no crisis to tackle, he would go out and find one.

My views on chairmanship and how boards should run are not driven only by experience of NEXT, however. In recent years I have been a non-executive director of two other major public companies, Aggregate Industries and Wm Morrison.

Of the two, Aggregate is by far the easier to comment on. It is a fine company and I am sad that my involvement there has come to an end, because it has been sold by an agreed bid to a Swiss company. There is always a tendency to assume that only the people in your own business have the pride and dedication that make it a good company. The people in Aggregate have that same quality, even though they operate in a much less glamorous, lower-profile sector than fashion retailing. Peter Tom has done a fantastic job as chief executive, and deserves every bit of the success that should result from a takeover that gives his shareholders a full price and his management team much greater opportunities to progress. And his chairman Lord Fowler (the former Conservative minister Norman Fowler) also deserves praise. While he does not have the range of business experience of a Michael Pickard or a Brian Pitman, he is another first-class chairman with an excellent style at board meetings.

By contrast, my involvement in the supermarket group Wm Morrison has turned out to be quite different to what I had expected.

Let me say first that this was the one non-executive directorship I really hankered after. I have known Sir Ken Morrison since the early 1980s when I was at Grattan – we were both part of a group of local businessmen and dignitaries who were trying to regenerate Bradford, a proud city whose heart had been ripped out by the demise of the textile industry. I had and still have the greatest admiration for Ken as the man who created a great supermarket chain out of a business founded by his father with an egg and butter stall in Bradford Market in 1899.

When Morrisons was given the go-ahead to make a £3 billion bid for Safeway – which was a substantially bigger business than Morrisons itself – I wrote to Ken and put my name forward as a potential non-executive director, because I was sure that if the bid was successful he would be looking to appoint someone to the post of non-executive.

Apart from the fact that I quite fancied getting involved in a different retailing market, and that, conveniently, Morrison's head office was less than 12 miles from my home, there was an additional challenge. Ken Morrison is reputed not to be impressed by non-executive directors.

Among the quotes attributed to him are: 'Two check-out girls represent better value than one non-exec!' and 'What is the difference between a supermarket trolley and a non-executive director? You can get more wine into a non-exec!'

It is irrelevant whether or not he actually made these remarks. The fact is he has acquired the reputation that he has never been convinced that non-executive directors add value to a company's management team.

After several weeks without a response to my letter, I forgot about it. Then out of the blue I had a call from Ken asking for a meeting to discuss the possibility of my joining the board. What followed has the makings of a classic corporate story that might one day be worth making into a film. It might also be the opening chapter of the next volume of my autobiography!

At the tender age of 72 Ken was the executive chairman of a business he had run for nearly 50 years, surrounded by a loyal team who would put everything on the line for him. Together they ran a tight ship in which every penny was accounted for. Then early in 2004 he made what many considered to be a most uncharacteristic decision: he decided to buy a company that was nearly three times bigger than his own pride and joy, with – arguably – a different breed of customers from those in his Yorkshire home territory.

At the May 2004 annual general meeting, Duncan Davidson of Persimmon Homes and I were elected to the board of Wm Morrison Supermarkets plc as the first two non-executive directors in its history as a public company. Altough we could both appreciate the logic for the acquisition – it was a 'property deal' to obtain over 200 good sites – we began to realise that absorbing the bigger business into the Morrisons format was not going according to plan. In particular, some aspects of the Safeway accounting systems appeared to be causing problems. Therefore it became apparent that both of us would have to spend more time in the business. I was prepared to do that, but unfortunately Duncan could not give the extra time and he resigned.

Maybe I should have followed suit – it would have certainly saved me from a very stressful six months. It never occurred to me that I should resign, however, because deep down I thought I could make a difference. It was the old 'there must be an answer to this problem' syndrome again. I tried to put myself in Ken's shoes: I would not like a 'young whippersnapper' like me encroaching on my personal fiefdom and telling me how to run my business. I decided to respect his feelings and tread carefully.

My first real surprise was when the auditors explained to me that they could not support the 2004/5 profit figure – there was a black hole of around £40 million. I took advice from our merchant bankers, who confirmed that, despite the fact that we were due to announce our preliminary results on the following Wednesday, we would have to issue a profits warning.

Since that time the situation has become increasingly difficult and – fuelled by the financial journalists who sniffed a good story – the so-called boardroom battle has been read about at every breakfast table in the land. This has been particularly upsetting because, whatever the rights or wrongs, no one benefits from this negative publicity; in particular, it is very disturbing for the tens of thousands of loyal employees who, without detailed knowledge to the contrary, have to believe that what they read in the newspapers is true.

I was appointed deputy chairman at the annual general meeting in May 2005 and was given authority by the board to look for additional non-executive directors and ensure that good corporate governance is introduced. It is an almost unique task. Usually a plc may be searching for a replacement for one retiring non-executive director, whereas we needed to recruit at least four. This presented me with the opportunity to look for four people of different expertise, background and personality who could gel together as a team to make a positive contribution to the company.

At the same time, I have to prove to the board of Wm Morrison Supermarkets plc that non-executive directors do have a good, positive contribution to make. Although this is no easy task, it is one I relish because it provides me with the opportunity to try out my ideas of corporate governance. More importantly in personal terms, it gives me something to get my teeth into.

It would be wrong for me to say any more than this about Morrisons at this delicate juncture, but what I can do is outline some of the general principles that I think should define the role of the non-executive director.

Every chairman now has to keep more than one eye on corporate governance – despite the fact that much of it is a waste of time, more to do with ticking boxes than actually making certain that the company is being run properly.

In my opinion, responsibility for ensuring that the company is being managed properly must lie with the senior non-executive director and his team of non-executives. They must have specific guidelines to follow, but in general their duty is to the shareholders and that is to ensure that the business is being run efficiently.

To achieve this there has to be a new breed of non-executive directors. At present, in my opinion, they fall into five categories. There are still the titled ones who have been invited to join the board because they look good on the letterhead. Then there's the 'I'll be on your board if you'll be on mine' gang. Third, there is the ex-chief executive who resigned 'to spend more time with his family' and accepts every new job offer he receives in order to supplement his inflated final-salary pension – before the truth gets out that he was actually fired for incompetence. Next, there is the full-time chief executive who is encouraged to take on non-executive directorships, despite the fact that he has neither the time nor the interest to do the job properly.

And last, there are the good ones. These are usually people who have held responsible senior positions in their first careers but for one reason or another have decided to retire from full-time work and take on a portfolio of part-time directorships. Business needs more of them.

If I am ever asked to chair yet another committee to add to the shelf full of reports from Cadbury, Greenbury, Hampel, Higgs *et al.* and compose a new code of corporate governance, I would make half a dozen major recommendations.

First, change the title of non-executive directors to 'independent directors', and call executive directors 'operating directors'. Independence of mind and a degree of distance from the internal politics and pressures of the day-to-day operations of the company are the key requirements. They are expected to be independent, so why not call them that?

Second, make the senior independent director the deputy chairman, to ensure that his or her authority is clear to everyone, internally and externally.

Third, ensure that there are an equal number of independent and operating directors. Balance is essential, and it is up to a skilled chairman to find consensus or exercise judgement if there is disagreement between the two groups.

Fourth, insist that the independent directors spend at least three days of every month in the business. They must have a good knowledge of how the business operates in order to make a worthwhile contribution at board meetings. There is no excuse for not knowing what the executive directors are talking about or not understanding the board report. In addition, they must know the second tier of management to satisfy themselves that there is indeed a viable succession plan. One of the ways in which we managed to get the NEXT independent directors to be more knowledgeable about the company was to ask them to adopt a store near their home or regular workplace, and to visit that store whenever they could to find out what was really happening.

Fifth, for the same reasons, no one – however wise or well connected they may be – should be permitted to have more than three public company independent directorships.

Sixth, I would make it mandatory that the annual accounts of every public limited company should include a signed statement from each independent director confirming that they have had access to all the relevant information to enable them to do their jobs efficiently.

Unfortunately, there have been a number of high-profile company disasters on both sides of the Atlantic that have made shareholders wonder what the non-executives have been doing – inevitably leading to the conclusion that non-execs are a waste of time. I believe that the power of independent directors has got to be increased to make them far more accountable for the efficient and honest running of the business.

The choice of chairman has to be agreed by both the independent and operating directors. The senior independent director has to ensure that there are sound reasons – which he is prepared to explain to shareholders – why the chairman was chosen for the job. He or she also has to ensure that the relationship between the chairman and chief executive is successful and is working in the best interests of the company. There cannot be any hard-and-fast rules about this relationship; each one has to be judged independently according to the circumstances, personalities and the needs of the business at that particular time. My working relationships with Michael Stoddart, David Wolfson and Brian Pitman during my 13 years as chief executive of NEXT were all quite different, but all worked remarkably well.

Current corporate governance 'best practice' says that a retiring chief executive should not become chairman. I am sure that there are many instances where this rule is appropriate, but I would argue that each case has to be considered on its merits. I believe that Simon Wolfson and I have a good, constructive relationship that has been built up over many years, and that it would have been wrong to implement the current code – and rule me out of the chairmanship – because the board of NEXT would have lost the services of someone with vast knowledge of the company and the industry. Likewise, if I had found it difficult to give up the reins and had tried to go on running the business from the chair, cutting across Simon's authority, I would have expected the senior independent director to have intervened and called for a new chairman.

In the case of chairmen, I believe that their title should be either 'full-time' or 'part-time' and not 'executive' or 'non-executive', which simply adds to the potential confusion.

Another example of the nonsense that finds its way into the rules is the fact that after nine years as a non-executive director, the individual is no longer deemed to be independent. What utter rubbish! Independence is a matter of wisdom, experience and integrity, not length of service. It is the senior non-executive director's job to assess and monitor an individual's independence, and they should be prepared to state their reasons for keeping each non-executive on the board at the annual general meeting.

In order to attract good people in their forties and fifties to take on independent directorships, the remuneration package has to be worthwhile, which means in many cases that it needs to be at least doubled. I would also make it mandatory that new independent directors have medical examinations every year to ensure that they are capable of doing the job.

Apart from monitoring the performance of the company, the independent directors must ensure that the company has a regularly updated strategic plan and a sensible succession plan, in case any of the senior people unexpectedly leave the business.

Finally, drawing directly on my own experience at NEXT, I would try to find a way to encourage senior managers of companies to retire when they have completed ten years in the job. That is the time to hand over to a successor who has been carefully identified and groomed.

If more senior managers agreed with me on all this, there would be a constant supply of good independent directors. But I doubt whether many people will agree with my stance on going voluntarily, well before your 'sell-by' date.

The lack of good independent directors leads me to the idea of starting a business that specialises in finding good managers who could be trained as independent directors and offered to institutional shareholders as candidates to sit on boards of companies in which the institutions have invested. The Bank of England set up an agency called PRO NED to provide a service of this sort, but I'm sure it could and should be done better. Part of the service would be to ensure that the independent directors are updated with the relevant information necessary to do their job. If anyone else out there thinks that this idea has potential, please feel free to contact me!

Before leaving the subject of corporate governance, I must say something about the various bodies that pass judgement on companies and their accounts, and advise shareholders what action they should take on resolutions put forward at the annual general meeting. They have probably helped to eliminate many sharp practices that used to go on, particularly the 'creative accounting' that was so popular in the 1980s. But I do question the rigidity of their stance on issues such as the nine-year maximum tenure for non-executive directors. They should at least make the effort to understand the particular case the company wishes to make as to why, in some circumstances, a long-serving director should be re-elected.

NEXT provides a good example of the harm that 'black-or-white' corporate governance dogma can do to companies whose directors are in fact genuinely trying to protect the interests of their shareholders. Some of our retail competitors are private companies who are not subject to the same rules of disclosure as plcs. These companies can offer top people in NEXT huge incentives to join them without the risk of incurring the wrath of the City, because they are not obliged to publish the details of such packages. I believe most strongly that NEXT's board has a responsibility to shareholders to try to avoid any of our star executives being enticed away in this way. This means that we have to be able to remunerate them fully, even if that causes some flak when the details are published.

NEXT recently introduced a unique 'risk/reward' scheme, whereby senior executives risk their own cash as well as bonuses due to them in a form of bet on the share price reaching a certain level in five years' time. If it does they make a great deal of money, but not at any cost to the company. The shareholders will be delighted if the target share price is achieved – and in fact everyone is happy with the whole scheme, except for certain regulatory bodies whose black-or-white rules are offended by it. To make matters even more bizarre, they will probably advise our institutional shareholders to abstain when a vote is taken on the scheme at the AGM.

As in so many things, good corporate governance often boils down, in the end, to nothing more than common sense, to which I would add picking the right people for the board, defining their roles, planning their succession and – either as a chairman or a non-executive director – being tough when you have to be.

Chapter 11

'Luck, guts and reading upside down'

A few years ago, I was invited to speak at the annual dinner of the Association of British Textile Manufacturers. I refused the invitation because, as I said in the Introduction, I really don't like making speeches. But they enlisted one of my senior managers to persuade me to do it, and eventually I agreed. I worked hard on my speech and after about six drafts I thought I had cracked it. It was called 'Why NEXT needs a strong UK manufacturing base', and as I enjoyed a good dinner and good company before the moment came, I was quietly confident that it was a first-class piece of work.

Minutes before I was due to be introduced, someone came up to me and said that everyone was looking forward to my speech, especially as last year they had endured a long, boring one from Rick Greenbury entitled 'Why Marks & Spencer needs a strong UK manufacturing base'.

I ripped up my masterpiece and slowly walked to the microphone, wondering what on earth I was going to say. When the applause died down I took a deep breath – and winged it:

'David Charles Jones, age 57, accountant, workaholic. Secret of success: taking advantage of luck when it came my way, having the guts to make difficult decisions when they had to be made, and being able to read upside down…'

I went on to deliver an entirely impromptu speech about my career. It was warmly received, but it was not an easy thing for me to do, because throughout my working life I have rarely looked backwards. It often surprised me that, although Kays had been a significant part of my life, the Kays years were almost totally forgotten as soon as I left to run BMOC. Likewise when I joined Grattan, my 20 years at GUS felt like a passing dream – or a nightmare, at least in respect of the final six months. When I had to sell Grattan to save NEXT from extinction, the fact that I had so little attachment to the past helped soften the blow. But nowadays I do occasionally allow myself to reflect on my career to date – and in many ways it still surprises me.

Hard as I try to detect some sign in my early life that indicated the path ahead, I honestly cannot find any trace of aspiring talent or ambition. My academic record, for example, was hardly one that would normally mark out a future recipient of honorary doctorates from the universities of Bradford, Huddersfield, de Montfort and Leicester.

But I think I succeeded chiefly because I actually liked work. Unlike many other clerks at Kays, I enjoyed balancing my agents' accounts and I got a real thrill when we slaughtered the previous year's profit figure. I relished sorting out the problems at Martland and Grattan. Most of all, I enjoyed making NEXT the success that it is today.

Everyone needs luck to succeed, but as I said in that speech, you have to take advantage of it when it comes your way. It was lucky for me that my predecessor as finance director of Kays was retired early. But I got his job because I had worked hard and put myself into a position to be considered as a possible successor.

It was luck that I was in the right place at the right time to become managing director of BMOC, and that Grattan needed a new chief executive exactly at the moment when I was at my most disgruntled with GUS. But by that stage, there were probably only a handful of people in the industry with my breadth of experience. It was luck that I met George Davies at the time that he was looking for a way of expanding the NEXT franchise and I was looking for a way of linking Grattan with a successful high-street brand. But the Grattan team was probably the only team in the industry capable of making the NEXT Directory the success it subsequently became. And it was luck that both Sears and Otto Versand wanted to acquire Grattan, enabling me to sell it at a price that kept NEXT afloat.

So yes, I have had a good share of luck – but I was able to take advantage of it because I worked hard to be in the right position to do so. And I had the guts to challenge some difficult people along the way and take some tough decisions, such as closing down over 100 NEXT stores. Latterly, it took some guts to accept the position of deputy chairman of Morrisons.

If I ever make a public speech again I would add two more reasons why I got to where I did: never allowing anything to defeat me – the more difficult the problem, the harder I worked to solve it – and selecting the right people and keeping them together.

That last reason is the most fundamental. In Kays I gathered a fantastic team around me. Its key members came with me to BMOC and onwards to Grattan and NEXT, where other very talented and loyal people came to join us. So don't let anyone tell you that one individual can make a business successful. You need a team of dedicated, like-minded people, and it was my greatest good fortune to have such a team.

And you need a few strokes of fate on your side: I was also very fortunate that my business career was linked to three generations of the Wolfson family – Isaac, Leonard, David and Simon – and I doubt whether anyone else in business today can claim a similar relationship. Like so many things in my life, it wasn't planned, it just happened. True, I planned that David Wolfson would become chairman of NEXT, but some people might say it was fate that brought us together in the first place.

Fate, or chance, has brought me into contact with all sorts of other fascinating people in different corners of the business world. Two I think of with special warmth are Adam Faith, a pop star from the swinging sixties, and Fran Cotton, one of the England and British Lions rugby heroes of the seventies.

In 1990, when NEXT and I were both at a very low point, I received a letter from Adam, who by then had advanced from being a pop star to being an accomplished actor and a not very accomplished financial adviser, in association with a gentleman called

Roger Levitt. Adam also wrote a share-tipping column in the *Mail on Sunday*.

His letter thanked me for allowing him to use our helipad. I knew nothing about this, but apparently he had flown up to Leicester to interview the then Chancellor, Nigel Lawson, who was a local MP for Blaby in Leicestershire. Adam wanted to return the favour by inviting me to lunch with him at the Savoy Grill.

I was in need of some light relief, so I agreed to go. But what on earth do you talk about at lunch with an ageing pop star? I did some research and found out that he had a daughter, Katya, who was the same age as my own daughter Alison. So there we sat in those splendid surroundings, at his personal table, interrupted by a succession of celebrities who wanted to shake his hand, chatting about our daughters.

We became good friends – and I still don't really know why. Perhaps he was a lonely person, who had lots of acquaintances but few real friends he could trust. I think that we became mates because he did not need me and never asked me for anything, while I never encroached on his fame. He did recommend his readers to buy NEXT shares at 9p, saying in his column that I had an eye for a good 'frock'. That was not instigated by me, I hasten to add, but if the readers followed his advice they would have done phenomenally well out of it.

Goodness knows what Adam was doing associating with Roger Levitt, who looked and behaved like a spiv in the mould of Walker in *Dad's Army*, with sleek black hair, a manicured moustache and an inevitable fat cigar. When Adam introduced me to him, Levitt treated me to a monologue about his own financial brilliance, how he should be a non-executive director of NEXT, and how he would make me a very rich man if only I would invest half a million pounds with him. He reminded me of those people who sell monthly share tips for £10 a time: if they're so good at spotting winners, you wonder why they don't just make a fortune investing their own money.

I would never have invested with Levitt anyway, but as I had no money at the time, the question didn't arise. I know a number of other people, some of them big names in the sporting world, who lost a bundle with him. He went bankrupt for millions and was tried for fraud and theft in 1993; after some smart work by his defence lawyers he pleaded guilty to a lesser charge of misleading the regulators, an offence that turned out to carry a sentence of only 180 days' community service, causing quite a furore in parliament and the media at the time.

I had lunch with Adam for the last time a week before he died of a heart attack, aged 62, in March 2003. He was in good form that day, optimistic about the future even though he had lost a lot of money on the paper value of his holding in the Money Channel, which had theoretically once been worth over £20 million. He was talking about reviving *Love Hurts*, the television sitcom series he made with Zoë Wanamaker, and he was excited about some new insurance venture relating to theatre tickets that I never understood. He was an eternal teenager – always full of energy and ideas and optimism. I have always liked the company of optimists: I was glad to have known him, and I was very sad when he died.

As for Fran Cotton, I first met him in 1983 at a benefit dinner I helped organise for David Hughes, a very popular Lancashire cricketer. I subsequently invited Fran and his business partner Steve Smith, another ex rugby international, to come over to Grattan for a social Friday lunch of fish and chips and red wine. At that time they were working for Bukta, which was part of the French Connection clothing empire. I got the impression that their relationship with Stephen Marks, the owner of French Connection, was not always a constructive one, and in due course they left to set up on their own as Cotton Traders, a direct mail-order business that sold merchandise by adverts in magazines, then distributed a series of small catalogues to people who had bought 'off the page'.

I did not see very much of them until 1987 when I bumped into Steve in the reception at NEXT. He was hoping to see a buyer about supplying lingerie from the Far East. In the nicest possible way I said I did not think that NEXT would be interested, but suggested he had a chat with John Wallis, who was thinking about increasing the Kaleidoscope range to include lingerie. As it turned out, John was so enthused by the Cotton Traders offer that we struck an agreement to distribute the Cotton Traders catalogue to Grattan customers and split the profit from the sales generated. Both sides did well out of this deal, and the volumes helped to establish Cotton Traders as a brand.

When Grattan was sold to Otto Versand, we decided by mutual consent to discontinue this joint venture; Cotton Traders was at that point moving forward quite steadily under its own steam. But in 1992 Fran and Steve came back to see me with a sad story of a large bad debt that was the subject of a court action and would take time to resolve, leaving them with severe cash-flow problems.

As with the story of Scorex and Jean-Michel Trousse I told in Chapter 4, I was uncomfortable being asked to make an investment decision on NEXT's behalf that might be influenced by a personal friendship. I asked my finance director – by this time it was David Keens – to look at it. He found a way of injecting enough cash into Cotton Traders to keep it afloat, with its debt to NEXT secured on a freehold property, while also giving us a one-third stake in the equity.

I became chairman of Cotton Traders, and it is a business that has given me an immense amount of enjoyment – not least because I enjoy the company of great rugby players. I have been on two Lions tours with Fran and Steve, as well as to the World Cup in Australia in 2003. On one occasion I was at Twickenham watching an England–Wales game with Fran and Steve and Tony Neary, who were all former captains of England, when they were asked by a gang of supporters for their autographs. A lot of them must have wondered why a Welshman called Jones had signed their pro-grammes as well!

I have walked around Sydney Harbour and the West Car Park at Twickenham with Fran and seen the way every rugby fan recognises and greets him. He is always happy to sign autographs or have his picture taken with a bemused small boy urged forward by a wide-eyed father. He never turns anyone down and is a much-loved pil-lar of English rugby, working tirelessly to improve the game with very little reward or thanks. I am certain that without Fran's support, Clive Woodward would have lost his job after his first, unsuccessful World Cup campaign. With all the knighthoods and gongs going around the sporting world these days, I am amazed that Fran has never been honoured in any way.

So sport and the good fellowship that goes with it have formed another important strand of my life, even though I was never much of a sportsman myself. It has been a huge pleasure for me to be a director of Leicester Tigers, which is most certainly the premier rugby union club in Britain. Unfortunately I have not been able to watch them play as much as I would have liked because my home is in Yorkshire, but many of the players have become good friends. My large collection of signed rugby shirts and other memorabilia is the by-product of the help that I have enjoyed giving to players who have been granted well-earned benefits.

It was also a fantastic honour to be invited to be president of Yorkshire County Cricket Club, that hallowed institution of my adopted home county. As with the Leicester Tigers connection, this has enabled me to meet many of today's great sportsmen, such as Michael Vaughan, an outstanding England captain, and many of yesterday's, including Brian Close, the most courageous batsman I ever saw, and 'Fiery' Fred Trueman, the finest fast bowler of my generation.

I sometimes dream of a day when I will ease back from all my other activities, sink into a comfortable chair, and devote myself to watching either the summer game or the winter one, with a glass of something refreshing in my hand.

Somehow I doubt that day will ever come. Most of the gang I have worked with all these years are already retired, having made good money on their NEXT shares, and they all tell me how much they are enjoying themselves. I don't doubt them and in a way I envy them. But in another way I don't, because I know that I can't retire – for two reasons, one physical, the other mental.

The physical reason is my Parkinson's Disease. Unfortunately for me, I cannot relax. I have to keep my mind active because if I don't, I become restless and I feel all my aches and pains.

The mental reason is perhaps a little more complex. In a career of over 40 years there is very little I have not done. I have negotiated small contracts and very large ones. I have bought businesses and sold them. I have sued people and been sued. I have coped with two unofficial strikes. I have learned how the City works. I have learned how to handle journalists. I have helped create tens of thousands of other jobs and I have had to make thousands of people redundant.

I have experienced bad times and good times. I have worked with inspirational people and learned so much from them. Wouldn't it be a waste not to use all that experience to help to create something that others can benefit from?

I now have a number of investments and interests that keep me busy – my wife would say that they keep me too busy! They cover a wide range of different activities, but they have one thing in common: they are fun.

In September 2001, three bright young men in their mid-20s asked me to help them prepare a business plan to present to a bank, in order to raise funding to set up a staff recruitment agency using the internet rather than traditional advertising media. I spent about four Sunday mornings with them and was so impressed by their ideas and enthusiasm that I decided to back them myself. Three years on, they have repaid my initial investment and the company now has an annual turnover in excess of £1 million, employing 25 people. We have a board meeting every month and I find it strange but interesting that, as chairman, I am the cautious one whereas they are just like me at their age – bursting with ideas, impatient, and obviously thinking that the old chap at the head of the table does not really understand.

By far my biggest private investments are associated with cars. I have yet to understand why I have this infatuation with the motor industry, because to this day I have no idea how a car actually works. Maybe I inherited the interest from my father and his experience as an apprentice at the Morgan Motor Company at Malvern. Wherever it came from, it has brought me into contact with some of the most talented people in the industry today.

In February 2003, a small company in which I had a majority shareholding had built and sold five Ronart Lightnings – a roaring beast of a two-seater sports car powered by a Ford Mustang V12 engine. I needed some advice about how to develop the business, and my elder son, Richard, suggested I had a chat with Lee Noble, who was the brains behind a sensational new sports car called the Noble M12. The car had been featured on the BBC's *Top Gear* programme and had received a rave review from Jeremy Clarkson, who apparently said that when he put his foot on the throttle 'my eyes hit the back of my head and my kidneys went down the exhaust pipe'. The car could go from nought to 60 miles per hour in three and a half seconds, though I have often wondered why on earth anyone would actually want to do that.

I met Lee at his factory near Leicester. He was very critical of the Ronart and really only wanted to talk about his own creation. But the man was clearly a genius, without any formal engineering training; his first job had been cleaning cars at a small garage nearby. He had designed and built an award-winning sports car that was faster round a one-mile track than any other car on the road at any price.

Lee and his business partner Tony Moy explained that their business needed capital to develop the next generation of the Noble, and Lee needed some managerial help to run a fast-growing business. I finished up buying 60 per cent of the company from Tony Moy. Today Noble Cars is a highly respected marque with a turnover in excess of £10 million and a growing number of companies wanting to buy it.

My involvement in Noble has led me to invest in another fast-growing company in the sector, making, among other things, body parts for Formula One race cars. It is the brainchild of a bright young engineer, Graham Mulholland, who is the only person I know who revises his sales and profit forecast upwards every time there is a pile-up at a Grand Prix.

I have also met a younger version of Lee Noble called Ewan Baldry, whose ambition is to build a car to win the Le Mans 24-hour race. Like all the other people I am helping, he is dedicated to his dream and works incredibly hard. He deserves a bit of financial assistance and what I hope is sound business advice from me to help him on his way.

I feel the same way about Alistair Griffin, a young man who finished in second place on the BBC's *Fame Academy*. He is a very talented singer and songwriter whom I have taken under my wing. All he needs is a little piece of good fortune and he will make it.

I will not bore you about the restaurant called The Grove that I have bought in Ilkley, or the computer technology company in which I have a large shareholding, which boasts that it has developed the best 're-boot' system in the world (whatever that means). Or the company in New Zealand that has developed a unique point-of-sale promotional system, which is thriving in South Africa and the Far East. Or the finance companies that a group of friends and I own in South Africa.

But I will tell you about the British film I have helped to produce. Early in 2004, a friend who advises a property development firm that I own jointly with my retired company secretary, Peter Webber, told me about a tax-efficient investment opportunity in film finance. I had invested some large sums in previous years on the advice of my tax accountants, Ernst & Young, so I was not immediately interested – until I met Julia Taylor-Stanley. Julia is a little powerhouse of incredible energy who had spent many years trying to get her pet project off the ground. She wrote the script, lined up the stars and was rushing around trying to raise the finance to make a film called *These Foolish Things*.

Maybe I have a weakness for people I think are dedicated, or maybe the real truth is that I am just a soft touch. Who cares? Initially I invested £200,000 in the film, but when I read the script and saw the list of stars she had lined up, I was prepared to invest more. I became, in effect, the production chequebook, particularly when other investors who had promised funds pulled out.

These Foolish Things is a pre-Second World War light drama, produced on a relatively low budget of £5.5 million (not all of it mine, I hasten to add) on location in Cheltenham. It was completed on time and within budget, but most important it features some really great stars. Ann and I had the enormous pleasure of having dinner one evening with Lauren Bacall, Terence Stamp, Angelica Huston, Julia McKenzie and Jos Ackland. I sat next to the legendary Miss Bacall, who was enchanting. I spent some time on the film set and can say that the whole experience was a highlight of recent years.

The film had a private showing at the BAFTA headquarters in Piccadilly in March 2005 and was very well received. It was also shown at the Cannes Film Festival in May and will be premiered in Britain in January 2006 – later than originally planned to avoid clashing with the 'blockbusters' that are due to be released before Christmas.

Whether *These Foolish Things* is a financial success remains to be seen. It seems to me, having studied the takings figures achieved by recent releases, that a film is either fantastically successful, making a huge profit for the producers, or a complete flop, losing the investors everything they have put into it. There is no middle way.

The rights to the film have been sold in seven countries including the UK, so I do not think I shall lose money, but whether it is a real financial success depends on current negotiations with the distributors from the USA. It is beyond doubt the riskiest venture I have taken on but, whatever the outcome, I would not have wanted to miss the chance to be part of it.

Perhaps the most satisfying of all the ventures I have been involved with are the ones for good causes. I have always believed that businesses and business people should make a wider contribution to the societies in which they operate, and I have been involved with a variety of charities since Grattan days, when we began a long connection with the Duke of Edinburgh's Award Scheme.

This happened through a retired GUS supplier called Bert Raphael, who rang me one day to say that Prince Edward was visiting Bradford and Leeds to promote the scheme and was hoping to visit Grattan. I thought that sounded splendid until I was told what it would cost us. I turned it down, but a week later I had second thoughts and decided to find out more about the scheme. It is an impressive story, and as one of Bradford's biggest and most successful employers I felt we should do our bit. I rang Bert to say that the prince was welcome to come.

I had never met a member of the royal family before and I was quite nervous on the morning of the visit. The prince was due at quarter to twelve, and I paced around my office repeating 'Good morning, your Royal Highness. Welcome to Grattan.'

He actually arrived at ten past twelve, and to my embarrassment he said 'Good afternoon' just as I said my rehearsed 'Good morning'. But he then apologised for being late and the tour went well – he was a delight to show round and had a good sense of humour. That evening I had a table at a gala fundraising dinner for the Duke of Edinburgh's scheme at the Queen's Hotel in Leeds. John Whitmarsh, Dick Swain, John Cutts, Mike Bottomley and their wives came along with Ann and me – and Dick won first prize in the £10-a-ticket raffle, which was a business-class return flight for the weekend to New York, with three nights in a hotel and tickets for *The Phantom of the Opera*.

In my rather tipsy state, I told one of the prince's entourage that if HRH could come up with eight more tickets for the show, I would personally contribute a five-figure sum to the award scheme, and the whole of my table would go to New York. He did come up with the tickets, and I subsequently discovered that in my enthusiasm I had mentioned my offer to two members of the entourage, who both claimed the donation from me. Pride would not allow me to do anything other than double it, which made that weekend in New York the most expensive of my life.

But it was the start of a long association with the Duke of Edinburgh's award scheme that continues and has taken me to many enjoyable events, including the last banquet on the royal yacht *Britannia* before its final voyage, and Prince Philip's 70th and 80th birthday celebrations. At the 70th, at Windsor Castle, we put on a NEXT fashion show. The 80th was a gala dinner co-sponsored by NEXT at the Royal Albert Hall with a glittering collection of stars. We even co-sponsored a garden party at Buckingham Palace, which I likened to flying on Concorde – enjoyable in itself, but the real bonus was being able to talk about it afterwards!

There have also been many amusing moments. I sat opposite Prince Philip at a dinner that we sponsored at St James's Palace and there was a rather large, loud American lady who tried throughout the meal to catch the royal eye. When she eventually succeeded she seemed to lose control and blurted out, 'I just love your house!' It was the only time I ever saw HRH lost for words.

On many other occasions I have handed out Gold Awards to young people. The usual procedure is that HRH talks to the recipients, then hands the certificates to whoever is presenting them and goes on to the next group. As he was chatting to my group, a tie caught his eye.

'What is that tie?'

'My school tie, sir.'

He turned to another award winner: 'And what is your tie?'

'My regimental tie, sir.'

Then to another: 'And yours?'

'It's a NEXT tie, sir!'

HRH laughed, turned to me and said, 'Another good customer!'

I am also the fundraising chairman of The Healing Foundation, a new charity of which Prince Edward's wife, the Countess of Wessex, is patron, and Chris Patten is chairman of the trustees. Its objective is to fund research to improve the treatment of all kinds of disfigurement, and I was amazed to discover how many people have to have operations for disfigurement caused by accidents, by illnesses such as cancer and meningitis, or at birth.

I did not intend to say yes when I was first approached by Chris Patten. But I thought it was a bit rude to say no to the last British governor of Hong Kong, so I decided to think about it for a couple of weeks before I declined. But then I visited the plastic surgery ward of the Leicester Royal Infirmary and saw so many examples of the physical and mental results of disfigurement that in the end I just could not turn down the invitation.

I remember in particular a little Asian girl called Bumicka, who was sitting on the floor playing with Lego. I was so captivated by her happy face that I failed to notice that both her legs had been amputated and she was terribly scarred from her neck to her knees. She had had a form of meningitis that would result in her having to be operated on several times a year to allow her body to grow despite the terrible scarring.

In October 2003, NEXT organised a charity ball to raise money for The Healing Foundation. It provides a story that neatly ends this chapter by connecting my love of sport and my commitment to fundraising with one of my earlier themes, my admiration for Philip Green.

I had managed to obtain two tickets for the Rugby World Cup Final in Sydney, and thanks to the generosity of the Cathay Pacific airline, I was able to auction a package for two people to fly to Australia for the final – which I was already planning to attend myself. There were two people bidding and when the amount reached £50,000 I went on stage to announce that I had actually arranged two packages, so that each bidder could buy one for £50,000. Of course they both agreed.

As a special treat I was then able to arrange for the four people who used the tickets to have a private lunch with Clive Woodward, the England coach, two days before the final. At this lunch I was asked if I could get hold of an England rugby shirt signed by all the players, for an auction at another event, in London a week after the final.

It was easy for me to obtain a signed shirt because I was very friendly with Dorian West, the Leicester Tigers hooker who was in the England squad. When we were back in the UK, Dorian handed me his Number 16 shirt signed by all the players. Fortunately it was still very clean, because the services of the reserve hooker had not been required in the final, despite some erratic line-out throws from the first choice. I had the shirt framed and inscribed 'Dorian West's Rugby World Cup Final Shirt'.

The ball was an amazing evening, with entertainment supplied by José Carreras, Bryan Ferry and the legendary James Brown. I noticed when we arrived that the auction lots included a red Ferrari and a Mini One among other prestigious items, and I started to worry about the wisdom of including a mere rugby shirt in such a high-class auction. I expressed my concern to the main sponsor, who must have told Philip Green, because when he came into the room he gave me his usual hug and whispered: 'Don't worry about the rugby shirt.'

All the items ahead of us in the auction went for prices way above their true value. I was cautiously optimistic that the shirt, which was the last item to be auctioned, would realise a good price – maybe as much as £25,000 to a really dedicated England fan. Jimmy Tarbuck was doing the auctioneering, and announced the shirt as the final lot to be sold. He asked for an opening bid.

'£250,000,' said a voice I recognised.

The audience started to cheer as Tarbie shouted: 'Sold to Mr Philip Green for £250,000!'

When the noise finally died down, however, someone else got up and declared he had put his hand up to bid £275,000, but the auctioneer hadn't spotted him. Jimmy Tarbuck apologised, but pointed out that the lot had been knocked down to Mr Green. Philip immediately told him to reopen the bidding.

'I have a bid for £250,000 from Mr Philip Green. Is there any advance on that?'

'Two-seven-five!'

Everyone's eyes were fixed on Philip. Philip looked at the shirt, turned to look at the other bidder, then looked at Jimmy and said quietly: '£500,000.'

Once again riotous clapping and cheering – and no more bids!

Since we launched The Healing Foundation's appeal in November 2002 we have raised over £5 million to fund research; £1 million of that has come in donations from NEXT and from me personally. I am thrilled to have been able to help.

As you see, I have a very full life, with a mixture of public company responsibilities, personal investments, charity work and sporting interests. With so much still to do, how can I possibly retire?

Chapter 12

'People just don't understand what it's like'

A s I said at the beginning…
Throughout the dramas of the 1980s and early 1990s I was able to keep my Parkinson's in check, largely by drugs and partly by willpower, and that is why I have said so little about it in the preceding chapters. I was very fortunate that my condition deteriorated very slowly, even allowing me to continue playing golf, and the only real problem was that my movements were rather slow when I was tired.

But by the mid-1990s the condition was becoming a lot worse. I began to experience more marked 'on' and 'off' periods. I had to start planning each day so that I was 'on' at exactly the right time to give a presentation to analysts or chair a meeting. I found that the best time for me was from 10 a.m. until 3 p.m.: any earlier and the body had not woken up; any later and I was getting tired. I had to learn to be very patient during my 'off' periods and relax as much I could, waiting for the 'on' periods to arrive.

I realize that to those who are not familiar with Parkinson's, all this talk about 'on' and 'off' periods may not mean very much. It is not difficult to describe the visible symptoms of the disease, but I have always been very reluctant to describe what it is actually like for the sufferer, from the inside. There are many reasons for this reluctance – I don't want sympathy, I don't want to be treated like an invalid, but principally it is almost impossible for anyone to understand what it is like unless you have the disease yourself.

Some years ago, long before it was public knowledge that I had Parkinson's, I was at a Sunday lunchtime drinks party and was chatting to a woman about nothing in particular when she suddenly said that she had just received some bad news. She had been diagnosed with Parkinson's.

'Don't worry about that, I have had it for 12 years!'

This was the first time I had admitted to anyone outside my family and close friends that I had Parkinson's. She and I have become good friends and draw strength from each other. Recently I bumped into her at the supermarket. I was having a good day, but unfortunately she was not.

'People just do not understand what it's like,' she said. She is absolutely right – only those people with Parkinson's will fully understand what I am about to describe. Those who have it know that no two days are the same: when you wake up you just do not know what the day is going to be like. Similarly, those who have it share the knowledge that no two Parkinson's sufferers have exactly the same daily experience. But however you experience it, this selfish disease takes over every day of your life.

I generally wake up about 6 a.m. My body is stiff and I am almost unable to move. If I am at home I ask Ann to move my legs out of the bed and pull me up. If I am away from home I have developed a technique of rolling off the bed onto the floor, then getting onto my knees before making a supreme effort to stand up. This can take anything up to half an hour to achieve.

I then take my first medication for the day – dispersible Madopar tablets that, all being well, get to the brain quickly. Depending on how stiff my body is, I either lie down to wait for the drugs to work, or check on my emails or play patience. The latter is the best therapy because it helps to get my hands and arms moving – and concentrating on the cards stops me thinking about how dreadful I feel.

About 30 minutes later my right foot starts to clench. This is the first indication that the drugs are working – the first highlight of my day, because I can now think about showering, shaving and getting ready.

Dressing is a trial and very frustrating because of the time it takes. I am not bad at putting on a shirt or trousers, but socks are difficult; at weekends I often go sockless. Buttons are a nightmare, and ties are such an impossible task that I rarely wear one.

From 9 a.m. to around 3 p.m. I am reasonably active, providing I take the right pills at the correct intervals. There are usually about 20 of them, a combination of Madopar, Amantanine, Selegiline and Pergoline. I try to balance the intake of drugs to suit the schedule for the day. If I have important meetings I tend to under-dose myself because by far the worst feature of Parkinson's is the involuntary shaking caused by the body receiving a higher dosage than it can absorb.

This is called dyskinesia and it is the nightmare that I live with every second of every day of my life. Some days I do not have any sign of it, but on other days I struggle with almost total immobility or involuntary twisting and turning movements of the limbs, mouth, tongue and jaw.

If I am scheduled to make a speech at a charity function, my team always has to have a reserve standing by in case I am unable to keep still. But sometimes it is not possible to have a stand-in, such as when I was honoured as Yorkshire Businessman of the Year in December 2004. At the precise time that they announced my name at the award ceremony, dyskinesia broke out with a vengeance. I could not keep still, and the circumstances were made more distressing by the fact that there was a screen at the far side of the room on which I could see myself as other people were seeing me. I took the opportunity to make an impromptu speech about Parkinson's, which received a very warm and sympathetic response.

But there are occasions when it is best not to try to speak in public at all. By far the most distressing time is when the shaking is accompanied by an inability to control my facial muscles, so that I develop a vacant stare and my speech becomes distorted.

Simple actions like standing up become difficult; I have to avoid low chairs. I now have to walk with a stick, an indignity I have delayed for as long as possible. I cannot put a jacket or coat on without assistance, and I don't have any plans for racing one of my Noble cars!

But I have to keep going – I have to make the effort to make the steep uphill trek home from the local station, or walk into Ilkley from home to buy a newspaper – because if I start to give up then it is all, in a different sense, downhill.

The worst time is when I wake up in the morning. I dread this so much that if I have an important day ahead of me, I just do not go to bed! This is not as drastic as it may sound, because I very rarely have a good night's sleep, mainly because I have great difficulty in moving or turning over on my side and suffer severe cramp in my arms and legs.

The fact that no two days are ever exactly the same makes it all worse still. Trying to plan for important events – including my daughter Alison's wedding – becomes a nightmare. At NEXT it was also very frustrating for my secretary June and her successor Stephanie, who would have to cancel meetings at short notice using an ever-increasing list of imaginative excuses.

I hate the mask-like stare that I invariably have on my face. It took four separate photo sessions to produce a photograph that I was happy to put on the cover of this book. I look at photographs of my children's weddings and wonder who the person is standing next to my wife. It is certainly not me; it's the other guy, the one who has Parkinson's.

There was an occasion when we were taking the family round Madame Tussauds in London – waxworks were not exactly my scene, and I was rushing through the rooms when I realised that I had lost Ann and the children. I stopped and looked back to see if they were coming. I must have been strangely motionless, because an American couple came up and stared at me intently. Then the woman complained to her partner: 'I can't find this one in the guidebook!'

I vividly remember the morning in March 1997 when we were due to announce NEXT's profits for the year to 31 January. I got up at 5.30, took the usual intake of drugs, and sat in my chair to wait for the body to start functioning. But nothing happened. I took more drugs – and still nothing. The drugs were not getting through to my brain. I could not shave or shower properly. It took me half an hour to put my shirt on. I had to give up on the tie and shoelaces.

In desperation, I rang Dick Swain and he came round to help me finish dressing. I took even more drugs in an effort to get my body moving, so that I could get to the meeting to present the figures.

At the precise time that I stood up to make my presentation the over-drugging took its vengeance. I could not stop shaking, my face was distorted, my voice was someone else's. I must have looked absolutely panic stricken. The next day, rumours were rife in exactly the way that I had dreaded all those years – retail analysts and financial journalists were saying that I must be ill. I could not admit I had Parkinson's, and fortunately no one asked me directly, so I used the (by now well-rehearsed) arthritis story again and blamed the shaking on a new drug I said I was trying out. I got away with it and the rumours stopped, but I knew that time was running out. Some time soon, the two David Joneses were going to have to meet in public.

Some people may accuse me of being irresponsible by continuing my career under the pressure of the disease. I argue in response that I kept my illness a secret for the right reasons, and that the success I achieved at Grattan and NEXT more than justified the decision. I am very proud of the fact that I was responsible for the turnaround of those two companies, and of the value I created for their shareholders in doing so. Having a numerical mind, I tend to measure my achievements by share prices: Grattan's went from 32p when I became chief executive in 1981 to £5.40 when we sold the company to NEXT in 1986. At NEXT we generated one of the most spectacular share rises of any British company in the 1990s, from 7p to £14, and it was all the more satisfying because so few people would have predicted that such a recovery could have been led by the 'grey Yorkshire accountant' who had been responsible for the sacking of NEXT's highly talented creator. But privately, what is most satisfying of all is that I achieved these things without giving in to this horrible disease.

Looking back, however, I would not advise anyone who is diagnosed with Parkinson's today to keep their condition a secret – because it can be hell. The strain of trying to hide the disease has often been worse than the disease itself. And why hide it anyway? There is certainly nothing to be ashamed about, and the disease now has a much higher profile as a result of publicity about Michael J. Fox and Muhammad Ali both suffering from it. I hope that my own lower-profile efforts to talk about the disease can add to this new openness.

We have not yet reached the day when Parkinson's sufferers are completely accepted by society – without embarrassed reactions and looking the other way – but slowly the barriers are being broken down. I recently made a speech at the launch of a book by Muhammad Ali's daughter Rasheda called *I'll Hold Your Hand So You Won't Fall*. It is a delightful book, written in simple language, which will help to increase awareness of the problems that people with Parkinson's face every day of their lives.

The beginning of this change in public attitudes towards Parkinson's was another reason why, early in 2001, I decided to come out as a Parkinson's sufferer. The timing was right from a business point of view: the chief executive's crown had been successfully transferred to my very able and well-trained successor. There was no need to continue to hide behind the arthritis story. From a personal point of view, Parkinson's was becoming increasingly difficult to hide.

And I had a growing urge to do something to help other people who had Parkinson's but had fewer means than I do to help themselves. I decided that with the help of my charity team at NEXT – Sue Myatt, Karen Bird and their wonderful band of helpers – I would host a NEXT Parkinson's Ball to raise money for Parkinson's charities and increase awareness of what a terrible disease it is.

Around 150,000 people in Britain have Parkinson's and most of them are ashamed of the fact. They resent being reliant on drugs to lead a 'normal' life and they hate the fact that their shuffling and shaking make other people shy away from them in embarrassment rather than reach out to help.

I wanted to use the means at my disposal to say to people with Parkinson's: I know what you feel like, because I've lived with it for over 20 years. It's a bugger. But don't give in to it, because with determination and support it's possible to have a very full and exciting life. My own life has been tremendously enjoyable, and I hope there's a lot more of it to come.

On an altogether higher plane, Pope John Paul II was a Parkinson's sufferer for his last 15 years, yet he maintained his spiritual mission and his charisma and authority right to the end.

And I wanted to say to people who don't have Parkinson's that those who do don't want pity or sympathy, but nor do we want to be treated like lepers. We just want to be treated as normal human beings who occasionally need a bit of help to do even the simplest everyday things.

Not long ago I was at a hotel dinner table with a group of friends when the hotelier came over to have a chat. I was shaking, and throughout the 20 minutes or so that he was talking to us he did not once look at me. Did it occur to him to wonder how I felt?

More recently I was queuing up to pass through the security check at an airport. I put my hand luggage on the conveyor. The security man told me to take off my jacket and put it on the conveyor as well.

'OK,' I said, 'but you'll have to help me take it off, please.'

'What's wrong with you?' he replied scornfully. 'Are you a f******
invalid?'

'No, but I do have Parkinson's Disease.'

He apologised rather sheepishly and helped me. Maybe this is not such a good example, because I probably did not look as if I needed help. But why hadn't his training warned him that people with Parkinson's (and lots of other illnesses) cannot automatically respond to even the simple request to take off a jacket?

In all the years I have had Parkinson's I have never asked 'Why me?' I have accepted it and got on with my life. It has never ruled me, though it has tried very hard to do so. On the contrary, in some ways I think it has actually helped me to lead a better life.

For a start, it made me more determined to succeed. I have this 'it's not going to get me down' attitude. I enjoy playing golf all the more, simply because I do not know how long I will be able to continue playing. I believe I appreciate more than most people those special moments with my family and friends.

I think that perhaps Parkinson's has made me a more generous person than I might otherwise have been. If I can assist someone who needs a bit of help, I try to do so – and it has made me want to make NEXT a caring company. We became involved in many charities in a modest way, and when times were bad I sometimes paid the donations personally to keep the relationships with the charities going.

Many of NEXT's donations were purposely unpublicised at the time they were given – we paid for the refurbishing of the staff common room after the school tragedy at Dunblane, for example – because we did not want to be accused of trying to gain commercial benefit. As long as we believed it was money well spent we had no reason to make it public

So I had a whole set of good reasons to tell the world about Parkinson's. But having made the decision, I had to find the best way to do so and to promote my fundraising ball.

I asked Alistair McKinnon-Musson, NEXT's financial PR man and a good friend, for his thoughts. I suggested that we ask Kate Rankine, a City journalist for the *Daily Telegraph*, to do a story about the fact that I had been diagnosed 20 years ago and had kept it a secret all this time. I wanted to ask Kate to write the article because I liked her work and because she was the only major journalist ever to have asked me point blank if I was ill. I hadn't exactly lied to her when she asked, but I had certainly been economical with the truth and this was an opportunity to make amends. Alistair agreed to speak to Kate.

At about the same time I had a routine chat with my consultant neurologist, Ernie Spokes. I told him about my idea of a charity ball and he suggested I got in touch with Mary Baker, the chief executive of the British Parkinson's Disease Society. A couple of weeks later I saw an interview with Mary on BBC breakfast television. That reminded me to make contact with her, but still I had done nothing much to move the project forward.

Then something rather strange happened. I was walking up Oxford Street – having dropped in to the Marks & Spencer store to look at its spring ranges – when I noticed a young, blind Asian woman getting herself in a tangle with the display units outside a newsagent's shop. Her white stick was caught in a paper rack and she nearly tripped over a National Lottery sign. The poor girl was getting very agitated.

There were plenty of people going in and out of the shop, but no one bothered to help her. I had walked past the shop, but I turned back to offer a hand. I held her arm and said quietly that I meant her no harm and would guide her out of the maze she was in. She was shaking and said something I could not hear – but I assumed that she was happy for me to help her. I asked where she wanted to go and she said she was trying to get to the Tube. I led her down the steps of Marble Arch station and handed her over to a London Underground official.

Feeling mildly saintly, I walked back up the steps – and spotted a poster advertising the British Parkinson's Disease Society. At the bottom of it was a telephone number. I called Mary Baker's office immediately and arranged to meet her the following day at the Royal College of Surgeons, where the society was holding a conference.

While I was waiting for her to come out of the conference hall, I looked round this impressive building and noticed a bronze bust of my old boss Sir Isaac Wolfson, who had been a benefactor of the college. He had been dead for a decade – he spent his last years in Israel, a victim of Alzheimer's – but it was nice to be reminded of him, and of his kindly interest in me. We had a brief imaginary chat and I told him I still had not received the ten shillings rise he once promised.

Then Mary appeared. Her positive, can-do attitude made an immediate impression on me. She agreed to help organise the ball, and in return I promised to donate part of the money raised to the European Parkinson's Disease Society, as she was shortly retiring as full-time head of the British society to become head of the EPDS.

And so the plan for the long-postponed meeting of the two David Joneses began to take shape. We would announce Simon's appointment as chief executive at the annual general meeting in May 2001, Kate would write her article shortly after that, and the invitations to the ball to be held in September would be sent out at the end of June.

Kate Rankine's interview with me appeared in the *Daily Telegraph* on Saturday, 28 May 2001. What she found oddest about my Parkinson's secret, she wrote, was the fact that I had not even told David Wolfson, even when we were working extremely closely together to rescue NEXT.

I explained that I had not told David until after he left NEXT because I never thought it was relevant. I knew I had the disease, but it was as if it was happening to somebody else. 'It wasn't me, if you can understand that.'

'Doesn't all the stress of being a chief exec make it worse?' she wanted to know. My job at NEXT actually made it better, I said, 'because you don't have time to think about it.' And there was no time for self-pity either. 'To be honest, I'm not that sort of person. The way I look at life is to say there's a damn sight more people who are worse off, and those are the ones that I feel sorry for. Not myself.'

She was even brave enough to ask me how the disease is likely to progress in the next five to ten years – to which the answer from my specialist is that whatever I die from, it won't be that. Finally, Kate decided to switch subjects, 'because there's a lot more to Jones than living with Parkinson's Disease...'

She was right: there is a lot more to me, and even as I approach the possibility of retirement from the chairmanship of NEXT, I have a full portfolio of business projects and sporting interests to keep me busy. But Parkinson's has become a bigger part in my life than it used to be for one very positive reason – because I am determined to raise as much money for it as I possibly can.

The NEXT Parkinson's Ball at the Grosvenor House Hotel in Park Lane was an outstanding success, raising over £300,000 for the two Parkinson's charities. When we were planning it, I told my team that I wanted Shirley Bassey to be the star attraction. They thought I was aiming too high, but I was not to be put off!

With the kind help of Eric Worral, a director of the Duke of Edinburgh's Award Scheme, I was able to sit next to Shirley Bassey at a very exclusive private dinner party at the Dorchester Hotel in Park Lane. The purpose of the dinner was to thank the three people whose companies had sponsored a gala night at the Royal Albert Hall to celebrate the Duke of Edinburgh's 80th birthday. Apart from Ann and myself there were the co-sponsors – Lord Kirkham, founder of the DFS furniture retail chain, and Sir Donald Gosling, founder of National Car Parks – as well as Shirley Bassey and Richard Stilgoe, who had performed at the Albert Hall gala. HRH and I sat on either side of Shirley, who was an absolute delight to talk to. She did not even mind being told that I had first seen her perform at the Gaumont Theatre in Worcester in 1964, on a double bill with Matt Monro.

I took the plunge and told her about the Parkinson's Ball. She promised to be there, provided she did not have a prior engagement. She didn't let me down!

One of the first of the 1200 guests to arrive at the ball was a fund manager who had successfully followed my career in Grattan and NEXT and had no doubt earned good bonuses by buying both companies' shares at the right time. He came up to me and said he was sorry to learn that I had Parkinson's, but in a way 'quite relieved'. Startled, I asked him why.

He explained that over the years he had seen me at various functions and had noticed me walking out of the room with a rather unsteady shuffle. He had concluded that I drank too much red wine, but he now realised that it was my Parkinson's that caused the slow exit. He laughed when I said that the moral of the story was that institutional shareholders obviously preferred chief executives of companies they invested in to have Parkinson's, rather than be alcoholics!

Our most important guest for the evening was HRH the Duchess of Gloucester, who is the patron of the British Parkinson's Disease Society, and it was my pleasure to welcome her. She is a woman of great warmth and I remember two lovely examples of this. As we approached the staircase down to the Great Room, I suddenly panicked because I did not know whether I should go first or follow her.

'Can I ask you something?' I whispered.

'Of course.'

'Do I go first, or do you?'

'Let's walk down together!'

Later in the evening, I made a speech and talked publicly for the first time about my illness. I got quite emotional and as I left the stage everyone stood to applaud me. When I got to my seat, the duchess was standing too, and ushered me to my chair.

'I can't sit down while you are standing,' I mumbled.

'Then let's sit down together,' she smiled. She is a very charming, gracious and considerate person.

Many people would say that the highlight of the evening was an amazing speech by Mary Baker. She delivered it without notes and with great feeling. Here is part of what she said:

Every one of you in this room is on a life's journey and it's a journey that you've been prepared for, by your parents, by your teachers at school, by your religious beliefs, by the people that you have met on your journey.

But there is one part of that journey that no one has prepared you for and that is the moment that you receive the diagnosis of a neurological illness. No one has prepared you for that.

Research shows that it is a watershed. Human beings are planners – think back to when you were at school. What career path would you take? Where would you live? How many children would you have? Where are you going for your summer holiday? Always planning. Some cynics say that we get more enjoyment out of the planning and the anticipation than the event itself.

But if you've got a degenerative neurological illness, that planning becomes terribly difficult, because it is unpredictable. You've lost control. But there is a way of reinstating that control and that is by the provision of first-class, clear, understandable information.

This is what the Parkinson's Disease Society does. It gives infor-mation, provides a map, for this very challenging part of the journey. Thankfully there are people – caring, talented people – who have made it their life's work to help to find that pathway.

There are researchers, scientists, surgeons, nurses, therapists and social workers. There is a great pharmaceutical industry that all the time keeps searching for the cure and in the meantime pro-vides all the drugs for therapy. There are ministers and members of parliament who listen and make it their business to try to understand and to try to improve the quality of life of those who suffer...

But some people have to make the journey because they have Parkinson's. Their courage and dignity and their sense of humour make them truly inspirational people. And such a person is your host this evening...

She went on to say very nice things about me – and the flattery worked, because that speech was a great inspiration to me to go out and raise more money for Parkinson's research and care.

It had the same impact on Tom Isaacs, whom I met at the ball. Tom had been diagnosed with Parkinson's at the very early age of 27 and has worked tirelessly for the cause ever since. During 2002 and 2003 he completed a 4500-mile, 365-day sponsored walk around the perimeter of England, Scotland and Wales, climbing Ben Nevis, Scafell and Snowdon on his way. I encouraged him every step of the way – by email, that is – and at least I managed to walk the final mile and a half with him. As if that wasn't enough, for an encore, two days after completing the walk he ran the London

Marathon in a very respectable time. So far he has raised over £350,000 for Parkinson's by his own efforts.

Tom and I got together with two other Parkinson's sufferers – Sir Richard Nichols, who had been Lord Mayor of London in 1997–98, and Air Vice Marshal Michael Dicken, who had coincidentally been private secretary to successive Lord Mayors of London during the 1990s. The four of us formed Movers and Shakers, a fundraising team to support a new charity called The Cure Parkinson's Trust.

The trust itself has five aims and a five-year timetable from now until 2010. We want to compel the drive towards a cure; to channel funds efficiently into specific projects coordinated by Parkinson's charities and other reputable research bodies; to change the stereo-typical misconceptions of Parkinson's and promote a more positive outlook for those affected by it; to create opportunities for deliver-ing key messages through public speaking and media coverage; and to connect and bridge gaps within the Parkinson's community in terms of funding, organisations and individuals

We have a close allegiance to the Parkinson's Disease Society in support of its excellent programme of research. But we also allocate funds, where appropriate, to projects coordinated by other rep-utable institutions such as the European Parkinson's Disease Society and the Michael J. Fox Foundation.

Between us, and including the NEXT ball in 2001, the Movers and Shakers have already raised more than £1 million for these objec-tives. Michael and Jenny Dicken, together with Richard and Shelagh Nichols, organised a Movers and Shakers dinner at the Mansion House in May 2004, and I went on to organise an event that turned into one of the best nights of my life, the Swing Low Sweet Charity Ball at the Battersea Arena on 20 November 2004.

The catalyst for the event was the England rugby team's fantas-tic victory in the World Cup in Australia. Rugby, as you will have gathered by now, is one of my passions, and I was lucky enough to be in Sydney on 22 November 2003 to see Jonny Wilkinson's win-ning drop goal against Australia in the last seconds of extra time, surely one of the greatest moments of modern sporting history. As a director and avid supporter of Leicester Tigers, I am also a great admirer of Martin Johnson, the former England captain, for whom the club was planning a benefit season in 2004/5. My idea was to hold another ball to celebrate the first anniversary of the World Cup victory for the benefit of Martin's chosen charities plus Movers and Shakers.

Thanks to the enormous energy of the NEXT charity committee, the ball was a glittering success. Fifteen of the winning England squad were there, and they and 1500 guests were entertained by Lionel Ritchie and some of our friends in the show business world who performed for free, including Tony Hadley, Shane Ritchie and Alistair Griffin. An early typescript of this book was auctioned for £50,000, and my friend Philip Green bid £150,000 for a Noble car that I donated. All told, we raised over £500,000 for Parkinson's.

My speech during the evening summed up everything I wanted to say. To end on a cheerful note – and to remind you that the proceeds of this book will also go to Parkinson's charities – I can do no better than to finish by repeating most of it here:

364 days, 13 hours, 7 minutes and 23 seconds ago, the most famous drop kick in English rugby history soared majestically between the posts.

Ian Robertson, a native of Scotland and the BBC Radio rugby commentator, gritted his teeth and shouted: 'England have won the World Cup!' That must have hurt! 37 seconds later the final whistle confirmed his prediction.

40,000 English supporters dressed in white rugby shirts – £39.99 from Cotton Traders – jumped into the air in celebration. 20,000 Australian supporters dressed in gold shirts were stunned. And 10,000 French supporters also dressed in the gold colours of Australia were physically sick! Ha! Ha! Ha! So much for the European Constitution – support your fellow members at all times!

In the immortal words of Max Boyce: 'and I was there!'

I jumped up and hugged and kissed my wife several times before realising that she had changed places with Peter Webber at the interval! Yuk!

This afternoon I was reliving that marvellous day and suddenly thought: 'What would have happened if that kick had missed? Or if Jason Robinson had missed that vital tackle on the Australian winger?'

No arise Sir Clive! No CBEs, OBEs or MBEs! No bestselling auto-biographies! But worst of all, no Ball!

Back in January I had the idea of combining the celebration of the first anniversary of this great win with a tribute to Martin Johnson, whose leadership was, in my view, the most important factor that won the Cup.

But even more important to me, it would give me the opportunity to introduce you to a new initiative set up by four people – Sir Richard Nichols, Air Vice Marshal Michael Dicken, Tom Isaacs and me, David Jones – to raise money to fund research to find a cure for Parkinson's Disease. All four of us have PD.

We have called our initiative Movers and Shakers, and between us have raised over £750,000.

Parkinson's can affect anyone at any age. It is not a killer, but it can ruin the quality of life. It is a physical disease. It affects every muscle in your body. People with Parkinson's are aware every second that they have it – there is no relief.

Parkinson's makes you shake or makes you slow or both. You take medication to allow yourself to move more freely. The medication can make you move too much, so that you cannot stop moving. The comfort band between these two extremes gets narrower until it no longer exists.

When I was told way back in 1982 that I had Parkinson's, I cre-ated in my mind two David Joneses – one who was the chief execu-tive of Grattan and then NEXT, the other one who had Parkinson's. For 20 years I was able to keep them apart, but now they are mov-ing closer together.

The Movers and Shakers are backing research being carried out by Stephen Gill at Frenchay Hospital, Bristol. Stephen has been treating a small number of people who have severe Parkinson's.

I am determined to raise the money so that Stephen can complete his research. I have made a significant personal financial commitment – but I need a little help from my friends.

Thank you for listening to me...

...and thank you, dear reader, for helping me to raise more money for Parkinson's. It's worth the effort, because I believe that a cure or an improved way of treating Parkinson's Disease is not far away. I certainly hope so, because I still have so many things to do.

If by any chance you would like to make a further donation, please send it to:

The Cure Parkinson's Trust
c/o Karen Bird
NEXT plc
Desford Road
Enderby
Leicester LE19 4AT

Alternatively, you can make a donation online at:
www.cureparkinsons.org.uk

Acknowledgements

I talked in Chapter 11 about the huge debt I owe to the loyal and talented team who have worked with me over the past four decades. Many of them have appeared in this story, but it would be remiss of me not to mention and thank them again.

John Whitmarsh, 'Uncle' Dick Swain, John Cutts, Mick Bottomley, Dave Fortey, Ray Sheward, Brian Young, Dick Stokes, Richard Clarke, Paul Skinner and others formed the original team at Kays in the late 1960s and early 1970s.

We were joined at BMOC in Manchester by Colin Tranter, John Williams, Sam Nelson and Phil Wise. When we crossed the Pennines to Grattan in Bradford we added Dave Abbott, Dave King, Barry Neate, Peter Lomas, John Brenton and Pete Storey to the crew.

At NEXT we were joined by Peter Webber, Andrew Varley, Bob Harrison, David Keens, Sue Myatt, Peter Ward, Julie Heath and Cristos Angelides.

A special thank-you to my two secretaries who have had to put up with me over the last 25 years, June Osborne and Stephanie Pemberton, and to my driver, bodyguard and case packer, Peter Ellis.

The support I have received from Sue Myatt, Karen Bird and the NEXT charity committee has been outstanding and together we have staged some truly incredible events.

Also in my charity work I am proud to have been associated with Mary Baker and Tom Isaacs of the Cure Parkinson's Trust, John Hart and Brendan Eley of The Healing Foundation, and Eric Worrall and his team at the Duke of Edinburgh's Award Scheme.

There have been many times over the last five years when I truly doubted whether this literary masterpiece would ever be completed – it would not have been without the patient prodding of my publisher, Nick Brealey, my editor, Martin Vander Weyer, and the printers, the Mohn Group.

Finally, my sincere thanks to Simon Wolfson for 'bending the rules' and allowing me to sell my story through the NEXT Directory and Retail Stores and thereby maximising the royalty contribution to the search for a cure for Parkinson's Disease.

Chronology

February 1943	David Jones born.
September 1953	David Jones starts at Kings School, Worcester.
October 1960	David Jones joins Kays of Worcester.
August 1969	David Jones appointed finance director of Kays.
September 1974	David Jones appointed assistant managing director of Kays.
January 1976	David Jones appointed managing director of BMOC.
January 1981	David Jones joins Grattan as chief executive.
March 1981	George Davies joins J. Hepworth & Sons Ltd to develop NEXT.
February 1982	The first NEXT stores open.
January 1985	George Davies becomes chief executive of Hepworths.
September 1985	NEXT buys Lord John and Werff.
January 1986	Hepworths changes its name to NEXT plc.
July 1986	NEXT and Grattan merge; David Jones becomes deputy chief executive.
May 1987	NEXT buys Combined English Stores.
August 1987	Liz Davies joins the NEXT board.

October 1987	George Davies succeeds Michael Stoddart as chairman.
January 1988	Launch of NEXT Directory; pre-tax profits (for a 17-month period) hit £122 million.
April 1988	NEXT buys Dillons newsagents and Preedys confectioners.
December 1988	George and Liz Davies are sacked; Michael Stoddart returns as chairman; David Jones becomes chief executive.
June 1989	Sir David Wolfson succeeds Michael Stoddart as chairman.
January 1991	Group loss after extraordinary items is a record £445 million.
April 1991	Grattan sold to Otto Versand.
January 1995	Group annual pre-tax profits pass £100 million.
February 1997	Simon Wolfson joins the NEXT board.
January 1998	Group annual turnover passes £1 billion.
May 1998	Sir Brian Pitman succeeds David Wolfson (now Lord Wolfson of Sunningdale) as chairman.
August 2001	Simon Wolfson succeeds David Jones as chief executive.
May 2002	David Jones succeeds Sir Brian Pitman as chairman.
January 2005	Group annual turnover reaches £2.9 billion; pre-tax profits reach £423 million.

Index

Index

the **CURE PARKINSON'S** trust

In January 2005 David Jones co-founded The Cure Parkinson's Trust with three fellow Movers and Shakers who are fighting their Parkinson's both for themselves and for everyone touched by the condition. The Trust was founded by Sir Richard Nichols, former Lord Mayor of London, Air Vice Marshal Michael Dicken and Tom Isaacs, who recently completed a year-long challenge to walk around the coastline of Britain.

The Cure Parkinson's Trust aims to raise £2.5 million over five years for research into finding a Cure for Parkinson's Disease, a degenerative neurological condition that progressively and restrictively affects a person's movement. Parkinson's Disease can affect anyone, at any age.

The Cure Parkinson's Trust believes that an effective antidote to curb the progression of the illness will be available within five years. An outright cure may be further away, but the Trust's mission is to act as a catalyst to help accelerate the drive towards a cure for this disabling condition, which affects 7 million people in the UK either directly or indirectly. There is genuine hope for a cure for this disease.

www.cureparkinsons.org.uk

the **CURE PARKINSON'S** trust
supported by
Movers & Shakers

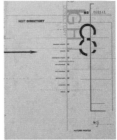

Error-free Software

WILEY SERIES IN
SOFTWARE ENGINEERING PRACTICE

Series Editors:

Patrick A.V. Hall, *The Open University, UK*
Martyn A. Ould, *Praxis Systems plc, UK*
William E. Riddle, *Software Design & Analysis, Inc., USA*

Fletcher J. Buckley • Implementing Software Engineering
Practices

John J. Marciniak and Donald J. Reifer
• Software Acquisition Management

John S. Hares • SSADM for the Advanced Practitioner

Martyn A. Ould • Strategies for Software Engineering
The Management of Risk and Quality

David P. Youll • Making Software Development Visible
Effective Project Control

Charles P. Hollocker • Software Reviews and Audits
Handbook

Robert Laurence Baber • Error-free Software
Know-how and Know-why of Program
Correctness

Charles R. Symons • Software Sizing and Estimating
MkII FPA (Function Point Analysis)